Advance Praise

"*Planning for the Success of Students With IEPs* centers the educator as a problem-solver who uses a systematic and support-based approach to educational planning, which is much needed in the contemporary context of supporting students with disabilities to be fully inclusive and participating members of schools. The wealth of information, strategies, and resources supports creative problem-solving aligned to: *What to teach? How to teach?* and *How to promote participation?* It will be embraced by educators of all types."

—**Mary E. Morningstar**, PhD, Professor, Department of Special Education, Portland State University

"This book provides concrete guidance to special educators engaged in the educational planning process who want to improve their ability to provide an inclusive and individualized education for students with disabilities. The author, James Thompson, identifies the ideal special educator as an effective problem-solver; he then describes how those skills can be used to plan, deliver, monitor, and evaluate the supports their students with disabilities require. This book is a must-read for those special educators who want to improve the academic success of students with disabilities. I am anxious to see what these inspired special educators will be able to accomplish and, even more so, the students with disabilities they will reach."

—**Colleen A. Thoma**, Professor, Department of Counseling and Special Education, Virginia Commonwealth University, coeditor of *Inclusion*

"If you want to be a great teacher of students with disabilities, first you need to forget what you have been taught. No, it's not impossible. No, you don't need a bottomless budget, a bigger staff, or a different credential. You do need to understand how to solve the problems that a disabled student faces every day. Here is a strong framework to support your inclusive problem-solving. This book is educator empowerment."

—**Sue Swenson**, President, Inclusion International

"This is *the* book on inclusive education. It provides an excellent framework for supports planning for students with any level of support needs. It is definitely a 'how to' book that offers many useful tools, but it also addresses the 'why' question of inclusive education, by including the philosophical, theoretical, and legal bases for inclusion. While providing detailed expert information from several leading authorities in the field, the book is highly readable, and will be useful for everyone from students to professionals. The discussion questions at the end of each chapter help the reader check for understanding and apply key concepts. It is an ideal book for training inclusive educators, or for general and special education teachers who aspire to include all students."

—**Kathleen Mortier**, PhD, Associate Professor, Department of Special Education, San Francisco State University, Extensive Support Needs Program

PLANNING FOR THE SUCCESS OF STUDENTS WITH IEPs

A SYSTEMATIC, SUPPORTS-BASED APPROACH

The Norton Series on Inclusive Education for Students with Disabilities

Michael L. Wehmeyer and Jennifer A. Kurth, series editors

The Series on Inclusive Education for Students with Disabilities is a publishing home for books that offer strengths-based approaches to understanding disability and that propose educational supports to enable all students, with and without disabilities, to succeed. Books in the series provide practical, research-referenced information for educators who teach students with disabilities in typical education contexts with their nondisabled peers.

Planning for the Success of Students With IEPs
James R. Thompson

Inclusive Education in a Strengths-Based Era
Michael L. Wehmeyer and Jennifer A. Kurth

Norton Books in Education

PLANNING FOR THE SUCCESS OF STUDENTS WITH IEPs

A SYSTEMATIC, SUPPORTS-BASED APPROACH

JAMES R. THOMPSON

W. W. NORTON & COMPANY
Independent Publishers Since 1923

Note to Readers: Models and/or techniques described in this volume are illustrative or are included for general informational purposes only; neither the publisher nor the author(s) can guarantee the efficacy or appropriateness of any particular recommendation in every circumstance. As of press time, the URLs displayed in this book link or refer to existing sites. The publisher and author are not responsible for any content that appears on third-party websites. Individuals and cases described in this volume are composite portraits representing no particular persons, living or dead.

Printed in the United States of America
First Edition

For information about permission to reproduce selections from this book, write to
Permissions, W. W. Norton & Company, Inc., 500 Fifth Avenue, New York, NY 10110

For information about special discounts for bulk purchases, please contact
W. W. Norton Special Sales at specialsales@wwnorton.com or 800-233-4830

Manufacturing by Versa Press
Production manager: Katelyn MacKenzie

ISBN: 978-1-324-01641-0 (pbk.)

W. W. Norton & Company, Inc., 500 Fifth Avenue, New York, N.Y. 10110
www.wwnorton.com

W. W. Norton & Company Ltd., 15 Carlisle Street, London W1D 3BS

1 2 3 4 5 6 7 8 9 0

This book is dedicated to students with IEPs and their families.

Contents

Figures and Tables

Acknowledgments

The contents of this book are based on a research project funded by Grant PR Award No. R324A180034 from the US Department of Education, Institute of Education Sciences, National Center for Special Education Research. The contents do not necessarily represent the policy of the Department of Education and endorsement by the federal government should not be assumed.

The research on which this book is based was carried out by a team of researchers, all of whom contributed in valuable ways and deserve to share credit as authors. The authors are:

1. James R. Thompson — University of Kansas
2. Virginia L Walker — University of North Carolina at Charlotte
3. Michael L. Wehmeyer — University of Kansas
4. Dave L. Edyburn — Knowledge by Design
5. Melinda R. Snodgrass — Illinois State University
6. Sarah R. Carlson — Vanderbilt University
7. Megan E. Carpenter — University of Kansas
8. Jessica A. Nelson — Missouri State University
9. Kristin Joannou Lyon — Lawrence Public Schools
10. Andrea P. Dinaro — Concordia University Chicago
11. Karrie A. Shogren — University of Kansas
12. Susan B. Palmer — University of Kanas
13. Nikki Michalak — Illinois State University
14. Selena J. Layden — Old Dominion University
15. Melissa Tapp — University of North Carolina at Charlotte

PLANNING FOR THE SUCCESS OF STUDENTS WITH IEPs

A SYSTEMATIC, SUPPORTS-BASED APPROACH

1

Special Educators as Problem-Solvers

Understanding Students by Their Needs for Support

What makes a great special educator? How would you answer this question? How would you expect your family and friends, school administrators and school board members, or even people chosen randomly on the street to respond? No doubt, some thoughtful answers would be offered; likely, there would be some cringeworthy ones as well. For instance, variations of "Bless your heart, being a special education teacher takes such great patience" have been uttered by well-meaning individuals since the field of special education first began. Simply declaring that one is majoring in special education in college is often enough to be deemed a worthy recipient of the golden badge of patience.

Although there are worse things than being admired for your bottomless reservoir of patience, some unwanted baggage lies below the surface of the "patience of a saint" ideal. That exceptional levels of patience are required does not reflect well on the children with disabilities whom the special educator teaches. To suggest that children, who may not learn, walk, communicate, and act in the ways that people expect, will inherently test the patience of people around them may say more about societal fear and rejection of children with disabilities than it does about the purported patience to teach them. Furthermore, aggrandizing patience above other desirable human qualities (creativity, optimism, integrity, self-confidence) can construe that the profession of special education is best suited for long-suffering people who are willing to resign themselves to teaching students who make only meager progress. In contrast, special educators who perceive their students' lives to be full of possibilities and take the education of their students very seriously are likely to bring a sense of urgency to their work that is not readily associated with patience. Certainly, patience with children is a virtue that all teachers should possess in good measure. It is not, however, what distinguishes great special educators.

Another misconception of the ideal special educator, particularly among school administrators of a certain ilk, is that of paperwork champion. A special educator who conscientiously completes the mountain of paperwork that comes with their job (Fowler et al., 2019) and can be counted on to dot every "i" and cross every "t" on their students' individualized education program (IEP) forms, may be quite successful in keeping their school district beyond reproach from a legal standpoint. Understandably, any school administrator or school board member would value that. But, although documenting compliance with the law must be done, avoiding legal trouble is not the pinnacle of accomplishment to which special educators should aspire.

There are plenty of other misguided notions about what constitutes an outstanding special education teacher, many of which, like the patience of a saint and the paperwork champion visions of excellence, have some truth to them. For instance, it is not wrong to suggest that special educators should be empathetic, have strong communication skills, be organized, be hard workers, be open to learning new ideas, seek out evidence-based practices, embrace cultural diversity and practice cultural responsiveness, and remain calm when faced with challenging circumstances. Like all professional work, special education requires multiple competencies that include dispositions, knowledge, and skills that are honed through formal education and practical experience. But, the sine qua non of truly outstanding special educators is their ability to identify and implement workable solutions to whatever challenges are impeding the education of their students. Students who are encountering difficulties learning and participating in general education classrooms need teachers who can figure out solutions. *A great special educator is an expert problem-solver.*

When the right supports are in place, there is high probability that the student, teachers, and classmates will have successful experiences in the general education classroom.

The premise of this book is that it is critical for special educators to possess a high level of expertise in analyzing student support needs in relation to classroom expectations, and top-notch skills for planning, delivering, monitoring, and evaluating the supports that their students require. The focus here is to describe and explain how a systematic approach to problem-solving (such as the Systematic Supports Planning Process or SSPP) can be used by special educators in collaboration with general education teachers to identify and arrange personalized supports that enhance the learning outcomes and the participation of students with IEPs in general education classrooms. Applying the SSPP empowers educators to provide supports that are thoughtfully aligned with a student's support needs. When the right supports are in place, there is high probability that the student, teachers, and classmates will have successful experiences in the general education classroom.

Problems, Problem-Solving, and Problem-Solvers

A problem occurs when there is a difference between an actual and a desired state of affairs. It is the difference between what is and what should be. Viewed through this lens, discovering a problem is not a negative event. Rather, discovering a problem reveals that people are practicing collective self-awareness. They know what they want to accomplish, and they are not content to bury their head in the sand and pretend that there are no ways to further their progress. A good understanding of a problem is a first—and necessary—step down the path leading to growth and improvement (Conn & McLean, 2018).

Problem-solving is a process that involves a series of actions or steps that are taken to find a solution to a problem. According to Conn and McLean (2018), the quality of problem-solving is most critical "when there is complexity and uncertainty that rules out obvious answers, and where there are consequences that make the work to get good answers worth it" (p. xiii). Problems cannot be wished away, and coming to a satisfactory resolution requires people to work together. McBride and Cutting (2019) indicated that problem-solving processes involve (a) defining and analyzing the problem; (b) identifying, prioritizing, and selecting alternatives for a solution; (c) implementing a solution; and (d) evaluating the extent to which the solution was successful.

Upon synthesizing the professional literature on problem-solving, Jonassen (2011) concluded that a person's competence in solving problems was the most important factor relevant to success across a wide spectrum of professional occupations. The World Economic Forum (2016) agreed, listing problem-solving as the most important skill needed for current and future jobs across nine economic sectors. Jonassen (2011) proposed a typology of different problems to be solved, and identified multiple components that can affect the nature of problem-solving in different contexts.

Although a deep dive into Jonassen's (2011) conceptual work goes beyond the scope of this book, it is useful to take a moment to consider his primary thesis. Namely, there is a continuum of problems to be solved, based on their structure, from well-structured to exceptionally ill-structured problems. The problems to be solved at the extreme end of the well-structured portion of the continuum have an irrefutable and knowable solution (such as solving a math problem). In contrast, the most extreme ill-structured problems are those for which a single correct solution does not exist due to a combination of conflicting assumptions, varied opinions, and diverse sources of evidence (e.g., achieving an international peace accord that all stakeholders can fully support).

Solving well-structured problems requires problem-solvers to complete a well-defined procedure. The path to an acceptable solution is known and a resolution will result if the process is followed correctly. Whether the well-structured problem is to solve an algebraic equation, bake a rhubarb pie that is tasty, or build the safest possible nuclear power plant, the steps to arrive at a resolution is not a mystery. That does not mean that people do not need to be highly knowledgeable and skilled to implement the steps and to move successfully through the process when the task is complex. For instance, in the case of building a nuclear power plant, if the execution of the process is flawed, the outcome could be truly disastrous. Although well-structured problems are characterized by predictable and verifiable solutions, success in completing complex tasks is contingent on having access to a team with a variety of competencies (Jonassen, 2011).

On the other end of the continuum are ill-structured problems, the most extreme of which may not have a solution (Jonassen, 2011). For instance, despite its pervasive presence in action movies set in outer space, developing the technology to travel at warp speed (traveling faster than light) is impossible based on the laws of physics. Not only would the energy required to get to warp speed be so immense that producing it defies all logic, but any spaceship traveling that fast would burn up long before it reached warp speed.

For other ill-structured problems for which full resolutions have yet to be figured out, however, there are logically feasible solutions as well as partial solutions available (Jonassen, 2011). For instance, it is likely that many of the most vexing social problems, which Rittel and Weber (1973) famously described as "wicked" problems (including gun violence and homelessness), may have multiple partial resolutions. Even when a sweeping, straightforward fix is out of reach, partial solutions may collectively reduce the extent of the negative consequences associated with a wicked, ill-structured problem (Jonassen, 2011).

Problem-solving in the context of special education involves coming up with resolutions to problems that are somewhere in the in middle of Jonassen's (2011) well-defined to ill-defined continuum. Contrary to what certain cynics might suggest, the difficulties that students with IEPs encounter in general education classrooms are rarely impossible to overcome. At the same time, it is naïve to suggest that all of the challenges that students with IEPs encounter in their classrooms can be resolved with little thought, effort, or expertise. Educators need a systematic process to identify supports that enable students with IEPs to participate and benefit from instruction in general education classrooms. Successfully implementing the process hinges on access to educators who have sufficient imagination to envision students with disabilities fully participating in general education classrooms, and who are willing to put in the hard work that is required to figure out solutions. Remember, a problem is a gap between *what is* and *what should be*, and the problem that the SSPP (the focus of this book) has been designed to solve is when there is a poor alignment between the expectations of a general education classroom and the characteristics of a student.

A systematic process is an approach to resolving a recurring problem in a strategic way. The SSPP is a systematic process to supporting students with IEPs in general education classrooms so that their education is meaningful, and providing supports in a manner that is workable for the student, educators, and fellow students. It involves (a) analyzing classroom requirements for student participation, and (b) identifying ways to support students that have a strong likelihood for success. The SSPP also encourages creative thinking and collaboration among educators. Creativity is essential because students and classrooms are unique, and solutions must be tailored to each situation. Collaboration is essential because the best ideas for supports are likely to emerge from multiple perspectives. Just as importantly, collaboratively coming to decisions on how to support a student will assure that all educators are invested in finding and using successful supports.

The SSPP: A Process to Plan and Deliver Supports

The SSPP assists educators in (a) identifying why students are experiencing difficulties in learning and participating in general education classrooms, and (b) arriving at solutions that address the difficulties that students encounter. Although the SSPP is fully described in Chapter 2, the focus of the remainder of this chapter is on the theory of disability on which the SSPP is based, how the SSPP promotes teacher creativity, and how the SSPP brings schools in alignment with legal requirements contained in the federal special education law (Individuals with Disabilities Education Act [IDEA], 2004).

Professionalism and Systematic Processes

The SSPP is a systematic process that garners educator expertise, stimulates creative thinking, and encourages professional collaboration. A major advantage of systematic processes are their replicability and sustainability (Barrett et al., 2005). High-level professional work is often systematic. For instance, architects use a multiphase development process when designing a new building; surgical teams follow protocols when performing heart transplants; and even professional sports teams have processes they go through to generate game plans and optimize opportunities for success. Thus, asking educators to approach their work systematically is consistent with expectations for other professions that require specialized knowledge (see Barrett et al., 2005).

The opposite of a systematic process is an amorphous process that relies on improvisation. Although ad-libbing a solution may work beautifully in a given situation, repeatedly doing so is not a good strategy. A major disadvantage of improvising continuously in any type of professional work is that success will be difficult to sustain (Barrett et al., 2005). For instance, if success hinges on a person who is particularly imaginative and competent, success will cease if that person leaves or forgets what they did to be successful. Amorphous processes are difficult to replicate and hard to evaluate because no audit trail is created. Determining what may have gone right or wrong depends on a retrospective analysis where key information may not be remembered. Important considerations and diverse perspectives are often discounted during the course of makeshift, informal activities. In contrast, systematic processes require documenting what was done during each step of the way, and those who approach their work systematically can rightly claim that they attempted to leave no stone unturned in their efforts to achieve their desired outcome (Conn & McLean, 2018).

Systematic processes, however, do not guarantee success, and they are not without potential pitfalls (Conn & McLean, 2018). For instance, a process that is poorly designed, poorly implemented, or poorly monitored can end up doing more harm than good. A particular concern for those working in education is that systematic processes can morph into rote, perfunctory actions (Milner, 2013). A narrow focus on getting tasks "checked off" can displace creative thinking and innovation (Conn & McLean, 2018), and, unfortunately, the field of education is replete with such examples. For instance, data from Kurth et al. (2019) suggested that processes put into place to facilitate the development of IEPs (for instance, drafting IEPs before meetings) supplanted efforts to collaborate with parents and students in developing educational plans that were uniquely tailored to a student's learning needs.

Another example of systemization choking innovation occurred in cases where educators were required by their school districts to teach scripted lessons from commercially produced curricula. Teachers reported that the rigidness in the scope and sequence of the scripted lessons thwarted their efforts to meet the diverse needs of students in their classrooms. It also prevented them from incorporating learning activities that were aligned with their teaching styles and preferences (Timberlake et al., 2017).

The phrase "thinking outside the box" might be an overused cliché, but it is critical that a systematic process not only allows for, but encourages, thoughtful consideration of alternatives that build upon and go beyond approaches that have been used in the past. This is especially true for a process that is intended to inform classroom supports for students with IEPs. In developing the SSPP, special attention was paid to offering educators a process that was highly systematic but at the same time encouraged creative problem-solving, such as considering approaches that might be new to both the educators and their students.

The Creativity–Systemization Nexus

Figure 1.1 shows four potential conditions that can occur in relationship to planning supports for children with IEPs in general education classrooms when creativity and systemization vary. The SSPP is intended to promote the type of professional practice that is characterized in Quadrant 1–Sustainable and

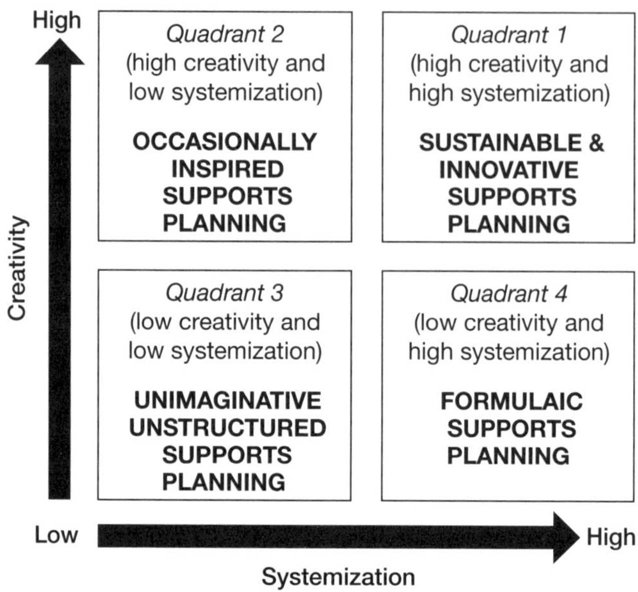

FIGURE 1.1: The Four Quadrants of the Creativity–Systemization Nexus

Innovative Supports Planning. Educators in this quadrant progress through a series of actions and steps that require them to thoughtfully consider each student's needs in relationship to classroom expectations. At the conclusion of the planning process, they arrive at individualized supports that address the misalignment between what the student is able to do and the learning and participation expectations in the classroom. The process, however, also requires educators to monitor and evaluate the supports over time and adjust as needed. The result is sustainable and innovative supports planning.

Quadrant 2–Occasionally Inspired Supports Planning reflects a state of affairs where educators are applying their creative problem-solving skills to identify and arrange supports for a student, but are doing so non-systematically. They do not document their ideas and decisions along the way. Therefore, determining how conclusions were arrived at is unclear. With no constraints placed on educator imagination, it is possible that truly inspired supports planning may occur. Perhaps, in some cases, the lack of structure for implementation will not pose a barrier; for instance, people will informally agree on what needs to be done and follow through on their commitments. But, as noted earlier, continual improvisation is not a good strategy for replicating success across students, and haphazard implementation can severely foil even the most inspired plans.

Quadrant 3–Unimaginative and Unstructured Supports Planning represents the worst of both worlds. These educators are most likely to quickly abandon any supports planning and implementation efforts. Integrating students with IEPs in these educators' general education classrooms will be perceived to be "unworkable" for the same reasons that have been given for years: a student is too disruptive to other children; the curriculum is not commensurate with a student's intellectual level; a student needs more individual attention than can be offered in the general education classroom (see Kurth & Forber-Pratt, 2017). Educators who operate in this quadrant not only lack the imagination to envision students with disabilities thriving in general education classrooms but they also lack ideas about how to begin creating inclusive classrooms and schools.

Quadrant 4–Formulaic Supports Planning encompasses cases where educators use a systematic process to plan and implement supports, but either their process does not sufficiently inspire them to think creatively and come up with good solutions, or they may lack the dispositions, knowledge, skills, or time/energy to implement the process with the creativity needed to generate solutions. Thus, the process is *formulaic*, characterized by educators going through a familiar routine with little commitment and enthusiasm. Documenting that a process was implemented does not guarantee that quality problem-solving has occurred; even the best systematic process can be implemented superficially and yield poor outcomes. A red flag that a formulaic approach has taken hold in supports planning and implementation is the presence of the same vague references to supports on school planning forms for multiple students, such as "accommodations and modifications will be made available to (insert student name) as needed." Without specifying what supports may look like in practice or who is responsible for implementing them, accommodations and modifications are little more than jargon that may reflect worthy intentions but offer no real direction for action.

Another red flag signifying the presence of formulaic planning is when there is evidence of a cognitive bias called the law of the hammer approach (McBride & Cutting, 2019). Poorly motivated, unimaginative problem-solvers tend to develop an overreliance on a single tool in which they are familiar (ergo, if all you have is a hammer, then everything looks like a nail).

For example, if the "hammer" is to rely on paraprofessionals to support students in classrooms, then every support need will be understood as something to be addressed by providing a paraprofessional. Does a student need academic supports? If so, provide a paraprofessional to support the student in completing classroom assignments. Does a student need social supports? If so, provide a paraprofessional to assist the student with classroom interactions. Does a student need support to organize their materials for learning? If so . . . (you've got it!) provide a paraprofessional to help the student get organized at the start of each lesson.

Another example is schools that develop overreliance on the special education teacher to plan and arrange supports. When an educational team assumes that it is the special educator's sole responsibility to come up with a solution when a student is having difficulties, they will not perceive contributing to supports problem-solving as a part of their job. When general educators do not share ownership of the supports that are put into place, the supports are much less likely to be successful. Educators who get stuck in Quadrant 4 will likely become cynical of the systematic process they are using. They end up going through the motions instead of problem-solving solutions to address the unique support needs of their students.

The SSPP is structured around three questions to assure that a focus on the student's interaction with the general education classroom and curriculum is maintained and to keep educators in Quadrant 1 (and away from Quadrants 2–4). The questions are *What to teach? How to teach?* and *How to promote participation?* Each of these will be discussed in detail later in this book. At each step of the SSPP there are critical questions to answer, essential actions to take, and supports to specify and arrange. As educators move through the SSPP, resources and suggestions that are embedded within the process are provided. Educators must make decisions based on their student's characteristics and the attributes of the classroom in which their student will be participating, particularly in regard to the learning activities the general educator uses during instruction. The SSPP was formulated on a social–ecological conceptualization of disability, and viewing students through a social–ecological lens is critical to implementing it effectively.

The Social–Ecological Model of Disability

Considering different conceptualizations of disability may seem like a topic that is overly esoteric or philosophical to be of value to educators who are seeking practical guidance in planning and implementing supports for students with IEPs in general education classrooms. However, the way in which disability is understood underlies all actions that educators undertake on behalf of students with IEPs, all laws and public policies, and all human services and social programs.

Therefore, the theoretical foundations, historical perspectives, and conceptual frameworks shaping contemporary understandings of disability need to be acknowledged. In the spirit of Kurt Lewin's (1943) famous maxim that "there is nothing as practical as a good theory," it is critical to consider the theory of disability that provides the conceptual foundation for the SSPP. If the foundation is fundamentally faulty, spending time and effort in implementing the SSPP will be fundamentally misguided. Conversely, if the conceptual foundation for the SSPP makes sense, putting it into practice will be logical and worthwhile.

What Is a Disability?

Traditionally, disabilities were understood to be pathologies within a person that were manifested as personal deficit traits. It was perceived that a person's deficits limited their capacity to meaningfully participate in school and society. Just like other pathologies or infectious disease that plague the human body, a medical model of disability called for efforts to eliminate the pathology so that people could be "fixed" or cured (Hogan, 2019). Medical model mindsets continue to be evident in today's world, but alternative conceptualizations have gained considerable traction over the past 30 years.

One alternative is the social–ecological model of disability, and it is the one on which the SSPP is based. In this model, disability is "characterized by a significant and chronic mismatch between a person's competencies and the demands of settings and activities associated with participating in an inclusive society" (Thompson et al., 2017, p. 31). Thus, disability is understood contextually through examining the interaction of the person within their environment. Disability is a state of functioning as opposed to a personal trait.

It has been argued that multiple models of disability have a place in interdisciplinary professional work involving people with disabilities (see Pledger, 2003). For instance, examining disability through a medical lens is helpful in situations where a biological intervention is effective. Phenylketonuria (PKU) occurs in about 1 of every 10,000 births, and children born with the condition experience a buildup of a body chemical called phenylalanine, which causes severe damage to the brain. However, damage can be prevented when PKU is identified at birth and the child adheres to a special diet (Dykens et al., 2000). The value of the medical model in this context is evident by the fact that PKU has been virtually eliminated as a cause of intellectual disability in developed countries over the past 60 years.

For people who are most interested in promoting the education and community participation of children and adults with disabilities, the social–ecological model provides an actionable way to understand disability because of the emphasis that is placed on "the fit" between people and their environments. According to the social–ecological model, a person's state of disability can be mitigated by adjusting the expectations of the environment and/or providing people the right supports. Supports function to reduce disparities between environmental demands and personal competencies, and a person's quality of supports can be evidenced by their status across an array of quality-of-life indicators (Thompson et al., 2009).

The SSPP and the Social-Ecological Model of Disability

Both the American Association on Intellectual and Developmental Disabilities ([AAIDD]; Schalock et al., 2010) and World Health Organization (WHO, 2001) proposed models of human functioning that are focused on the interaction between people and environments. Figure 1.2 provides a graphic depiction of understanding disability through a social–ecological conceptualization. The figure shows that the social–ecological model emphasizes (a) providing personalized supports to address any gaps that people experience between their personal competencies and environmental demands, and (b) designing environments that are optimally accessible or universally designed.

As shown in Figure 1.2, personal competence is an amalgam of health, wellness, and physical strength and vitality; intelligence and learned skills (i.e., adaptive behaviors); challenging behaviors; motivation; and anything else that influences successful functioning. It is a holistic construct and is influenced by the combination of the relative strengths and relative limitations a person possesses (Thompson et al., 2017). Environmental demands include the intellectual, physical, emotional, and behavioral demands that are associated with the different settings and activities in which the individual participates. Just like personal competence, environmental demands are unique to each environment.

Alternately, "misalignment" signifies that the competence of the person is not in alignment with the demands of the settings and activities in which they want to participate. Of course, everyone has moments in life where their competencies are not well aligned with environmental expectations and when they experience difficulties participating. However, experiencing time-limited, acute

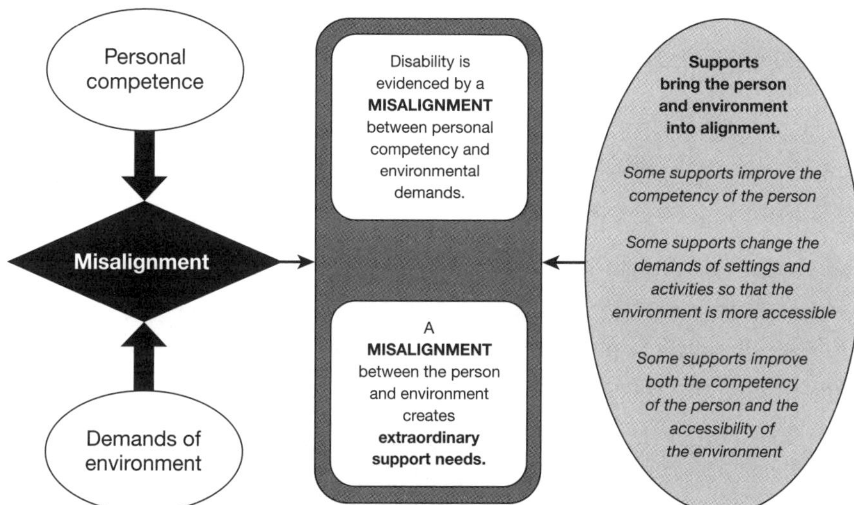

FIGURE 1.2: Social–Ecological Model of Disability: Supports Address the Misalignment Between Personal Competence and Environmental Demands

difficulties is not evidence of a disability. Disability is present when a person experiences chronic difficulty in meeting environmental demands, and the difficulties are of a magnitude that most other people in society do not experience.

Figure 1.2 shows that according to the social–ecological model, disability is evidenced by the misalignment of a person and their environment. Thus, disability is understood contextually, as a state of functioning characterized by extraordinary support needs that most others in society do not experience to the same extent.

Educators who endorse the social–ecological model are called to provide students with disabilities with the supports they need to effectively address the misalignment they experience with their school environment. Supports can be offered that improve the competence of the student and/or change the demands of settings and activities to make them more accessible. Providing the right types of supports to students requires educators who understand their students' strengths as well as limitations, recognize what is required to participate in activities within classroom and school settings, and can identify supports that bridge the divide between student competencies and environmental requirements. The SSPP was specifically designed to assist educators in identifying, arranging, and delivering personalized supports in general education classrooms. Based on a social–ecological model of disability, when a student is not successful in the classroom, the solution is to adjust the demands of the environment and/or introduce more effective supports.

Inclusive Education: What Is It, Exactly?

Haug (2017) pointed out that, depending on who is speaking, the phrase "inclusive education" can mean just about anything. It might be used as a buzzword in a school district's policy documents that call for a system-wide, unequivocal embrace of all students from subgroups that have traditionally been marginalized due to disability diagnoses, sexual identity, racial identity, family economic status, and so forth. It might be used at the school level to describe modest efforts to integrate students with certain disability labels, by including them in nonacademic general education activities and settings (lunch and free-play periods) for a portion of the school day. Inclusive education is something that few educators oppose in spirit and that almost every school district will claim to practice. Yet, the reality is more complicated.

Because the term "inclusive education" is used differently across school districts and people, it can require a mental stretch to reconcile its implementation versus its description in educational journals and professional writing (see Chapter 1 of Kurth & Gross, 2015). For this reason, it is difficult to draw conclusions about a school's relative inclusivity toward students with IEPs when information is based solely on a school's self-report. For an unbiased evaluation of a school district's inclusivity, a checklist of verifiable criteria, such as those provided by Kluth (2010) or Villa and Thousand (2016) can be useful, especially when completed by an outside party. But even these well-designed checklists, which include items such as "Within each unit of study, content and materials differentiation routinely occurs with students being offered multiple options for taking in information . . ." (Villa & Thousand, p. 70), may not provide a full picture. The people participating in a school district, school, or classroom on a daily basis are the only ones who really know how inclusive their school district, school, and classroom are for students with IEPs.

Data on the educational placement of students with IEPs have been collected by the US Department of Education since the 1977–78 school year and are summarized annually in a report to the US Congress. These reports shed light on how the inclusivity of the nation's schools has changed over time. For those preferring to view the glass as half full, a cursory examination of year-to-year data clearly shows that schools in the United States have become more inclusive. Direct comparisons over time are difficult, however, because early reports used terms such as "special classroom" and "resource room" to identify placement categories rather than the more recent and more precise categories like "percentage of time in regular class."

The people participating in a school district, school, or classroom on a daily basis are the only ones who really know how inclusive their school district, school, and classroom are for students with IEPs.

Data shown in Figure 1.3 from the *41st Annual Report to Congress on the Implementation of IDEA* (US Department of Education, 2020) reveal that separate educational settings have become less common but are still employed for all disability populations to varying degrees. Only 5 of 12 disability groups have a majority of students who spend 80% or more of their school day in a general education classroom. Thus, there is still a long way to go before the claim can be made that most US schools display the capacity to educate a wide array of students with IEPs in general education classrooms. Students with a primary diagnosis of autism, deaf-blindness, intellectual disability, or multiple disabilities are especially at risk of not having access to general education settings for a large portion of their school days.

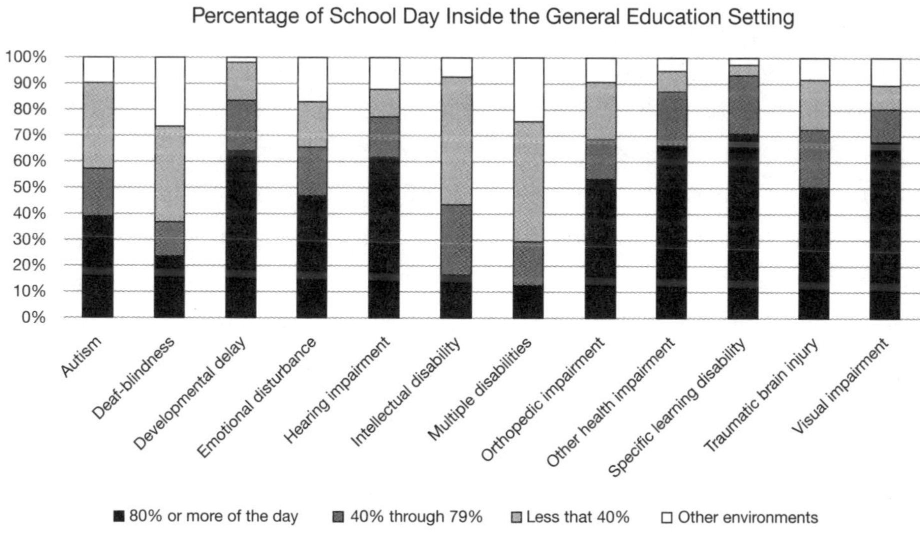

FIGURE 1.3: Placement Data From the 41st Annual Report to Congress on the Implementation of the Individuals with Disabilities Education Act, 2019

Individual Education Plans and Inclusive Education

The types of special education services that are provided to students in the United States and many other countries (for Canada, see Tremblay & Belley, 2017) are detailed in a planning document called the individualized education program (IEP). An IEP is a legal document that details goals and objectives for the student along with supplemental aides and services. In the United States, once a student is found eligible for special education services, the educational team must develop an IEP within 30 days.

It is important to acknowledge that students with IEPs are a subset of students with disabilities. That is, not every student with a diagnosed disability is eligible for an IEP, but every student with an IEP will have been diagnosed as having a disability. In the United States there are 13 different disability categories under which a child may be determined to be eligible for an IEP, and each category has specific criteria associated with it. The scope of students eligible for the special education services specified in IEPs varies over time and across localities within and between countries. For instance, Riser-Kositsky (2019) reported that the percentage of students with IEPs varies from just under 10% to slightly over 19% of the public-school population within different US states. Because all educational practices advocated in this book are applicable to students with IEPs, this is the population for whom the book targets. However, many of these practices may also be useful for students who are struggling in schools but do not have IEPs. Also, it is absolutely critical to acknowledge the reality that students with IEPs are a heterogeneous population. Although there are problem-solving strategies that are applicable to all students with IEPs, actual supports need to be determined on an individualized basis.

Although the educational experiences of all children are important, content relevant to student populations other than those with IEPs is beyond the scope of this discussion. Thus, for the purpose of this book, the definition of "inclusive education" will be a simple one. Inclusive education involves

- educating students with IEPs in age-appropriate, general education classrooms in the same neighborhood schools they would attend if they did not have IEPs;
- providing them with effective instruction based on the core

curriculum as well as personal learning goals that are outside the core curriculum;
- providing them with the supports they need to successfully learn from and participate in general education classroom activities.

The Legal Basis for Inclusive Education

The Education for All Handicapped Children Act was the original title of the landmark federal education law, signed by President Gerald Ford on November 29, 1975. It mandated public schools in the United States to provide a free and appropriate education to students who were determined eligible for services under 1 of 10 different disability categories. Since then, there has been a consistent stream of big and small changes to the law as a result of legislative amendments and updated federal regulations. For instance, since its enactment, the number of disability classifications covered under this law has expanded from 10 to 13; educators have been required to initiate school-to-adult life transition planning on or before students reach the age of 16; greater emphasis has been placed on assuring students' access to the general education curriculum; and the law was renamed the Individuals with Disabilities Education Act or IDEA (IDEA, 2004).

Despite IDEA's many changes, there have also been many constants. One of the most critical and enduring legal requirements is that any student who is eligible for services under IDEA must have an IEP that is developed by a team that includes parents and educators. Today, in many instances, students are also active participants on their IEP team. The IEP specifies learning goals for a student and stipulates the school-district services deemed necessary to support the student's learning goals. Among the most important requirement is that the IEP team must specify the supplementary aids and services to be provided to support a student's education *in the least restrictive environment* (LRE). The LRE provision requires educating students with IEPs alongside same-age peers in general education classrooms and settings to the maximum extent.

Although interpretations of what comprises "the maximum extent" will vary, it is clear that the spirit of the law is for educators to make concerted efforts to remove barriers to participation in general education classrooms and design educational activities and spaces that are accessible to all children. The quality of supplementary aids and services available will have a tremendous impact on IEP planning-team decisions regarding placement (such as what constitutes the LRE for the individual student). Per IDEA, "[s]upplementary aids and services means aids, services, and other supports that are provided in regular education classes, other education-related settings, and in extracurricular and nonacademic settings, to enable children with disabilities to be educated with nondisabled children to the maximum extent appropriate" (IDEA, 2004, §300.42).

When supplementary aids and services are individualized and comprehensive, the general education classroom and other general education settings are more likely to be identified as the LRE. Conversely, when supplementary aids and services are only superficially considered, separate educational settings are more likely to be viewed as necessary.

The Relationship of "Supplementary Aids and Services" to "Supports"

As discussed, specifying and providing supplementary aids and services is a legal requirement of IDEA when developing an IEP. Specifically, IDEA requires that IEPs include a statement of the supplementary aids and services that are needed for a student to make progress toward individualized learning goals, to make progress in the general education curriculum, to participate in extracurricular and other nonacademic activities, and to interact with other children. Whereas "supplementary aids and services" is a legal term from IDEA, "supports" and "support needs" are conceptual terms associated with the social–ecological model of disability that was discussed earlier.

Supports have been defined as "resources and strategies that aim to promote the development, education, interests, and personal well-being of a person and that enhance individual functioning" (Schalock et al., 2010, p. 18). Everyone uses a variety of supports in daily life; for example, a GPS on a mobile phone serves as navigational support to travel to a destination efficiently and safely. However, the supports needed by children with IEPs are more intense. They differ in regard to type, frequency, and duration compared with the supports needed by most children from the general population. Support needs refer to "the pattern and intensity of support a person requires to participate in activities associated with typical human functioning" (Thompson et al., 2009, p. 135). Support needs refer to a student's persistent needs, and are not a point-in-time description of a need for a particular type of support.

For students with IEPs in general education classrooms, "supports" and "supplementary aids and services" can be considered to be interchangeable terms. Both terms are focused on using resources and strategies to address the mismatch between student characteristics and the demands of general education settings and learning activities. In this book, the term "supports" will be used because it is less legalistic and serves as a reminder that the purpose is to enhance student engagement and learning. If engagement and learning are not enhanced, then whatever is being provided is not functioning as a support.

The purpose of the SSPP is to provide educators with a practical resource that enhances problem-solving in regard to identifying and providing supports. It assumes that supports that are truly useful in enhancing student engagement in classroom learning opportunities are most likely to be identified when there has been thorough and thoughtful consideration of student support needs in relation to classroom and school demands. The SSPP is described in detail in Chapter 2.

Key Ideas From This Chapter

- Expert special educators have great problem-solving skills. They can recognize when student competencies and classroom demands are poorly aligned and are able to identify what supports a student needs to be successful.
- A problem-solving process to identify and arrange supports needs to encourage both systemization and creativity. Without a systematic process, efforts will be haphazard and success will be inconsistent. Without creativity, solutions run the risk of being formulaic and ineffective.
- A social–ecological conceptualization of disability is useful to educators because understanding disability as a mismatch between the person and the environment (specifically, between the student and the classroom settings and activities) provides a clear direction for their work. The work of educators is to identify and arrange the supports their students need to be successful in classrooms and schools.
- The Systematic Supports Planning Process (SSPP) is intended to assist educators in identifying supports for students with IEPs that bring better alignment to student competencies and classroom

expectations. Applying the SSPP is an approach to creating inclusive classrooms and schools that successfully educate children with diverse characteristics and learning needs.

Questions for Discussion

1. It was suggested that reframing a problem as an opportunity for positive change is a critical step to succeeding in educational settings. Can you think of a problem in schools today that might be frustrating to teachers, students, and/or school administrators, and reframe it as an opportunity for positive change?
2. Professional work is of vital importance to others in society. Among the hallmarks of professionals is their specialized knowledge and their autonomy over how their work is completed (Milner, 2013). For example, medical doctors are universally considered to be professionals because they possess knowledge about healing that others do not have, and they typically conduct their work with a great deal of autonomy. Many people have voiced concern that teaching has been deprofessionalized over the years (see Milner, 2013). How would using a systematic process such as the SSPP help build a case that teachers are skilled professionals engaged in professional work?
3. In this chapter, inclusive education was defined as (a) educating students with IEPs in age-appropriate, general education classrooms in the same neighborhood schools they would attend if they did not have IEPs; (b) providing them with effective instruction based on the core curriculum as well as personal learning goals that are outside the core curriculum, and (c) providing them with the supports they need to successfully learn from and participate in general education classroom activities. Data from the US Department of Education, however, show that an inclusive educational experience remains elusive for many students with IEPs. Why do you think including students with IEPs in general education classroom is so important, and why is it so elusive?

2

The Systematic Supports Planning Process

Your Roadmap to Success

The SSPP provides a framework for educators to organize their thinking in regard to identifying and arranging individualized supports that are aligned with each student's pattern and intensity of support needs. It is focused on educator practices at the individual student level and directs attention to what content is taught, how content is taught, and how to support a student's participation in classroom learning activities. An overview of each phase of the SSPP is provided in this chapter, as well as a discussion of how the SSPP can be used in concert with the principles of universal design for learning (UDL)—toward the goal of assuring that meaningful instruction is provided in the general education classroom to all students, including those with diverse learning needs.

The SSPP: Questions, Actions, and Supports

Expanding the capacity of general education classrooms to educate the vast majority of students with IEPs should not be viewed as a purely noble cause grounded in human empathy and a desire to create educational spaces where everyone belongs. Although ethical arguments for expanding inclusive educational opportunities are important to consider, educators should be aware that there is a legal basis that compels school districts to clearly document their efforts to offer general education classrooms as a placement where students with IEPs can be successfully educated. In addition to the Individuals with Disabilities Education Act (IDEA) requirement that IEPs specify the supplementary aids and services to be provided to support a student's education in the least restrictive environment (LRE), in March of 2017 the US Supreme Court issued a unanimous opinion in *Endrew F. v. Douglas County School District* that made it clear that schools must make concerted efforts to provide general education classrooms that have the capacity to educate students with IEPs.

The *Endrew F.* decision held that students have the right to more than a merely *de minimis* (a Latin expression meaning "insignificant" or "unimportant") education. The Court's ruling effectively created a higher substantive standard for the education of students with IEPs than previously required. According to the Court, all students have the right to make progress in the general education curriculum on appropriately ambitious and challenging learning goals (Turnbull et al., 2018; US Department of Education, 2017). Compliance with the spirit of the *Endrew F.* judgement compels educators to carefully consider ways in which students with IEPs can learn general education curricula content alongside their same-aged peers. The SSPP provides a means to document that educators have carefully considered how supports can be arranged to enable students with IEPs to access general education curricula and classrooms.

Figure 2.1 illustrates a supports-based approach to inclusive education that was developed over multiple years through research with teacher teams who were in the process of including students with IEPs in general education classrooms (Thompson et al., 2020; Thompson et al., 2018; Walker et al., 2014). The process is structured around three overarching questions:

1. What to teach?
2. How to teach?
3. How to promote participation?

Subsequent critical questions impel educators to gather specific information that is relevant to a student's learning characteristics and the general education context. This information is used to inform essential actions that result in identifying individualized supports and creating a plan for supports implementation. Although the SSPP is a uniform process applicable to all students, the supports that emerge from applying the process are individualized to each stu-

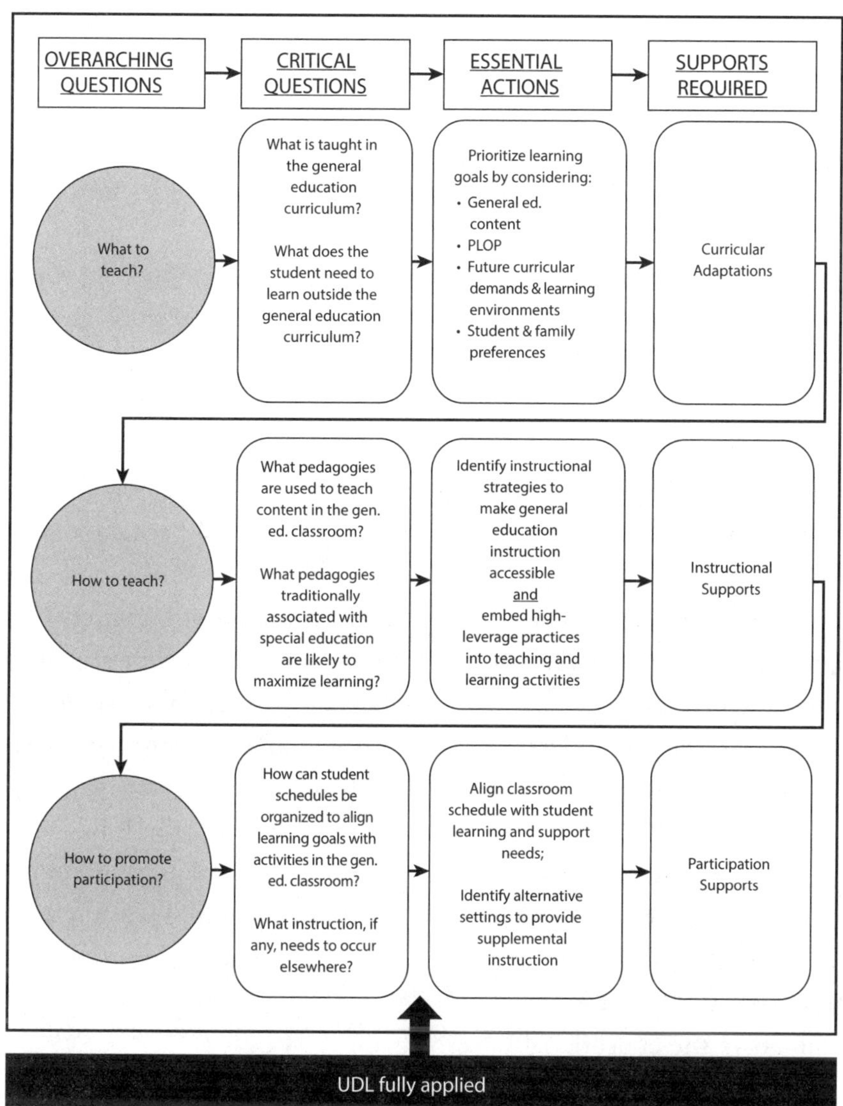

FIGURE 2.1: The Systematic Supports Planning Process

dent's unique needs and circumstances. Applying the SSPP will be most effective in schools embracing the universal design for learning (UDL) framework. The UDL framework provides a structure for curriculum and instructional design where intentional efforts are undertaken to provide students with multiple learning paths (Nelson, 2021).

What to Teach?

"If everything is a priority, then nothing is a priority" is an axiomatic truth. Occasionally, a well-meaning educator will express thoughts along the lines of "I want my students to learn it all. I don't want to set any limits on their learning." But this sentiment ignores the importance of prioritization. It's true that providing all students with access to the general education curriculum and basing their education on the same learning standards as the general population of students provides them the opportunity to learn everything that is taught in the classroom. However, just because all students have access to the entire scope of the curriculum does not mean that every student will experience the same learning outcomes. Moreover, having high expectations for all students does not mean having the same expectations for all students. Prioritization is critical because identifying a subset of learning goals that are the most important for a student to achieve is likely to result in more learning. Unfocused efforts run the risk of overwhelming students with information and can result in only superficially addressing content that students need to learn. Setting priorities for instruction for students with IEPs does not mean the students will not learn anything that has not been specifically targeted as a learning outcome. In reality, prioritizing learning goals happens all the time in classrooms among students with and without IEPs.

Setting instructional priorities signifies that a set of learning outcomes has been specifically targeted for a student, and educators are going to make a concerted effort to teach the student what is most important (for that student) to learn. To prioritize learning goals, the educational team must consider a student's present level of performance, the general education content being taught, future curricular demands and learning environments, and student and family preferences. Curricular adaptations, the first major category of supports for students shown in Figure 2.1, will be the outcome of this phase of the SSPP.

Curricular adaptations are any adjustments to the general education curriculum that enhance a student's learning by making the general education curriculum accessible and/or incorporate additional content that is important for a student to learn.

Curricular adaptations are any adjustments to the general education curriculum that enhance a student's learning by making the general education curriculum accessible and/or incorporate additional content that is important for a student to learn. Curricular adaptations can include supplementary content that builds on the general education curriculum, streamlined or simplified content within the general education curriculum, and alternative content that is outside what is taught in the general education curriculum. Chapter 4 of this book is devoted to a detailed description of how education teams can identify curricular adaptations to best assure students with IEPs are provided meaningful learning goals that reflect high expectations for their achievement.

How to Teach?

The second overarching question posed in Figure 2.1—"How to teach?"—focuses on how to offer the student the best opportunity to achieve the prioritized goals that were identified in the first phase of the SSPP.

Separate special education classrooms have been justified based on the claim that children with IEPs require pedagogies different from children without IEPs (Kauffman & Hornby, 2020). There are a few teaching techniques that would likely be limited to a narrow student population. For instance, cued speech is a technique to teach oral speech to students who are deaf and hard of hearing; see Gardiner-Walsh et al., 2020). However, most pedagogies can be applied successfully across an array of children within the context of the general education classroom, such as applied behavior analytic practices (Schwartz et al., 2005). There is no evidence that instructional methods used with students in general education classrooms are inherently ineffectual with students with IEPs. A diverse classroom guarantees that students will have different degrees of competence in academic learning before instruction is initiated as well as after it is delivered. This does not mean that instruction cannot be delivered in ways that are meaningful to all students.

The inconsistency between teaching practices that have been traditionally advocated for general educators and those advocated for special educators can be stark. A bridge between these two educational worlds needs to be built, and collaboratively using a systematic planning process like the SSPP can help build it. General educators most commonly focus on teaching the conceptual basis of material followed by instruction in the more practical applications of knowledge. To give one example, math educators stress the need for conceptual learning—such as understanding the relationship between quantity and numbers, or understanding problem-solving strategies—as a foundation for learning computational processes (Lambert & Tan, 2017; Thanheiser & Jansen, 2016). In contrast, there is a long tradition in special education to teach specific skills that have a practical application—such as identifying denominations of money and coins, or learning measurement units such as cups, quarts, and gallons—in lieu of teaching underlying concepts (Hord & Bouck,2012).

Fortunately, this gap in instructional practices is beginning to close. Research over the past several decades has made it clear that students with even the most significant cognitive disabilities can meaningfully access and benefit from instruction that focuses on conceptual knowledge (see Afacan et al., 2018; Browder et al., 2006; Courtade et al., 2013). Although achievement in conceptual knowledge will certainly vary considerably among students with IEPs, it also differs significantly among students without IEPs. Denying students access to instruction on conceptual content that is associated with the general education curriculum has the potential to severely limit students' future academic growth because conceptual knowledge provides the foundation for higher-level academic learning. This does not mean that instruction focusing on teaching and learning of more precise skills should be completely abandoned. It certainly should not. The charge to educators, however, is to find the right combination of pedagogies to teach conceptual as well as practical skills, and to manage instructional efforts so that all students are instructed in ways that will enable them to flourish as learners.

The SSPP process of arriving at instructional supports is consistent with the concept of differentiating instruction within a general education classroom (Lawrence-Brown, 2004; Tomlinson, 1999, 2017). Whereas differentiated instruction is typically used to refer to class-wide efforts to provide varied instructional approaches that meet the diverse learning needs of a group of students (see Tomlinson, 1999, 2017), instructional supports refer to the teaching methods, strategies, and materials that a specific student needs to maximize their learning in the general education context.

Providing instructional supports to differentiate instruction is the polar opposite of a one-size-fits-all mentality to classroom teaching and learning. Instructional supports can include any teaching approach; its defining feature is its relationship to the core instruction that is provided in a classroom. Instructional supports are evidenced by instructional adaptations and alternative adaptations. Instructional adaptations are "individualization of the way the teacher teaches and/or the way in which the student practices and demonstrates learning" (Janney & Snell, 2013, p. 78). Alternative adaptations are "learning activities that are coordinated with classroom instruction but are designed to address individualized learning priorities using student specific methods and/or materials" (Janney & Snell, 2013, p. 83). It is possible that in one subject a student will need few, if any, instructional supports, but in another subject this same student may have a significant need for them. Chapter 5 of this book is devoted to a detailed description of how educational teams can identify, arrange, and deliver instructional supports to meet the needs of diverse learners.

How to Promote Participation?

The third overarching question in Figure 2.1—"How to promote participation?"—is focused on how to support students so that they are fully engaged in classroom learning activities. The first critical question concerns promoting participation, specifically, how to align classroom schedules with student needs. A simple planning matrix, as is shown in Table 2.1, provides a starting point to identify ways in which individual learning goals can be addressed during different parts of the school day. It is focused on identifying when and where a student may need supports that most others in the classroom will not need. As can be seen in this example, the target student has two individualized communication goals that are unlikely to be shared by many (if any) other students. When considering how learning opportunities related to these goals can be distributed across the school day, multiple opportunities for the student to learn and practice these skills are identified. From there, the supports the student needs to make progress on these goals can be planned. Of course, the communication goals are relevant throughout the day, and there may be other teachable moments that occur. The planning matrix identifies the times of the day where there is certain to be targeted instruction and when progress monitoring data will be collected.

There are obvious advantages to teaching and learning practical skills within the context of participating in general education classroom activities, a practice termed "embedded instruction" (Jameson et al., 2007). Initial learning of skills will be enhanced because the skills are being taught through distributed practice, which is practicing emerging skills over relatively short, frequent sessions, versus massed practice, which is practicing emerging or newly learned skills in relatively lengthy, infrequent sessions. Also, the generalization of skills that a student masters will be enhanced because the skills are being applied

TABLE 2.1 Communication Goals and Supports Across the School Day

	CLASS SCHEDULE											
IEP GOALS	Arrival	A.M. work	Language skills	Reading	Music or art	Recess	Math	Lunch	Science/social studies	Writing	Reading	Departure
Communication learning goals												
1. Use simple sentences to express needs, feelings, ask/answer questions, make choices, relate recent events	x	o	x	x	o	x	o	x	x	x	x	x
Communication partners for Goal 1	A		B	C		D		E	A	C	F	B
2. Respond to and initiate interactions with peers	x	x	x	x	x	x	o	x	x	o	x	x
Communication partners for Goal 2	G	H	I	C	C	D		E	G		F	F

Note. x = goal is instructed and assessed during time frame; o = goal not assessed during time frame; A = Classroom teacher; B = Paraprofessional; C = Peer 1; D = Peer 2; E = Peer 3; F = Peer 4; G = Peer 5

in natural settings. Additional information about the application embedded instruction is provided in Chapter 5.

The matrix in Table 2.1 provides a good starting place for determining ways to support students' engagement with their individual learning goals throughout the school day. Table 2.2 provides an example of how to generate ideas for supporting students as they engage in specific learning activities that are applicable to the entire class. In this example, the general education teacher has planned several learning activities associated with her instruction focused on the Lewis and Clark Expedition. These include individual assignments to be completed in and out of the classroom, small-group work within the classroom, and whole-class instruction.

Table 2.2 shows that a variety of initial supports can be tentatively planned. A screen reader or a technological support will provide the student access to the reading assignment, whereas peer support will be needed for the student to be fully engaged in small-group learning activities. The adult supports delineated in the table are also critically important. Notice, (a) the special educator will create adapted materials for the timeline assignment, (b) the paraprofessional will provide supervision and guidance on completing the time line as well as monitoring the student during class time, and (c) the general education classroom teacher will be proactive in soliciting the student's participation during whole class instruction.

Table 2.2 indicates this student requires mostly *accommodations*, that is, supports that provide access to content taught in the general education curriculum and classroom but do not change the difficulty level or the performance expectations. There are also several *modifications* that are implied and explicitly mentioned; these change what is expected of the student during or following a classroom activity. The expectations on the timeline assignment are modified for this pupil by providing slides with description of events to sequence, versus requiring the student to both generate descriptions and sequence key events. Also, the quiz that the student will take at the end of the unit has been modified to remove short-answer expectations. Table 2.2 shows that accommodations and modifications can be incorporated within the same learning activity. For instance, allowing the student to provide oral responses is an accommodation (support that allows the student to meet expectations) for the quiz, but limiting quiz items to only "true/false" questions is a modification (change in expectations).

Note that Tables 2.1 and 2.2 show two aspects of planning that need to be aligned to provide the supports the student needs. Attempting to identify supports without taking the context of classroom schedules and learning activities into consideration runs the risk of generating unworkable supports that are very difficult to implement and, are therefore, ineffective.

Also, aligning supports with classroom schedules and activities allows situations to be identified when a student's needs may not be best met in the context of the general education classroom. When this occurs, exploring

TABLE 2.2 Learning Activities and Supports for Lewis and Clark Expedition

LEARNING ACTIVITIES	
Read textbook (individual); students are assigned reading that they are expected to complete during the class time devoted to it as well as at home for homework.	
Read maps, charts, tables, and draw conclusions from material (small group); students are given a packet of maps, charts, and tables, as well as an agenda for small-group work that includes questions that need to be answered. Students are expected to extract and/or synthesize information from maps, charts and/or tables; come to consensus on conclusions; and submit a group project stating their conclusions and reasoning. Class time will be allotted for this small group assignment.	
View class presentation and participate in discussion by asking questions and providing comments (whole class). Class time will be allotted for this class-wide presentation.	
Create a timeline by sequencing critical events on a printed or electronic timeline (individual). Class time will be allotted for this individual work, but students have option of also working on assignment at home.	
Take a quiz consisting of T/F, multiple-choice, and short-answer essay questions.	

alternative options for instruction outside the general education classroom is needed. Although the SSPP is designed to plan supports in inclusive classrooms, it does not require that students with IEPs must spend their entire school day in the same setting where the majority of their classmates without IEPs are educated. As Brown et al. (1991) famously pointed out, being "included in" is not equivalent to being "confined to" a general education classroom. Many students, with and without disabilities, receive supplemental instruction that goes beyond the instruction offered to the entire class, and it is often provided to students individually or in small groups outside the general education classroom. Supplemental instruction is a common practice in schools that have adopted multitiered system of support (MTSS) frameworks (Fuchs et al., 2012).

	SUPPORTS FOR TARGET STUDENT
	Textbook is electronic; thus, student can use a screen reader to access textbook content; student will have same reading assignment as others in the class. Parents will review summary questions at the end of reading assignment with student to promote comprehension.
	Student will have a peer buddy to support participation in the small group. Paraprofessional and teacher will also monitor the student's participation to ensure active engagement. The agenda requires students to take turns and share group work facilitation roles and responsibilities; the only roles and responsibilities the student will be exempt from are those of note taker and scribe.
	Student will have a set of printed question scripts to support participation in the large-group discussion and a graphic organizer to take notes during presentations, as well as a peer buddy to support participation in the large group. Teacher will make a point to solicit the student's input at least one time during each presentation.
	Special educator will provide student with PowerPoint slides that list 10 events. Student will sequence the events and type in a comment for each slide to create the multimedia presentation, and the classroom paraprofessional will monitor and offer verbal assistance as needed.
	Student will take quiz orally with teacher; questions will be limited to T/F and multiple choice.

Supplemental instruction provided individually or in a small group in a separate setting can be an important means to support students in achieving their learning goals. However, a word of caution is in order: Students with IEPs should not be routinely removed from the general education classroom more often than other students who are receiving supplemental instruction. Doing so can easily devolve into designating separate learning spaces for students based on disability characteristics and be used as a rationale to circumvent the hard work of increasing the capacity of general education classrooms to educate a diverse student population.

Participation supports are evidenced by their function. Specifically, their purpose is to promote the full engagement of a student in learning activities within the general education classroom as well as other school settings. Participation supports may include combinations of accommodations, modifications, personal assistance, and technologies—whatever is put into place to promote meaningful engagement and efficient participation in group learning activities. Chapter 6 is focused on how participation supports can be identified, arranged, and implemented.

Universal Design for Learning (UDL)

The bottom portion of the diagrammatic illustration of the SSPP indicates that UDL should influence all aspects of the SSPP. The reason for including UDL in the figure is simple and straightforward: If learning settings and activities are universally designed from the outset, the effort required to identify and arrange individual supports will be significantly reduced and the SSPP can be implemented more successfully.

The founders of the Center for Applied Science and Technology (CAST) integrated knowledge from the fields of neuroscience, brain science, education, educational psychology, and special education to develop the UDL framework (Meyer et al., 2014). The major premise underlying the UDL framework is that effective instructional planning can eliminate, or at least greatly reduce, many of the learning difficulties that students experience. By providing multiple pathways to success, students can follow the path that is best for them. As multiple authors have pointed out (see Israel et al., 2014; Meyer et al., 2014; Nelson, 2021), the UDL framework is based on three core principles.

- **Providing multiple means of representation.** Because there is not just one means of representation that will be optimal for all students, educators should design instruction to offer access to content through multiple avenues. These might include presenting alternatives to access information auditorily, visually, and tactilely instead of relying on a single representation; promoting understanding across languages; and providing multiple options for activating or supplying background knowledge.
- **Providing multiple means of engagement.** Because there is tremendous diversity in how students can be engaged or motivated to learn, educators should design instruction to account for the many ways to motivate students to fully participate and to get all they can from instructional

activities. To do this, teachers might provide students with choices for how to participate in a lesson or activity, actively teach and support students' learning of self-regulation skills, optimize the relevance of materials and lessons so that students acquire a sense of ownership of their learning goals, and foster learning communities for students who work best through collaborative and shared-learning activities.

- **Providing multiple means of action and expression.** Because students can indicate what they have learned in various ways, educators should design instruction that provides different opportunities for students to demonstrate their progress and growth. Some examples include providing multiple media for communications, varied opportunities for practice, and multiple approaches students can use monitor and assess their own progress.

Taken to the logical extreme, it may seem that there would actually be no need for the SSPP (nor for this book, for that matter!) if all school settings and activities were designed from the outset to be universally accessible to all. It is clear that applying the UDL framework can be extremely useful in reducing barriers to learning for students with diverse needs, including those with IEPs. However, applying the UDL framework will not completely relieve students of the need for individualized supports or release educators from their responsibilities to plan and implement supports for students. Even the most enthusiastic proponents of the UDL framework have unequivocally asserted that UDL is not a panacea for all of the educational barriers encountered by students with IEPs (see Nelson, 2021). Therefore, applying UDL goes hand in hand with supports planning, but it does not supplant the need to plan individualized supports.

The ways in which UDL principles can be applied to the design of instructional goals, methods, materials, and assessments to build in flexible paths for learning is explained in greater detail Chapter 7. The chapter also includes practical steps that educators can take to immediately make their schools and classroom more universally designed. For now, it is sufficient to highlight that applying the UDL framework to expand the capacity of general education classrooms to educate a more diverse array of students is essential to implementing the SSPP. When efforts are made to apply the UDL framework to schools and classrooms, it is likely that identifying and arranging specific supports for individual learners will proceed more efficiently and effectively.

Key Ideas From This Chapter

- The SSPP provides educators with a means to carefully consider how supports can be arranged to enable students with IEPs to access general education curricula and classrooms. It is structured around three overarching questions: *What to teach? How to teach?* and *How to promote participation?* Applying the SSPP generates three categories of supports: curricular adaptations, instructional supports, and participation supports.
- UDL goes hand in hand with planning individualized supports for students. The more educators incorporate the principles of UDL in their classrooms, the less challenging it will be to identify and arrange individualized supports.

Questions for Discussion

1. The SSPP directs users to move through the following problem-solving sequence:

    - First, ask "What to teach?" to identify curricular adaptations.
    - Second, ask "How to teach?" to identify instructional supports.
    - Third, ask "How to promote participation?" to identify participation supports.

Is it important to ask and answer these three questions in this sequence? If so, why does this sequence make the most sense? If not, why would it make better sense to ask the questions (and uncover the needed supports) in a different order?

2. How would you respond to a teacher colleague who suggests that schools should not have to apply UDL principles nor identify and arrange individualized supports because:

    > We are responsible for getting through everything in our grade-level curriculum. We can't put in all the extra time and effort it takes to create individualized supports or to apply the UDL framework for just a few kids. Isn't that what special education is for?

3

Assess for Success

Using Assessments to Inform Supports Planning

What assessment information is useful to IEP teams planning supports for students being educated in general education classrooms? To answer this question, a distinction needs to be made concerning assessment information that is "absolutely essential," "useful," and "probably not particularly useful." By and large, there is little assessment information that is *absolutely essential* to have before efforts are undertaken to support a student with an IEP in the general education classroom. This does not mean that students who have been educated in separate settings should be placed into a general education classroom without any thought or communication among educators. However, elevating any type of assessment activity as a prerequisite to inclusive education carries the danger of allowing educators to dawdle. The wisdom underlying the adage "If you want to learn to swim, jump in the water" is applicable to inclusive education. A school staff aspiring to become proficient in inclusive education should start by including students with IEPs in general education classrooms.

In sharp contrast, a "probably not particularly useful" assessment does not provide much insight for purposes of planning supports. For instance, it is unlikely that traditional diagnostic information collected for purposes of determining eligibility for special education services will be of much practical value for planning supports. Collecting and reviewing information from norm-referenced assessments that were not designed to explicitly focus on measuring student support needs will not be a good use of time. Assessment that documents deficits (deficit-based assessments) may serve a necessary gatekeeping function for services, but won't offer much insight regarding supports that a student needs. Although the extent of a student's deficits have a reciprocal relationship to intensity of support needed, understanding student deficit areas is not the same as understanding student support needs (Thompson et al., 2009).

Finally, "useful" assessment information is that which informs the planning, implementation, and evaluation of supports without the pretense of being absolutely essential to have before students are placed in general education classrooms. Useful supports assessment involves collecting information that informs decision-making about how to best support a student. Assessment information with direct relevance to maximizing learning and participation in the general education classroom will be valued by educators because the information is actionable. In this chapter, five types of useful assessments are identified along with ways that educators can apply the information that is gleaned from them.

Classroom Assessment

As was discussed in Chapter 1, the SSPP is grounded on a social–ecological model of disability where disability is understood as a state of functioning due to a mismatch between a person and their environment. Because of the importance of the environment to the SSPP, collecting information to better understand the demands of the general education classroom is every bit as important as assessing the characteristics of a student. The form shown in Figure 3.1 can be used to gather an initial overview of the characteristics and demands associated with classroom activities and settings. It is similar to other classroom inventories published elsewhere in the professional literature since the late 1980s (Wadsworth & Knight, 1999; Janney & Snell, 2013). IEP teams may find that it is best used as a template to create a more specific classroom assessment tailored to the context of their schools and classrooms.

The form in Figure 3.1 was developed to provide a structure for educators to compile a broad overview of the classroom context in which the student with the IEP will be operating. Although this template assumes that students are currently receiving instruction in the general education classroom, it can easily be modified for students who have not yet started attending general education classrooms.

FIGURE 3.1 General Education Classroom/Instruction Assessment

Section 1: Contextual Information

Target Student: *Olivia*
Grade: *3rd*
General Education Teacher: *Ms. Wilkerson*
Special Education Teacher: *Mr. Barker*
Number of Students in Classroom: *22*
Number of Adults and Roles: *1 general education teacher; 1 paraprofessional*

Focus of class:

☒ Reading and Language Arts
☐ Writing
☐ Social Studies
☐ Science
☐ Other, please describe: ____________________

Describe the physical arrangement of the classroom and/or the features of remote instruction if it is used:
The classroom consists of six round tables where three to four students complete independent and small group work. Currently, Olivia sits with two other peers and the paraprofessional. Ms. Wilkerson's desk is placed at the back of the classroom where she can easily monitor students during independent and small-group work time. There is a laptop cart and SMART board at the front of the classroom. Students access the laptop cart multiple times a day to complete various reading activities. The SMART board is primarily used for whole-group lessons and to display ClassDojo points.

Describe the individuals who were in close proximity to the target student in the classroom:
☒ Peers
☐ Special education personnel (e.g., paraprofessional/teaching assistant)
☒ General education teacher
☐ Other
☐ Not applicable—target student not present or instruction to all class members is remote

continued

FIGURE 3.1 *continued*

Describe the class-wide behavior-management supports:
Ms. Wilkerson uses ClassDojo to award points to students for demonstrating the school-wide behavioral expectations (Be safe, Be respectful, Be responsible). Once students accumulate a specific number of points, they earn a reward from the prize bin.

Section 2: Student Interactions

	CLASSMATES	TARGET STUDENT
Frequency of interactions	The peers at Olivia's table interacted frequently (over 30 times).	Olivia interacted with her peers once and with the paraprofessional over 10 times.
Topic of interactions (task related or social)	Olivia's peers were primarily engaged in off-topic conversations (e.g., plans for the upcoming winter break, what they did over the weekend). Occasionally, peers would ask Ms. Wilkerson questions about the reading activities.	The one time Olivia interacted with her peers was to greet them when she arrived in the classroom. Interactions with the paraprofessional were specifically related to the reading activities.
Form(s) of communication used by target student during interactions	Speech	Communication app on iPad

Section 3: Classroom Activities

	What are the activities and tasks in which students are expected to participate?	What are students doing during these activities and tasks?	How is the target student currently participating?	What current supports are in place for the target student?
Whole group	Ms. Wilkerson presents key concepts of the lesson and directions for small group- and/or independent-work activities on the SMART board. She also reads aloud to the entire class while asking comprehension questions about the stories' characters to check for student understanding.	Most students appear to be engaged as evidenced by their responses to questions and bodies facing in the direction of the teacher.	Olivia does not respond to questions posed by the teacher but appears to be engaged otherwise.	No supports observed.
Small group	Students work in small groups to describe characters (e.g., traits, motivations) in assigned stories.	Most students are collaboratively writing notes in a brainstorming document online.	Using the communication app on the iPad, Olivia is working with the paraprofessional to answer comprehension questions about the characters in the stories.	Paraprofessional support; different learning activity (responding to comprehension questions).

continued

FIGURE 3.1 *continued*

	What are the activities and tasks in which students are expected to participate?	What are students doing during these activities and tasks?	How is the target student currently participating?	What current supports are in place for the target student?
Independent work	Independent reading of assigned stories.	Most students are independently reading assigned stories online.	Olivia listens to the story being read to her by the paraprofessional.	Paraprofessional support; same learning activity with the accommodation of having the story read aloud.
Other	Not applicable	Not applicable	Not applicable	Not applicable

Student Interest/Preference Assessment

Going hand in hand with assessing classroom demands is the need to assess the characteristics of the student. Student assessment can cover many areas, but should always include efforts to obtain a good understanding of a student's interests and preferences. This information will provide insights into ways that students prefer to be supported, their strengths, and what motivates them.

A library search of the professional literature using a variety of descriptive terms that are related to the topic of assessing student interests and preferences (including student interviews, interest inventories, preference assessments) generated an expansive list of peer-reviewed articles that spanned multiple decades. The vast majority of these articles, however, were focused on specialized topics, such as identifying living-arrangement preferences after high school for the purpose of transition planning (see Kellems & Morningstar, 2010) or assessing preferences for reinforcement when planning interventions based on principles of applied behavior analysis (see Carr et al., 2000).

Many family-interview protocols are available that allow for the participation of the student. These protocols often include items where student "likes and dislikes" or "reinforcers" are identified (see Giangreco et al., 2011). A simple

Google search for student preference assessments similarly provided an eclectic assortment of professional resources focused on developing preference assessments (see Chazin & Ledford, 2016) as well as practitioner-created interview scripts and checklists for use with students. Some of these were free to download and others carried a price tag. Finally, interviews and surveys can be distributed to teachers, family members, and even peers to gather information about what other same-aged students prefer (Parrish et al., 2012).

Although good ideas can emerge from looking through existing student preference and interest assessments, a search for a definitive student interview form will likely yield diminishing returns. Students are so diverse in terms of their characteristics (age, interests, communication competencies) and there is an endless range of purposes for which these tools can be tailored. Educators may find that the best course of action might be to develop their own core set of interview or survey questions. Key to this end is to focus on gathering information to better understand (a) ways in which a student would prefer to be supported and (b) what might motivate a student. Figure 3.2 provides a starting point for educator teams wishing to develop their own assessment protocol.

When assessing student interests and preferences, it is critical that educators attempt to have a genuine conversation with the student and to build rapport. A willingness to venture "off script" based on the way the conversation evolves is advisable. Additionally, educators conducting interviews with students should consider personalizing questions based on what they know about their student's personality and background, and the way in which the student is comfortable interacting with adults. Finally, it is important to remember that preferences change over time. Therefore a preference assessment should always be considered ongoing; it is critical to attend to how student interests evolve and useful to periodically revisit these types of assessments to assure information is current (McConaughy, 2013).

Student–Classroom Fit Assessment

According to IDEA, a student's IEP must include a statement of the child's present levels of academic achievement and functional performance (PLAAFP). The most commonly used acronym for the PLAAFP statement is called the PLOP (present levels of performance). On IEPs, the PLOP is intended to provide a basis for setting instructional goals as well as for documenting progress from

FIGURE 3.2 Student Interest and Preference Assessment Interview

1. What is your favorite thing about school?

Seeing friends and holidays.

2. What do you not like so much about school?

Homework. When kids make fun of me. I don't like the bus rides.

3. What are some of your hobbies or interests?

Video games. Collecting Pokémon cards. I also like making maps.

4. Do you ever have problems at school with teachers or classmates or at certain times of the day? Tell me about these.

Some of the kids can be mean to me during recess and before school on the bus. I tell the teachers and bus drivers, but they don't do anything about it.

5. What kind of rewards would you like to earn for good behavior or good school work?

I don't need to be the best in the class, I just want to get good grades and pass. I like the stickers and other stuff in Mrs. Clay's prize box, but I don't need them to try my best.

6. In school we learn a lot of different things and do a lot of different activities. I am going to ask you to rate some things we do at school from 1 to 3, with a "1" meaning you really don't like it at all; a "2" meaning you don't like it too much, but also don't really dislike it; and a "3" meaning that this is something you enjoy at school.

Subject/activity	1	2	3	Subject/activity	1	2	3
Having a story read to me and the other students				Learning about social studies (like history)			
Practicing reading in small groups				Working on project with a small group of students			
Practicing reading in large groups				Writing activities			
Reading silently by myself				Art projects			

Subject/activity	1	2	3	Subject/activity	1	2	3
Having a teacher explain how to do a math problem	☹	**😐**	☺	Participating in PE	**☹**	😐	☺
Working on math in small groups	☹	😐	**☺**	Working on computers	☹	😐	**☺**
Working on math in large groups	☹	**😐**	☺	Music class	**☹**	😐	☺
Working on math problems by myself	☹	**😐**	☺	Lunchtime	☹	**😐**	☺
Learning about science	☹	😐	**☺**	Hanging out with friends during free time	☹	**😐**	☺

7. Are there any activities that you wish you had a chance to participate in but you don't have the opportunity?
I wish I could be part of Drum Club after school. They told me I couldn't because I didn't know how to play the drums, but I think I can.
8. Is there anything else you would like to tell me about how you're feeling about school?
The teachers are nice.

---

year to year. It often takes the form of a brief synopsis of a student's academic achievement as measured by standardized tests and/or in relation to grade-level expectations. For example:

> Chris's scores on the California Reading Achievement Test indicate he is reading 2 years below grade level, with relatively higher scores in comprehension and a relatively lower scores in decoding. His KeyMath3 scores indicate that achievement in mathematics is well below grade level across all subareas.

For the purpose of supports planning, PLOP summative statements found on IEPs are unlikely to be very helpful, but this could vary based on a school district's approach to IEP development. What is needed for the purpose of supports planning is to gather information that relates the student's current functioning in relation to classroom demands and expectations. There is a need to (a) identify where there is and is not a good alignment between the classroom and the student so appropriate supports can be identified and (b) identify a student's relative strengths on which to build supports.

It is critical for educators to acknowledge that relative strengths can occur in the same domain as relative weaknesses. For instance, take the case where a student's communication skills are not fully commensurate with the interactions that occur in the classroom due to the student's difficulties in expressive and receptive language. Being aware of this student's relative limitation in communication skills would be important when teachers provide oral instructions to the student during the school day. This would be true whether they be individual instructions or group instructions. Oral instructions for this student will need to be more explicitly communicated (using simpler sentences and allowing the student time to process) compared to most other students. Therefore, educators providing more explicit oral instructions is a type of support for this student.

However, it is just as important to recognize this student's relative communication strengths. For instance, noting that this student was friendly, outgoing, looked for the best in others, and seemed to bring out the best in others during personal interactions is as useful to developing a support plan as the student's relative limitations in expressive and receptive communication skills. Because of relative strengths in social communication, peer supports may be a particularly valuable support strategy for this student. Therefore, peer support to assure the student understands oral instructions could be another type of support for this student, one that builds on the student's relative strengths as much as it compensates for relative limitations.

As with the student preference form presented in the prior section, educators are encouraged to edit Figure 3.3 to meet their information needs when assessing student skills in relation to classroom expectations. As can be seen, this form is intended to provide a practical description of the student's current skills juxtaposed against an overview of classroom expectations. This format allows educators to identify and compare important discrepancies between the two. It is structured around curricular areas and includes key aspects of classroom participation, but could be just as easily structured around a general education classroom daily schedule. For example, one could substitute "Times of the day" for "Participation & curricular areas" in the first column of the form.

This form can be considered a means to assess PLOP, classroom expectations, and support needs assessment at the same time. The first column focuses on describing a student's current skills and thus is conceptually consistent with information included in a PLOP statement. The second column focuses on classroom expectations and therefore is a type of classroom assessment. The third column focuses on identifying the fit between classroom expectations and student functioning, and therefore provides an approach to identify student support needs. As alluded to previously, evidence of a chronic mismatch between the person and the settings/activities of their environment is an indication of unmet support needs. The information gleaned from this skills assessment can inform ways to adapt classroom settings and learning activities and make them accessible to all learners. It can also identify personalized supports a student needs to fully benefit from general education classroom instruction.

Functional Behavioral Assessment

Some students may require supports to address their behavioral needs. In many instances, such as the case presented in Figure 3.3, existing school-wide or small-group behavioral supports may be sufficient to address these needs. However, when a student engages in persistent challenging behavior that significantly interferes with learning or social opportunities, the IEP team should consider conducting an assessment (or a series of assessments) to understand why challenging behavior is occurring so that appropriate behavioral supports can be identified. Assessment that is focused on understanding the purpose or function of challenging behavior is most commonly referred to as functional behavior assessment (FBA). When conducting an FBA, the IEP team should keep in mind that challenging behavior can serve a number of functions or purposes for the student. For example, challenging behavior can be maintained by escape from undesirable or difficult activity. For example, a student who disrupts a classroom during math instruction and is sent to the principal's office as a consequence may have learned that disruptive behavior provides a ticket for avoiding math class. Challenging behavior can also be maintained by access to preferred toys or activities, attention from peers or adults, and/or access to or escape

FIGURE 3.3 Student Skills in Relation to Classroom Expectations (8-year-old in third grade)

Participation & curricular areas	Description of current skills & strengths	
Communication	*Articulation issues due to unresolved cleft palate; easily frustrated when not understood; hesitant to communicate at times; strong vocabulary and understanding of language; volume can be very loud or very soft.*	
Socialization	*Relatively good interactions with peers on a one-to-one basis; very hesitant to interact in large groups, especially noisy groups; may act out when fearing that peers are teasing or rejecting in some way.*	
Executive functioning	*Can become easily frustrated; can say "no" as a first response when asked to try something new, sometimes with verbal aggression, physical aggression and self-harm. When experiencing success and becomes "into it", shows strong perseverance.*	
Academic subjects (reading, writing, math, science, social studies)	*Reading is a relative strength area, as his skills are at or just slightly below grade-level expectations including strong comprehension skills (also, he reports that he enjoys reading). His writing skills are below grade-level expectations, and he is easily overwhelmed by writing tasks as evidenced by tearing up his paper or scribbling or drawing. In math, he is able to complete the exact steps of different computations when they are taught, but rarely recalls the steps later. He has not demonstrated understanding of foundational math concepts, such as grasping the magnitude of differences in quantity. Mental arithmetic is very difficult for him and he does best when allowed to calculate on his fingers, paper, or with a calculator. He is curious about the content taught in other subjects (social studies, science) and responds best when content is taught as a story (the story of a historical event or person, the story of how something in nature works).*	

	Description of classroom expectations	Where supports might be needed to address potential discrepancies
	Expectation of oral communication and reading to exhibit knowledge and understanding of subject; small-group work in which group communication is expected; social communication also critical to small-group work.	*Support for (a) oral summations in small or large groups; (b) multiple ways to express self, especially understanding of subject; (c) educating educators and peers about speech idiosyncrasies.*
	Participation in whole-group activities such as games to reinforce information and physical activities; peer time at end of day as well as at indoor and outdoor recess.	*Support for (a) peer interactions, especially in large groups; (b) recognizing when choosing not to participate is and is not an option; (c) educating teachers to notice when peer interactions are frustrating and deteriorating; (d) instruction to improve social skills.*
	The classroom-management system focuses on respect for others and self; classroom rules and routines are explicit and provide structure for student self-management; students can go to a calming area in back of classroom (teachers can also send students there).	*Supports for (a) understanding classroom rules and routines; (b) handling frustration in a productive way, including ways to de-escalate (e.g., visual reminders inside desk or a secret signal from teacher); (c) opportunities for breaks; (d) getting off to a good start on assignments to build his strength in perseverance on tasks.*
	Reading workshop approach is used in the classroom and requires discussion with teachers and peers, as well as making choices of how to express understanding of material. Short writing assignments are embedded in practically all academic instruction and introduced throughout the school day, and students are expected to try their best to respond to the writing prompts. Math is taught daily using teacher instruction and computer-aided instruction, and the curriculum is very sequential (current learning closely tied to past learning). Other academic content is most often taught through whole-class introduction of topic, small-group-project work, and individual work on assignments to demonstrate learning.	*Supports for (a) oral reading or expression will be needed (perhaps recording self in private for teacher or in hallway with teacher); (b) writing assignments—he will need more than just the writing prompt given to all students in order to get started on the assignments and to organize his ideas; strong and immediate reinforcement for completing these assignments may also be needed because they will make him anxious and he likely will not want to do them; modifications will also be needed; (c) math assignments—he will need support to complete assignments on his own, and require some additional instruction in order to understand the concepts behind the operations (for instance, he can learn the steps of long division, but needs to understand the concept of dividing a whole part into separate parts); (d) for other subjects, he will require some additional monitoring to stay engaged.*

continued

FIGURE 3.3 *continued*

Participation & curricular areas	Description of current skills & strengths	
Nonacademic subjects (music, art, PE)	*These are not subjects that he particularly enjoys, mostly because he is insecure about his performance (i.e., he reports that he is not good at it). For instance, the physical structure of his mouth, throat, and lungs make it difficult for him to produce volume and sounds needed in music.*	

from sensory experiences. As such, the goal of conducting an FBA is to generate a hypothesis about the behavioral function so that supports which directly address or match the behavioral function can be identified (O'Neill et al., 2015). If the FBA outcomes suggest that a student's disruptive behavior is maintained by adult attention, for example, the IEP team might identify strategies to teach the student an alternative and appropriate way to obtain attention (such as raising hand during class) and strategies to prevent the disruptive behavior from occurring (for instance, scheduling more teacher attention during times when the student tends to engage in the behavior).

The FBA process requires teams to carefully examine the relationship between challenging behavior and the environment. This can be done both directly and indirectly. The most common indirect FBA methods include behavior-rating scales and structured interviews. These methods do not involve observing the student but instead require gathering information from respondents who are familiar with the student. Respondents can include general educators, special educators, paraprofessionals, family members, or the student whose behavior is being assessed. If challenging behavior occurs in general education classrooms, it will be especially important to collect information from

Description of classroom expectations	Where supports might be needed to address potential discrepancies
Participation and effort are expected of all students, but there are not strict standards for performance. Options to do some art projects with peers are occasionally offered.	*Supports for (a) understanding that he is not in competition with peers in these subjects, and accepting that students excel in different ways would help him benefit and enjoy these classes; (b) educating peers that it is important to be sensitive to the feelings of others who may be struggling in these subject areas; (c) providing choices on how to complete assignments and participate in activities (e.g., allowing students to choose if they wish to cut out their own shapes or use shapes that are precut to create a picture; allowing instruments such as rhythm sticks to participate in a group song); (d) Strategic grouping in small-group activities to provide better opportunities for success.*

adults who are present in those settings. But, teams should also consider information from others who can speak to the student's success in other settings. A number of rating scales are available that can provide the team with insight into the behavioral function of challenging behavior. For instance, Paclawsky et al.'s (2002) *Questions about Behavioral Functioning* provides an excellent starting point. Likewise, several interview protocols are available, including *Functional Assessment Checklist for Teachers and Staff* (March et al., 2000), and *Functional Assessment Interview* (O'Neill et al., 2015). These methods can assist the team in gathering the following information: (a) environmental events that predict when challenging behavior will occur (i.e., antecedents), (b) an operational description of the behavior, and (c) consequences that maintain challenging behavior. Although these indirect methods are helpful in providing the team with preliminary information about behavioral function, they should be conducted in conjunction with direct assessment methods.

Direct FBA methods involve directly observing the student in order to further develop the hypothesized behavioral function identified through the indirect FBA. Again, the purpose of directly observing the student is to understand the antecedents that predict challenging behavior and the consequences

FIGURE 3.4 ABC Chart Example

Student: *Jamie* Observer: *Ms. Yates (paraprofessional)* Date: 11/12/22

Setting: *Math class*

Observation time/routine: *10:00–10:20 a.m./independent work*

Time	Antecedent	Behavior	Consequence	Notes
10:00	Teacher hands out math worksheet.	Jamie says, "I hate math. It's so hard!"	Teacher says, "Try your best."	Jamie drew pictures on worksheet until 10:05.
10:05	Teacher says, "Keep working, Jamie."	Jamie places head on table and says, "I don't know how to do this."	Teacher says nothing and walks away from Jamie.	Jamie kept head down until 10:07.
10:07	Teacher says, "You need to sit up and do your work."	Jamie walks across the room and sits on the bean bag chair in the reading corner.	Teaching gestures to Jamie's math worksheet.	Jamie sits on the bean bag chair for 2 minutes before returning to seat.
10:12	Teacher says, "Keep working, Jamie."	Jamie says, "I don't understand this stuff. It's hard!" and pounds both fists against the table.	Teacher says, "Just try your best."	Jamie stares at the worksheet until 10:15.
10:15	Other students turn in their worksheets to the teacher.	Jamie rolls eyes and leans back in chair.	Teacher says nothing. Students continue to turn in their worksheets.	Jamie sits in chair without working until the end of the class period.

that maintain it. Although there are different types of direct observation protocols, one of the most common is the antecedent-behavior-consequence (ABC) chart in which the observer records each behavioral incident and the antecedents and consequences specific to each incident. Figure 3.4 provides an example of a completed ABC chart for a student who engages in nonparticipation during math class.

By closely examining data from this ABC chart, team members can identify patterns across the recorded incidents to generate or update a hypothesis about the behavioral function. In this example, data suggest that the student's challenging behavior is maintained by momentary escape from the math task. In other words, when the student does not follow the teacher's directions, he is usually able to avoid completing the math assignment for a few minutes. Once the team has identified the behavioral function through FBA, behavioral supports planning can begin. It should be noted that in cases where challenging behavior is dangerous or the FBA does not produce a clear hypothesis regarding the reason why the problem behavior is occurring, the team should collaborate with a professional who has expertise in behavioral assessment and intervention, such as a school psychologist who has special training in applied behavior analysis (ABA). The goal of an ABA collaboration is to develop a plan of action to assess the challenging behavior in an ethical and effective manner.

Standardized Support Needs Assessment

The assessments reviewed so far in this chapter are helpful when planning supports based on information that is gathered about a student's specific needs within a particular context. It is also useful to get broader, more comprehensive information on student support needs that is applicable to contexts that are beyond the student's immediate classroom experiences. Such information can be gathered through standardized support needs assessment instruments.

Thompson et al. (2009) defined support needs as a psychological construct reflecting "the pattern and intensity of support a person requires to participate in activities associated with typical human functioning" (p. 135). A "psychological construct" is a label for something within a person that cannot be directly observed but that affects their behavior and functioning. Through observing multiple behaviors, the construct is inferred. For example, "anxiety" is a psychological construct. If someone is expressing that they are very worried or concerned about something, is hyperventilating, has an increased heart rate, and can't concentrate on anything other than their current worry, these behaviors are evidence that the person is experiencing a high level of anxiety. Support needs, like other psychological constructs, such as intelligence, motivation, empathy, and self-esteem, are documented by observing numerous behavioral markers in combination. Just like more widely known constructs, people's support needs can be relatively high or low in terms of intensity and quantity, but cannot be measured by a single item or observation.

Since the early 2000s, there have been multiple scales developed that purport to measure the support needs of children and adults. Thompson and DeSpain (2016) reviewed eight support needs assessment scales for which psychometric information (i.e., results of data analysis that provide indication of assessment reliability and validity) had been published in peer-reviewed literature. Reviews of professional literature by Arias et al. (2020) and Vilaesca et al. (2017) did not uncover any new scales since Thompson and DeSpain's 2016 review. Thompson and DeSpain noted that the eight scales varied considerably in amount and quality of published psychometric information, as well as in other types of information that were available about them (e.g., sample protocols, reports that summarize results).

The only standardized scale that has been targeted specifically to assess the support needs of children below the age of 16 is the Supports Intensity Scale-Children's Version or SIS-C (Thompson et al., 2016). Therefore, because this book is about planning and implementing supports for students in K–12 schools, this instrument will be highlighted here. Interested readers are encouraged, however, to compare and contrast different support needs assessment scales as they vary considerably.

The SIS-C

The SIS-C, originally developed for English-language users, has also been translated into Spanish, Catalan, Italian, Dutch, Icelandic, and Portuguese. Both the English version and translated versions have shown strong psychometric properties (Thompson et al., 2018). The scale consists of two sections. Section 1 documents extra supports that are needed to manage 19 different medical conditions and 13 separate problem behaviors. Section 2 consists of 61 items, the ratings from which generate standard scores that indicate a student's relative intensity of support needs compared to other students with intellectual disability and developmental disabilities (IDD) of the same age.

The standardization sample of the SIS-C was composed of over 4,000 children ages 5 to 16 with IDD. Its norm-referenced scores must be interpreted based on the age and disability groups represented in the standardization sample. However, in terms of traditional psychometric indicators of reliability and validity, the SIS-C has proven to be quite robust in regard to children from different disability populations, for instance, children with autism spectrum disorder (ASD) without intellectual disability, as well as children with a primary disability of physical disability. There is evidence that SIS-C is also valid for measuring the support needs of children slightly older and younger than the 5–16 age range (Shogren et al., 2016; Shogren, Wehmeyer, & Thompson, 2017; Thompson et al., 2018; Thompson et al., 2020). Regardless of age or disability diagnosis, the SIS-C can provide an overview of the nature and intensity of the extra support a student needs to fully participate in a wide range of life activities at school, within the community, and at home.

Exceptional Medical and Behavioral Needs

Of particular interest to educators may be the sections of the SIS-C that are focused on identifying extra supports needed due to medical conditions or challenging behaviors. Table 3.1 lists these the items along with brief descriptions. Each exceptional medical and behavioral item is rated on a 3-point scale: 0 = no extra support needed because the medical condition or challenging behavior is not an issue for the student; 1 = some support required (e.g., monitoring or occasional assistance); and 2 = extensive support needed (e.g., regular assistance required to assure the health and safety of the student and others).

It was stated earlier in the chapter that most assessment information is not absolutely essential to collect before undertaking efforts to support a student with an IEP in a general education classroom. Some of the items in Table 3.1, however, may be an exception to this rule. Although the SIS-C only provides a quick screening of a student for the presence of medical conditions and challenging behaviors that require extra support, if a student needs support for medical vulnerabilities such as "protection from infectious diseases due to immune system impairment" or for challenging behaviors such as "prevention of suicide," it would be important for educators to know about these support needs right away. Some medical conditions and challenging behaviors will influence the types and intensities of supports a student requires throughout a school day. For instance, providing the correct supports to "protect from infectious diseases" and "prevent suicide" could literally be a matter of life or death.

TABLE 3.1 Exceptional Medical and Behavioral Supports Needs Assessed on the SIS-C

EXCEPTIONAL MEDICAL NEEDS	EXCEPTIONAL BEHAVIORAL NEEDS
Inhalation or oxygen therapy Needs a nebulizer, oxygen, and/or CPAP	**Prevention of emotional outbursts** Screams, curses, throws objects, threatens physical violence, demeans others, cries excessively, and so on (extreme incidents, not just becoming angry)
Postural drainage Needs positioning to help drain mucus in the lungs	**Prevention of assaults or injuries to others** Hits, punches, kicks, bites, or intentionally harms others
Chest PT Needs chest physical therapy to help with drainage of secretions (e.g., chest percussion for cystic fibrosis)	**Prevention of property destruction** Defaces property, breaks windows, damages furniture, sets fires, and so on (e.g., fire setting, breaking furniture)
Suctioning Needs suctioning of secretions (e.g., suctioning a tracheotomy)	**Prevention of stealing** Steals/takes other people's property, shoplifts, and so on (deliberately or otherwise)
Oral stimulation or jaw positioning Needs physical assistance or oral stimulation to help with feeding	**Prevention of self-injury** Engages in head banging, eye gouging, skin picking, cutting, and so on
Tube feeding Needs a nasogastric or gastrostomy tube for feeding	**Prevention of pica** Ingestion of inedible substances such as paper
Parenteral feeding Uses an intravenous tube for feeding	**Prevention of suicide attempts** Attempts to hurt oneself with the intention of suicide
Turning or positioning Needs assistance with repositioning or turning in chair or bed to prevent sores	**Prevention of emotional outbursts** Screams, curses, throws objects, threatens physical violence, demeans others, cries excessively, and so on (extreme incidents, not just becoming angry)

EXCEPTIONAL MEDICAL NEEDS	EXCEPTIONAL BEHAVIORAL NEEDS
Dressing of open wound(s) Needs assistance with the cleaning and dressing of open sores	**Prevention of assaults or injuries to others** Hits, punches, kicks, bites, or intentionally harms others
Protection from infectious diseases due to immune system impairment Needs precautions to prevent infectious disease due to weakened immune system (e.g., HIV, chemotherapy, cancer, hepatitis, multiple sclerosis)	**Prevention of sexual aggression** Attempts nonconsensual sexual behavior with others; could include violent and aggressive sexual assault
Seizure management Needs assistance with seizure precautions and management (e.g., helmet, bite block, controlled environment, timing seizures, PRN prescriptions)	**Prevention of non-aggressive but inappropriate sexual behavior** Exposes self in public places, inappropriate touching or gesturing, masturbates in public places, exhibitionism, stalking, and so on
Dialysis Uses peritoneal dialysis or hemodialysis	**Prevention of wandering** Runs away, wanders off with the risk of getting lost or potentially injured
Ostomy care Needs assistance with ostomy (e.g., colostomy, tracheotomy, or any other stoma)	**Prevention of substance abuse** Engages in excessive consumption of alcohol, misuses prescription medication, uses illegal drugs or other toxic substances (e.g., sniffing glue, paint)
Lifting and/or transferring Needs assistance for lifting and transferring to and from chair, bed, and so on	**Maintaining mental health treatments** Needs assistance to comply with prescribed mental health treatments (e.g., taking psychotropic medication, interacting and working with mental health specialists)
Eating disorders Needs assistance to manage eating, including the refusal to eat	**Prevention of truancy** Prevention of missing school for reasons other than health or family death

continued

TABLE 3.1 *continued*

EXCEPTIONAL MEDICAL NEEDS	EXCEPTIONAL BEHAVIORAL NEEDS
Therapy services Needs assistance in implementing recommendations regarding therapies	**Other(s)—List all that apply:** Needs assistance to prevent or manage any exceptional challenging behaviors that are not accounted for in the previous items. Some other behaviors to consider may include (but not limited to) obsessive behaviors, anxiety-related behaviors, and food-seeking behaviors
Allergies Needs assistance to avoid triggers for allergic reactions, and managing allergic reactions	
Diabetes management Needs assistance managing diabetes, including monitoring blood sugar levels and administering insulin shots if needed	
Other(s) List all that apply: Needs assistance to manage any exceptional medical conditions that are not accounted for in the previous items	

Note. Adapted from: Thompson, J. R., Wehmeyer, M. L., Hughes, C., Shogren, K. A., Seo, H., Little, T. D., Schalock, R. L., Realon, R. E., Copeland, S. R., Patton, J. R., Polloway, E. A., Shelden, D., Tanis, A., & Tassé, M. J. (2016). *Supports Intensity Scale—Children's Version User's Manual* (p. 22, Table 3.1). American Association on Intellectual and Developmental Disabilities. © AAIDD. Used with permission.

Supports Needed to Participate in Daily Life Activities

Section 2 of the SIS-C is the standardized portion of the SIS-C. Each of the 61 items requires rating the extent of extra support that a student needs, which most other students the same age do not need, to successfully participate in a life activity. The life activities represented on the SIS-C are intended to have universal properties. That is, they were designed to be applicable across different age groups of childhood as well as cultural and geographic populations (Thompson et al., 2016). A few examples of SIS-C items are supports needed to use the toilet; move around the neighborhood and community; protect self from physical, verbal, and/or sexual abuse; make and keep friends; and communicate personal wants and needs.

It is important to highlight that the referent for all SIS-C items are community settings that are accessed and valued by the majority of the population. Examples include the general education classroom rather than a separate special education classroom, and a single-family home, or apartment in a residential neighborhood as opposed to a special residential facility for children with disabilities. If a student is not currently participating in such community environments, respondents are asked to envision the support that would be needed if the student were to be actively involved in such settings. This is the same for any life activity to which the student has not yet had an opportunity to participate (Thompson et al., 2016).

Although this might initially appear to introduce an untenable degree of subjectivity into the assessment, studies investigating the psychometric properties of the SIS-C have confirmed that the scales' reliability and validity is strong regardless of the extent of respondents' experiences in directly observing the student in specific settings and activities (Hagiwara et al., 2019). It is a requirement, however, for respondents to have known the child being assessed for at least 3 months and to have had recent opportunities to observe the child participating in one or more environments for several hours per setting. One advantage of envisioning students in activities in which they haven't yet participated is that it may serve to stretch people's imagination and thinking in regard to what is possible and achievable with the proper supports in place (Thompson et al., 2016).

SIS-C items are distributed across the following seven subscales: Home Life Activities; Community and Neighborhood Activities; School Participation Activities; School Learning Activities; Health and Safety Activities; Social Activities; and Advocacy Activities. For purposes of planning supports in school, educators are likely to be most interested in results from the School Participation Activities and School Learning Activities subscales. Table 3.2 lists items from these subscales along with brief descriptions. Each item is rated on three dimensions: (a) type of support (e.g., amount of physical assistance), (b) daily support time (hours and minutes devoted to support), and (c) frequency of support (how often support is needed). Each dimension is rated on a 0–4 scale with higher numbers indicating more-intense support needs. Thus, scores for each item can range from 0 (i.e., ratings for all three dimensions reflecting the lowest possible score) to 12 (i.e., ratings for each dimension reflecting the highest possible score). Averaged ratings across the three dimensions are used

TABLE 3.2 Items and Short Descriptions from SIS-C Subscales "C" and "D"

ITEM	SHORT DESCRIPTION
1. Being included in general education classrooms	Supports to participate in a general education classroom setting during structured as well as unstructured times.
2. Participating in activities in common school areas (e.g., playground, hallways, cafeteria)	Includes support to visit and use common school areas such as hallways (to get to and from classes and/or other business), playgrounds (for informal/unstructured play as well as organized activities that might be part of a class or cocurricular activity), and cafeterias.
3. Participating in cocurricular activities	Supports to participate in cocurricular activities, such as school clubs and teams.
4. Getting to school (includes transportation)	Supports to get to and from school.
5. Moving around within the school and transitioning between activities	Supports to move throughout the school during structured as well as unstructured parts of the school day and to transition between activities and classes.
6. Participating in large-scale test-taking activities required by state education systems	Supports to participate in state-level assessments, including high-stakes tests. Includes implementing reasonable accommodations and modifications.
7. Following classroom and school rules	Supports to participate in the school community without violating classroom or school rules.
8. Keeping track of personal belongings at school	Supports to manage personal belongings at school, such as getting and retrieving things from school lockers, keeping and spending lunch money, keeping possession of text books, etc.
9. Keeping track of schedule at school	Supports to be at the right place at the right time and engage in classroom routines (e.g., settling down and paying attention when teacher begins lesson).

ITEM	SHORT DESCRIPTION
10. Accessing grade-level curriculum content	Supports for participating in classes where content is tied to state- and district-curriculum standards and objectives.
11. Learning academic skills	Supports for learning content that is associated with core academic subjects such as reading, writing, mathematics, science, and social studies.
12. Learning and using metacognitive strategies	Supports to learn and use metacognitive strategies (i.e., use of mnemonics, learning strategies, test-taking and study strategies, clustering) to complete school assignments and promote independent learning and generalization of skills.
13. Completing academic tasks (e.g., time, quality, neatness, organizational skills)	Supports to complete assignments in core academic subjects such as reading, writing, mathematics, science, and social studies (e.g., teaching students to use specialized technology, determining reasonable accommodations).
14. Learning how to use and using educational materials, technologies, and tools	Supports to learn and use educational materials (e.g., worksheets, books), technologies (e.g., computers, calculators), and tools (e.g., scissors, pencils).
15. Learning how to use and using problem-solving and self-regulation strategies in the classroom	Supports to learn and use problem-solving and self-regulation strategies for social, personal, and behavioral purposes, such as time management, self-instruction, and self-reinforcement techniques, while in classroom settings.
16. Participating in classroom evaluations, such as tests	Supports to participate in evaluations within the general education classroom, for formative or summative assessments of learning goals and objectives.

continued

TABLE 3.2 ***continued***

ITEM	SHORT DESCRIPTION
17. Accessing the health and physical education curricula	Supports to learn health (e.g., how to prevent illnesses, basic first aid, healthy nutritional practices) and physical education (e.g., exercise, participation in individual or team sports or games) skills.
18. Completing homework assignments	Supports to identify homework assignments, organize materials and time to complete assignments, secure homework for submission, and submit homework to the proper teachers at school.

Note. Adapted from: Thompson, J. R., Wehmeyer, M. L., Hughes, C., Shogren, K. A., Seo, H., Little, T. D., Schalock, R. L., Realon, R. E., Copeland, S. R., Patton, J. R., Polloway, E. A., Shelden, D., Tanis, A., & Tassé, M. J. (2016). *Supports Intensity Scale—Children's Version User's Manual* (p. 24, Table 3.2). American Association on Intellectual and Developmental Disabilities. © AAIDD. Used with permission.

to calculate standard scores for each subscale and a composite standard score, the Support Needs Index (SNI). The SNI "reflects a child's overall intensity of support needs" (Thompson et al., 2016, p. 16).

The SIS-C is completed by interviewing at least two respondents who know the student very well. It is the interviewer's responsibility to integrate information from multiple respondents. A respondent can be a parent, relative, guardian, direct support staff, work supervisor, teacher, or any other person who knows the student being evaluated and understands the child's support needs. Additionally, the student with the disability whose support needs are being assessed may also serve as a respondent. The interviewer can also serve as one of the respondents but must be conscientious to make sure their opinions do not carry more weight than those of other respondents who provide information. Although two respondents are required for an SIS-C assessment, the goal is to incorporate the insights from as many people as needed to get accurate ratings. Oftentimes, different respondents will have better insights about supports needed in different settings. For instance, educators will have insights that parents do not have regarding supporting the student in school learning and participation activities, and parents will have insights that educators do not have in regard to supports needed by the student in home life activities.

When a SIS-C assessment is completed, the results should be used to inform support planning activities. Disseminating the results to parents as well as appropriate school personnel (*e.g.*, a case worker in situations where a child is the ward of the state) in a user-friendly report is likely to impact the usability of the information in a positive way. Appendix A is an example of a report that an educator can create to share assessment results and provides the type of additional explanation and reflection that makes completing a SIS-C assessment worthwhile.

Key Ideas From This Chapter

- Useful supports assessment involves collecting information that provides answers to questions about supporting students in ways that maximize their learning and participation in general education classrooms. If an assessment activity or scale doesn't contribute to better decision-making, then it isn't relevant for planning supports. There are five types of assessments that are useful for the purpose of informing supports planning.
- Classroom assessment to gain an overview of the physical, behavioral, social, and learning demands inherent to being a student in a classroom;
- Student preference and interest assessment to understand ways in which a student would prefer to be supported and factors that might motivate a student to do their best work;
- Student–classroom fit assessment to identify where there is and is not a good alignment between the classroom and the student, and to identify supports that can compensate for student vulnerabilities as well as build on student strengths;
- Functional behavioral assessment to provide a structured data-gathering process to plan behavior supports to be used at school;
- Standardized support needs assessment to gain a comprehensive perspective of student support needs applicable to contexts within and beyond the student's classroom experiences.

Questions for Discussion

1. In this chapter, it is stated that "Supports assessment involves collecting information that answers important questions and informs decision-making." Provide examples of one or more important questions that (a) classroom assessment, (b) student interest and preference assessment, (c) student–classroom fit assessment, (d) functional behavioral assessment, and (e) standardized support needs assessment might answer.
2. Appendix A provides an example of an Educator Generated SIS-C Supports Needs Report as a means to share standardized support needs assessment information with family members. What are some other ways educators might share results from assessments with family members and among educators?

4

Curricular Adaptations

The Power of Knowing What to Teach and What Students Will Learn

In Chapter 2, the Systematic Supports Planning Process (SSPP) was introduced as a supports-based approach to inclusive education. It provides educators a process to plan and arrange individualized supports that are aligned with a student's pattern and intensity of support needs. As previously discussed, the SSPP structure asks educators to answer the overarching questions *What to teach? How to teach?* and *How to promote participation?* This chapter is focused on answering the *What to teach?* question. Determining what to teach requires setting priorities for student learning and identifying ways in which the standard curriculum should be modified to align with a student's needs. "Curricular adaptations" are defined as any adjustments made to the general education curriculum to enhance a student's learning. The goal is to make the general education curriculum accessible and to incorporate additional content that is important for a student to learn.

This chapter will identify when curricular adaptations are needed and how to implement them. It begins with a discussion of curriculum and how educators can identify opportunities to teach students content and skills associated with prioritized learning goals. It covers the relationship between curricular adaptations and IEP goals. The importance of addressing the learning standards that drive instruction in general education classrooms is discussed. The chapter concludes with guidance on prioritizing learning goals that fall outside the general education curriculum.

The Multiple Layers of a Curriculum

Understanding what comprises any type of curriculum is analogous to peeling back the layers of an onion. What may seem relatively straightforward at first glance is actually multilayered and nuanced. Dictionaries define curriculum as a set of courses offered by an educational institution or within an area of specialization (https://www.dictionary.com/browse/curriculum; https://www.merriam-webster.com/dictionary/curriculum). Although perceiving the curriculum as a vessel for courses is not necessarily incorrect, course titles and sequences only impart a surface understanding of what is being taught to students.

Courses and course structures provide the means to organize content; therefore, it is the content that gets targeted for teaching and learning that is the essence of a curriculum. Focusing on content taught rather than courses offered introduces a vast layer of complexity to understanding any type of curriculum at any level of education. Because human knowledge is virtually unlimited, content associated with any subject or field of study can be taught and learned at multiple levels of scope and depth. For instance, content within the field of biology can be taught in a way that provides a general overview for beginning learners, but it can also be taught at a level so specialized that it would be nearly incomprehensible to anyone without advanced knowledge and expertise (e.g., next generation DNA sequencing).

Whatever the curriculum, identifying content knowledge is not simply a matter of pinpointing topics to be covered. It also requires that learner expectations be specified in relation to the content. Writing learning standards for a curriculum is a painstaking process that demands specifying the breadth and depth of knowledge and/or the performance competencies that instruction is intended to produce. What to include and what to leave out of a curriculum is rarely clear cut, and arriving at a consensus that is satisfying to all stakeholders is a challenging undertaking (Kelly, 2009; Riley, 2018).

Recognizing the Seabed of Opportunities Within a Multidimensional Curriculum

In addition to the complexity inherent in specifying the scope, depth, and performance standards associated with the content included in a curriculum, most educators consider details regarding student activities and assignments to be important curricular components. For instance, a writing curriculum may call for teaching and assessing writing across subjects and over time, and a reading curriculum may specify the educational materials that will be used (Great Schools Partnership, 2015).

Understanding a school's curriculum becomes even more complex upon considering the different subtypes of curricula that are evident within schools. For instance, Kelly (2009) pointed out the importance of:

a. distinguishing the total curriculum (the total program offered by an educational institution) from curricula associated with a particular subject or area of study;
b. acknowledging differences between the planned curriculum (what is written in syllabi and other formal documents) and the received curriculum (what students actually are taught);
c. separating the formal curriculum (learning activities that are compulsory and aligned with specific content standards) from the informal curriculum (learning activities without a specific focus or agenda, such those occurring during lunch or through voluntary, cocurricular learning activities); and
d. understanding the hidden curriculum (that which is not overtly taught, but that students are encouraged to learn due to the ways in which schooling is planned and organized, e.g., social expectations).

Although fully understanding the multidimensional nature of a K–12 curriculum may appear overwhelming, its expansiveness offers students a wealth of opportunities for participation and learning. The challenge for inclusive educators is to recognize occasions when a student's learning priorities can be addressed in the context of the curricula taught to the general student population and to take advantage of these opportunities when they arise. Of course, in order to recognize opportunities to teach priorities, student learning priorities must first be established.

Accessing the General Education Curriculum Through the Learning Priorities Prism

A self-evident truth that was introduced in Chapter 2 bears repeating: If everything is a priority, then nothing is a priority. Prioritizing learning goals for students with IEPs is essential because some potential learning outcomes are more important than others, and trying to address too many priorities at once displaces attention and effort away from those that are most important. Prioritization focuses on the most critical learning outcomes so that educator energy can center on developing and implementing effective curricular adaptations, instructional supports, and participation supports.

Identifying Learning Priorities

Students with IEPs are a heterogeneous group, and it is impossible to recommend how many learning objectives should be prioritized without knowing the nature of a student's goals or distinct needs. Regardless of individual differences, learning-goal prioritization should consider

- **A student's present level of performance in academic subjects.** Years of research findings show that academic achievement in the early grades predicts achievement in the later grades (see Rabiner et al., 2013). It is not difficult to understand how a failure to master foundational academic skills in the early grades leads to students falling further behind over time, discouragement with schooling, and a lack of commitment to academic growth. In contrast, developing foundational academic skills in the early grades dramatically increases a student's opportunities for success in subsequent grade levels and in their later life. For instance, if a student is not learning to read or is not developing basic numeracy skills in the early elementary school grades, a focus on accelerating academic growth in those areas must be a high priority.
- **The communication skills a student needs to functionally interact within their environment.** Although the developmental concerns in academic skill acquisition mentioned in the previous bullet are often closely related to language development (see Duff & Tomblin, 2018),

there are students who enter school without a reliable means to communicate to others about their basic wants or needs (I am thirsty, I am hurt), let alone communicate thoughts, feelings, and information. Because functional communication skills are essential to developing personal agency, nothing can be a higher priority than supporting students to acquire a functional communication system. This may involve learning and practicing modes for communication other than speech, such as those promoted in the field of augmentative and alternative communication (AAC).

- **The social and behavioral skills a student needs to be successful in future settings and activities.** Social norms and mores require students to demonstrate certain social and behavioral skills to participate in culturally valued environments. All students need to understand and model acceptable behavior in class so as not to disrupt their own learning and safety, or the learning and safety of others. Therefore, the behavioral and social skills essential to be a productive member of a classroom community may be a top priority for some students because success in future settings and activities depends upon it.
- **The learning priorities of the student and the parents.** In the example of the student interest/preference assessment discussed in Chapter 3, it was noted that these types of assessments could include input from family members. There are also a variety of person-centered planning processes (see Shogren, Wehmeyer, & Thompson, 2017) designed to secure the input of the people most important in a student's life. These can be used when setting both short- and long-term future goals and plans. Whatever methods are used, collaboration with students and parents is essential. Arriving at consensus regarding student learning goals can go a long way in assuring the "social validity" of the curricular adaptations and other supports developed through the SSPP. Social validity refers to the degree of acceptability and buy-in from the people who are intended to be the beneficiaries of the services being offered. Educators who do not try to understand the perspectives of parents or the learning preferences of their students miss the opportunity to gain credibility with the families and students. Learning goals that are reinforced in the home can have a tremendous impact on student achievement, as can tapping into

a student's motivation. The extent of student motivation has consistently been found to be a major predictor of school achievement (Kriegbaum et al., 2018).

There are more ways to inform learning goal prioritization than are provided in this short listing. What must not be forgotten is that establishing learning priorities is an essential first step to identifying curricular adaptations.

The Prism of Learning Priorities

To identify learning priorities, teachers, students, and parents must thoughtfully consider what is being taught in the general education curriculum, and what the student needs to learn that is not explicitly included in the general education curriculum. Analogous to the way in which a prism separates white light into a spectrum of component colors, coming to consensus on learning priorities is essential to identifying component learning goals that provide a focus for instruction, drive the development of curricular adaptations, and assure that proper attention is given the areas for learning that are the most important and urgent for a student.

Who Needs Curricular Adaptations?

It is safe to say that almost everyone needs curricular adaptations during the course of their K–12 schooling, if only in minor ways. Take the case of a fifth grader named William who was doing quite well in all his subjects—except his handwriting was illegible. Whether writing short answers to questions on his classroom quizzes or completing an essay assignment that required producing a rough draft, proofreading it, and developing a final draft, William would submit written output that everyone (including William) struggled to read. When confronted by his teacher regarding his undecipherable work and a concern that his handwriting had become worse over the course of the school year, William indicated that legible handwriting was not a concern to him. "I can always type it out if it is something important," he said. "Besides that," he informed his teacher, "they now have speech-to-text programs on phones and computers, and I can just talk into a device and print it out if needed. The important thing is for me to express myself, and today there are lots of ways to do that besides writing on paper."

In one sense, although William was being a bit cheeky by dismissing his teacher's concern, he was correct. He had decent keyboarding skills, and if he were a student with a physical disability that prevented him from writing legibly on paper with a pen or pencil, allowing him to keyboard all of his assignments or use speech-to-text software would most certainly be a reasonable accommodation. Additionally, penmanship had long disappeared as a focus of the fifth-grade curriculum at William's school. However, his teacher knew her educational research. Much of the in-class writing in K–12 schools is still done on paper, and when handwriting is very poor, teachers tend to form more-negative opinions about the quality of what a student is communicating (Klemm, 2013). Furthermore, William's teacher was confident that William could write legibly if he slowed down. She was also sure that writing legibly with relative fluency (i.e., automaticity) was a skill William was capable of mastering. Her response to William quickly cut to the chase. "Being able to express yourself is important; however, it is just as important for me to be able to understand what you are expressing. You can do better. Starting now, whenever you turn something in that I can't read, I will return it, and you will need to do it over again."

Although William did not have an IEP, his teacher made a curricular adaptation on his behalf. She assessed that William needed to become more proficient in skill that was outside the general education requirements of his grade level—namely, legible handwriting. Although she did not formally create an alternative learning goal or put her instructional plan in writing, the implementation plan and learning outcome were perfectly clear to William. As it turned out, it was also effective. Having to rewrite three assignments was all it took. William not only turned in legible written work to his teacher for the rest of Grade 5, but he did so in subsequent grades as well.

Another example of a curricular adaptation for a student without an IEP is apparent in the case of a first grader named Julia. Julia had a noticeably advanced vocabulary by the time she turned 3. She was always interested in books, and although her parents and older siblings provided her some guidance, she seemingly taught herself to read. Although Julia did not mind participating in her class's reading lessons and activities, for 3 days a week Julia left the classroom during the reading instruction time to go and work with the school librarian or with a retired teacher who continued to volunteer at the school. These educators guided Julia in selecting books to read that were at the third-grade level, which was the level commensurate with her reading skills. They also devoted time to discussing with Julia the books she had read the previous week, using probing questions that were aligned with the skills associated with third-grade readers. Julia might be asked to (a) describe the characters in a story; (b) identify different genres of fiction; (c) determine the main ideas as well as key details from nonfiction texts; and (d) make inferences and summarize material. In Julia's case, the curricular adaptations were made because her advanced skills rendered the scope of the first-grade general education reading curriculum a poor match for her.

The cases of William and Julia illustrate that curricular adaptations are not just for students with IEPs. Clearly, students can require curricular adaptations at one time but not need them at another. For instance, in William's case, the intervention was so effective that future educators did not need to target handwriting legibility as a future learning goal. In Julia's case, she remained an advanced reader for the remainder of her K–12 schooling, but several classmates caught up with her as they moved through the grades. By the time she reached high school, the college preparatory curriculum was sufficiently aligned with her educational needs.

Curricular Adaptations and Students With IEPs

Whereas curricular adaptations for students without IEPs may be introduced informally, curricular adaptations that are made for students with IEPs should be specified during the IEP planning process. As mentioned in Chapter 1, providing supports to students with IEPs is conceptually consistent with the IDEA's legal requirement of providing supplementary aids and services. When curricular adaptations are designated for different courses or subjects, the IEP goals should mirror the curricular adaptations and clearly indicate what progress the student is expected to make.

Figure 4.1 poses two questions used to determine if curricular adaptations are needed. If the answer is "Yes" to both questions (Quadrant A), curricular adaptations are called for because, as in the case of William, even though everything being taught general education curriculum is relevant to his education, there is also content (i.e., legible writing) outside the general education curriculum that needs to be learned.

Curricular adaptations are needed for students in Quadrant B because the scope of the general education curriculum is not a good match and specific

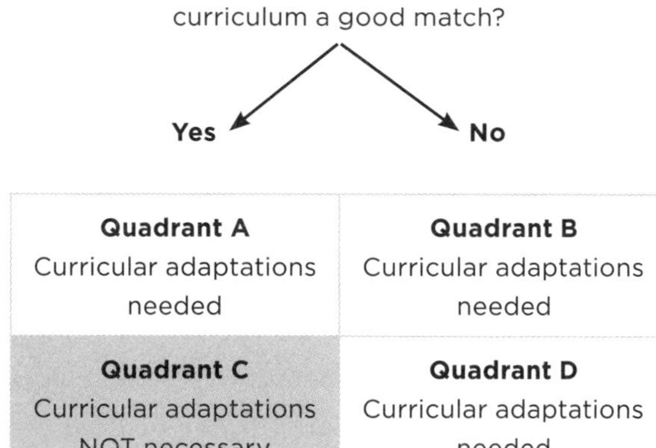

FIGURE 4.1: Determining the Need for Curricular Adaptations

content outside of it has been identified as a priority for teaching and learning. If the demands of the general education curriculum are too expansive for a student, and a student also has learning priorities that are outside of it, that student will be in Quadrant B. In contrast, no curricular adaptations are needed for Quadrant C students. For them, the scope of the general education curriculum is a good match and there is no content outside of it that is a priority for teaching.

Julia's case was consistent with Quadrant D. The scope of the general education curriculum was not a good match for her because she already read well above the first-grade level. Although she needed advanced reading instruction that was commensurate with her current skills, her reading instruction was clearly related to content taught in the general education curriculum. Julia had no learning priorities that fell outside the general education curriculum.

Curricular adaptations are often associated with the concepts of modifications and accommodations (Special Education Guide, 2021). Modifications are curricular adaptations that fundamentally alter the standards for performance that are expected following instruction. A modification example would be where a grade-level math expectation is to solve multidigit addition problems but the curricular adaptation for a student is to correctly identify a set of numbers. In contrast, accommodations are evident when the same performance standards are maintained but the process of teaching or student evaluation is different, as when a student is allowed extra time to finish a test. Because the concepts of accommodations and modifications are also relevant to how students participate in learning activities, they are discussed in Chapter 6, which focuses on participation supports.

A Curricular Adaptation Decision-Making Process

Figure 4.2 illustrates the decision-making process educators should undertake to identify curricular adaptations for students with IEPs. Specifically, the figure illustrates how prioritizing learning goals as the result of curricular adaptations does not mean that the entire general education curriculum or other content taught in schools are taken away from the student with the IEP. To the contrary, the entire curriculum and all of the associated learning activities are still taught and available for the student to learn. Curricular adaptations prioritize instruction based on the most important learning outcomes so that they do not become overshadowed by instruction on less significant learning goals. However, curricular adaptations do not remove opportunities to learn other content in the general education curriculum that has not been prioritized. As illustrated in Figure 4.2, the answer to the question "What to teach?" is: (a) first and foremost, teach content and skills that have been prioritized within and outside the

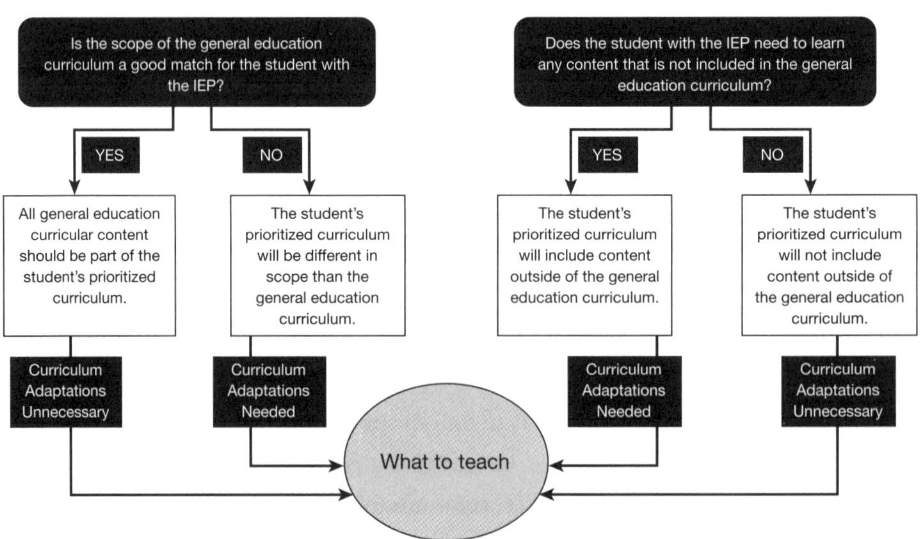

FIGURE 4.2: Determining What to Teach Students with IEPs

general education curriculum and are reflected in curricular adaptations; but (b) don't deny a student the opportunity to learn additional content and skills that are being taught in the general education curriculum that have been designated to be important for all students at a grade level to learn.

Why General Education Curriculum Must Be the Foundation for What to Teach

Although the general education curriculum may have been poorly defined prior to the education reforms of the early 2000s, state education agencies have since undergone multiyear processes defining content standards to establish the foundation for the general education curriculum for all students. A majority of states have adopted the Common Core Standards (CC Standards). The Common Core State Standards Initiative (2021) takes pains to explain that their work is concerned with learning standards and that they are not providing a curriculum. It is up to states, school districts, and schools to figure out how to package and deliver the CC Standards content. Nevertheless, like any other comprehensive content and achievement standard document, the CC Standards set the instructional agenda and expectations for each grade level.

Honest Questions and Respectful Answers

Some educators may question why the general education curriculum should be given such primacy in relationship to the education of students with IEPs. Their questions usually follow along these lines:

- Aren't students who meet the criteria for eligibility for special education services by definition, different learners than their peers?
- If so, don't these differences mean they aren't able to succeed in the general education curriculum? Instead of setting them up for failure in general education classrooms, why not teach them something they can be successful in learning?

These are honest questions that deserve respectful answers.

The first point to be made is that meeting criteria associated with one of the 13 disability categories defined under IDEA does not make students with IEPs different learners, it means they have unique needs for support. The educational needs of students with IEPs are met by providing them with the supports they need, not by teaching them completely different content from that given to students without IEPs. Educators should strive to provide classrooms that have the capacity to educate all students, including those who have relatively more-intense support needs in relation to their learning. When a student with an IEP is not learning in a general education classroom, the problem lies not with the curriculum being taught but with the absence of proper supports to facilitate the student's learning.

In response to the second question, it must be pointed out that students with IEPs can and do make progress toward the same general education curriculum standards as their peers without IEPs. There are two types of standards associated with the general education curriculum: content standards and achievement standards. Content standards refer to the knowledge and skills students should learn at each grade level (Quenemoen & Thurlow, 2019). For instance, a content standard for the seventh-grade social studies curriculum might be for students to compare and contrast everyday life in different periods and places around the world and to identify how some things change over time while others stay the same. Successful learning in regard to this content standard can be defined differently for different students. What might be evidence of significant success for one student in relationship to a content standard would just as clearly suggest unsatisfactory progress for another. Therefore, in regard to content standards, all students (including students with IEPs) can be successful because success is defined individually.

Achievement standards are different. They refer to how well students demonstrate the breadth and depth of information within the content standards (Quenemoen & Thurlow, 2019). These standards are assessed through standardized tests containing items that sample student performance across a content area. Assessments of achievement standards include items that are aligned with the most basic level as well as the most advanced level of mastery, with items of all difficulty levels in between. Assessments of achievement standards are used for accountability purposes; therefore, student performance assessments are considered to reflect the quality of education provided in a classroom, school, and school district. Should very few students meet the benchmark for success identified in the achievement standard, the quality of education is called into question. The wisdom of using standardized test scores to reflect the quality of instruction at a school is hotly debated (see Cramer et al., 2018; William, 2010).

Data over multiple years and across many different schools have shown that students with IEPs have achieved at levels that meet or exceed grade-level benchmarks. So, the answer to the question, "Can students with IEPs be high achievers when taught the general education curriculum" is a resounding "Yes!" Students with IEPs, however, are less likely to meet performance criteria than are students without IEPs (Quenemoen & Thurlow, 2019). However, being a member of a group that is statistically less likely to meet performance criteria is not a justifiable reason to deny students the opportunity to learn as much as they can.

State education agencies are allowed to exclude 10% of students with IEPs from standardized assessments that are aligned with achievement standards, although the excluded students must be evaluated using an alternate assessment to document their progress. But, 90% of students with IEPs are held to the same grade level of expectations as the rest of the student population (Quenemoen & Thurlow, 2019). Debates continue regarding how many students with IEPs should be included in assessments that are designed to measure grade-level performance standards (Great Schools, 2010).

Of course, when students with or without IEPs do not meet the benchmarks associated with achievement standards, it does not mean that they did not benefit from access to the general education curriculum or from participation in general education classes. The students who did not meet yearly benchmarks may have fallen even further behind if they'd been denied access to the general education curriculum. Clearly, neither students with or without IEPs could be successful on achievement tests based on the general education curriculum if denied the opportunity to learn the content on which the test is based.

Excluding all students with IEPs from the general education curriculum and from yearly assessments measuring progress toward state achievement standards may increase a classroom's or school district's standardized test pass rate. But, if all students with IEPs were automatically denied access to the general education curriculum throughout their schooling, it is likely that only very few of them would meet achievement standards. Thus, excluding students with IEPs in the effort to make a school district's standardized scores look better to an external audience would do great harm to the large number of students with IEPs who meet grade-level benchmarks. Moreover, excluding any group of students does nothing to improve instruction to a group of students who were not excluded.

The huge cost of excluding students with IEPs from the general education curriculum is that it denies them the opportunity to learn content and develop skills that society has said is important for all children to learn. When instruction for students with IEPs is grounded outside the general education curriculum, there is ample evidence to suggest that learning expectations are lower. Personal curricula based solely on IEP goals have shown to be consistently associated with low expectations (Shriner & DeStefano, 2003).

Before the movement to access the general education curriculum gathered steam in the early 2000s, it was common for students with IEPs to receive instruction targeted to deficits that were identified during an eligibility assessment. In this model, learning goals and objectives on IEPs were separate from the general education curriculum and usually consisted of isolated skill objectives that led to isolated instruction (Shriner & DeStefano, 2003). In contrast, instruction for students with IEPs that is grounded in the general education curriculum and provided in general education classrooms is not only more highly valued by society but is also associated with higher achievement (Kurth & Mastergeorge, 2012; Quenemoen & Thurlow, 2019).

The general education curriculum must be the starting point, the bedrock for what to teach students with IEPs. To do otherwise results in expectations for their learning and achievement that are far lower than what is expected of peers without IEPs. Lower expectations result in lower achievement. Put another way, when students with IEPs are told to not shoot for the stars, they will surely miss.

The Case for Curricular Adaptations Unrelated to the General Education Curriculum

Designating the general education curriculum as the foundation for student instruction and curricular adaptations does not mean that curricular adaptations for learning goals unrelated to the general education curriculum are unimportant. Returning to the earlier discussion on learning priorities, many students will benefit from learning goals that are clearly outside the general education curriculum because successfully accomplishing these goals is essential to the quality of their future lives. The challenge for educators is to identify which goals outside the general education curriculum should be prioritized. Several guidelines follow.

The Now and the Future

One consideration is to assess the relative application of different learning goals in relation to current and future settings and activities. Self-determination skills, communication skills, skills related to personal and social behavior, and effective study skills are examples of areas of instruction that have been shown to benefit many students with IEPs. These skills are typically only touched upon (if included at all) in the general education curriculum. As learning goals, they offer a great amount of practical utility for current and future environments. A student's most valuable learning experiences may be connected to learning goals that are outside the general education curriculum, directly relevant to their current life experiences, and directly applicable to their future success.

A student's most valuable learning experiences may be connected to learning goals that are outside the general education curriculum, directly relevant to their current life experiences, and directly applicable to their future success.

Although educators should consider the future when developing learning goals outside the general education curriculum, they should resist the temptation to peek so far into the future that practically anything can be justified. For instance, it is undoubtedly a problem that many adults with autism spectrum disorder (ASD) and intellectual disability (ID) are unemployed or underemployed (Butterworth et al., 2015). This fact, however, does not mean that second graders with these disability diagnoses should have IEP goals related to developing positive work habits and behaviors that will be taught via classroom jobs (e.g., watering the plants). All students in the second grade may benefit from opportunities to take on responsibilities that come with an ongoing job or task, but because second graders are not going to be eligible to seek employment for 10 years, it doesn't make sense to displace instruction from the general education curriculum for instruction on work-related skills. There will be future opportunities to focus on learning goals related to vocational skills, such as when the student is actually of vocational age.

Student and Family Input

Student and family preferences are another consideration for whether to develop curricular adaptations to address learning goals outside the general education curriculum. This was mentioned earlier in the chapter but bears repeating. Simply asking families and students about learning priorities is often all that is needed. The parent who shares, "I wish he could learn to keep track of his things. He lost so many materials last year, it seems as if we were replacing something every other day. One day it was library books, the next day it was folders. He's lost his lunch ticket at least once a week and we must have replaced enough markers, pens, and pencils for an entire classroom!" is pleading for someone to work with their child toward learning organizational skills. Fortunately, there are evidence-based strategies and systems for getting organized and keeping track of personal items that have been effective for students with organization challenges (Langberg et al., 2018). Devoting instructional time to teaching organizational strategies—like using binders and folders for each class and assignment, or introducing a due-date checklist—and then collaborating with parents to reinforce the use of strategies at home each evening, could turn out being the most valuable skills a student learns all year.

Functional (or Not)

Choosing learning goals outside the general education curriculum that parents and students do not embrace can be a waste of time. In an often-cited article titled "I can identify Saturn but I can't brush my teeth," Ayers and colleagues (2011) raise the question on whether the focus on accessing the general education curriculum has displaced more meaningful instruction on self-help skills, life skills, and other types of functional skills. Few would argue that how to brush one's own teeth would be more valuable to future success in life than identifying the planet Saturn on a model of the solar system.

But instruction in brushing teeth would likely only be meaningful if it were a priority of the student and the family. If the student or family indicated that independence in teeth brushing was of importance to them, then it would certainly be reasonable to prioritize it as a learning goal and to initiate a curricular adaptation. A teacher could develop a task analysis of the steps involved in teeth brushing, research the adaptive equipment that could be used to facilitate the brushing process (e.g., if the student had a physical disability that made gripping or controlling a toothbrush difficult), choose the best equipment, and make sure identical materials were used at school and home. Additionally, the educator could proceed to systematically teach toothbrushing at school and request that the family repeat the same teaching procedures at home: in the morning, after meals, and before bedtime.

On the other hand, if the family had no input and the teacher on their own had decided that toothbrushing was needed, the instruction could be waste of time. If the student used a different style of toothbrush at school than at home, generalization from home to school might not occur. Moreover, if the family continued to brush the student's teeth, whatever skills were developed at school would likely be lost over time because the student did not practice them. The same outcome would occur for any of the traditional life skills taught in a functional curriculum. Shoe tying, tie tying, fingernail polishing, French toast–making and so forth, are all skills that will vanish if they are not practiced in the home and supported by the family.

Guidelines (in a Nutshell)

Learning goals outside the general education curriculum are most justifiable when the outcome of the learning is applicable to a student's current and future life, and is endorsed by the student and the family. Once identified, alternative learning goals should be incorporated into the student's IEP as curricular adaptations. Although not directly related to the general education curriculum, instruction in the areas of self-determination, study skills, organization and personal management skills, communication, social-emotional competence, self-help skills, daily living, and vocational skills are all potentially excellent areas to target for curricular adaptations.

Confusing Curriculum With Placement

Applying the decision-making process shown in Figure 4.2 is consistent with the intent of federal laws. The IDEA (2004) requires involvement and progress in the general education curriculum for all students with disabilities. The Every Student Succeeds Act (ESSA, 2015) requires that all students have access to and make progress in the general education curriculum. Although these laws require that all students have access to the general education curriculum, they do not require students to spend time in general education settings. Students can be taught the general education curriculum in any setting and need not ever step foot in an inclusive classroom. Conversely, students can be taught many skills that are outside the general education curriculum within the context of a general education classroom (Rydak et al., 2013).

Data from the US Department of Education (2020) indicated that the amount of time spent in general education classrooms varies considerably by disability group:

> More than 8 in 10 students reported under the category of speech or language impairment (87.2 percent) were educated inside the regular class 80% or more of the day. Less than 2 in 10 students, or 17 percent, reported under the category of intellectual disability and 13.3 percent of students reported under the category of multiple disabilities were educated inside the regular class 80% or more of the day. (p. xxvii)

The continued segregation of large numbers of students with IEPs in separate classes and schools is perplexing considering the many instructional advantages general education settings offer over self-contained settings. The advantages for teaching general education content in general education settings are self-evident. Because students with IEPs will get exposure to instruction on the full range of the education curriculum offered in the general education class, they have the opportunity to learn content beyond their targeted learning goals. Additionally, when taught in the general education classroom, students gain exposure to the other types of school curricula. For example, the social, cultural, and other expectations of same-age peers is taught daily in schools in the hidden curriculum, according to Kelly (2009).

The general education classroom is often the best setting to teach alternative learning goals. For instance, a student who is developing functional communication skills will find it extremely advantageous to be surrounded by peers who have strong communication skills. If placed in a separate classroom with only those who also have extensive communication needs, the opportunities to engage in conversations will be limited. Strategies for embedding alternative curricular content in general education classrooms have been validated (Rydak et al., 2013) and are discussed in Chapter 5.

Although it would seem that access to the general education curriculum and access to a general education placement would be closely related, in practice this is not necessarily the case. Students can be offered the general education curriculum within and outside the general education classroom. Instruction on content outside the general education curriculum most often does not require removal of a student from an inclusive classroom. Despite the continuation of separate special education classrooms and schools, McDonnell and Hunt (2014) have documented that including students with IEPs in general education settings provides multiple benefits to them in terms of academic and social outcomes.

Key Ideas From This Chapter

- The multidimensional nature of the general education curriculum provides students with IEPs ample opportunities to learn content within and outside of it.
- Prioritizing learning goals is essential to identifying curricular adaptations. Curricular adaptations can address learning needs related to content within and outside the general education curriculum. Curricular adaptations should be clearly communicated to all IEP team members and documented in the IEP.
- The emergence of state-level content and achievement standards has clarified what access to the general education curriculum entails. The general education curriculum must be the foundation for what to teach students with IEPs. To do otherwise results in expectations for their learning and achievement that are far lower than what is expected of students without IEPs.
- Designating the general education curriculum as the foundation for student instruction and curricular adaptations does not mean that curricular adaptations for learning goals unrelated to the general education curriculum are not important. For many students, successfully accomplishing alternative learning goals is essential to their future learning and quality of life.

Questions for Discussion

1. Michaela is a seven-year-old who is diagnosed with ASD. She engages in echolalia on a regular basis, and she has a communication goal of maintaining a short conversation with others. Write a learning goal for Michaela and identify times during a school day when she could practice holding a short conversation.
2. A mother thinks it's great that her son with Down syndrome is learning about civics in the ninth-grade social studies general education class, because his older brother took that same course last year and she is familiar with the textbook, the vocabulary that will be introduced, and the assignments. She wonders what he'll possibly be able to get out of the class. What are some key concepts that a student, whose cognitive skills (including academic achievement) are significantly lower than other ninth-grade classmates, could learn in this class? What are some ways this student might be able to demonstrate his learning that may be different than the ways in which most other students demonstrate learning?

5

Instructional Supports

Personalizing Instruction for Student Success

Chapter 4 focused on determining what to teach as the basis for making curricular adaptations. Curricular adaptations provide the instructional destination. Instructional supports, on the other hand, provide the means of transport to that destination. Instructional supports are the teaching methods, strategies, and materials that a student needs to maximize their learning in the general education classroom.

This chapter begins with a discussion of the concept of differentiated instruction and how it aligns with the concept of identifying instructional supports to meet the needs of students with IEPs. Several of the most important and well-researched instructional strategies for students with IEPs are described, with special attention paid to how to incorporate these into group-learning contexts. Following that, the importance of collecting progress-monitoring data to evaluate the effectiveness of instructional supports is discussed. The chapter concludes by pointing out that it is just as important for educators to reject educational interventions that research shows are unlikely to be successful as it is to implement evidenced-based educational practices.

Differentiating Classroom Instruction and the Zone of Proximal Development

Students come from racially, ethnically, culturally, and linguistically diverse backgrounds. They vary considerably in regard to their present levels of achievement and preparedness to learn grade-level content. It is an ongoing challenge for teachers to meet the learning needs of a diverse population of students in a classroom. Since the early 1990s, there has been a particularly strong emphasis on preparing teachers to differentiate instruction to meet the challenges posed by student diversity (Dee, 2010). ASCD (formerly known as the Association for Supervision and Curriculum Development) has published over 600 articles or other products on differentiated instruction, and there is a profusion of books, manuals, and software available on the topic from other publishers as well (Delisle, 2015).

Differentiated instruction is not a definable collection of instructional methods. Rather, depending on which author one chooses to read, it's either a philosophy or a framework for instruction (Taylor, 2017). In the absence of additional information about how teaching and learning are occurring in a classroom, it is difficult to discern what teachers are actually doing when they claim to be differentiating instruction.

The ideals underlying differentiated instruction are not controversial. Only the most inflexible educators would reject the goal of providing classroom instruction that considers student diversity in personality, talent, background, and achievement history. Because students vary in terms of the rate and depth at which they learn material, good teaching requires respecting student differences and acknowledging that not every student should be taught in the same way. Although proponents of differentiated instruction are correct in asserting that one size of instruction does not fit all, the fact that an educator is using multiple instructional methods and materials does not guarantee that the educator is meeting the needs of all of their students—nor any of their students for that matter.

For the ideal of differentiated instruction to become a reality, teachers must demonstrate that they understand what their students are able to do and use that knowledge to align student learning goals accordingly. Educators who truly differentiate instruction pay close attention to aligning the difficulty level of a task, resources, and support to each student's current level of learning, understanding, and competence. They also consider factors such as student motivation and preferences (Tomlinson & Moon, 2013). These teachers understand that it is neither realistic nor desirable to expect a classroom of students to all achieve the same outcomes. But they also know that it is feasible and laudable to have high expectations for achievement class-wide and to develop instructional plans to bring out the best in all students.

The great Russian developmental psychologist, Lev Vygotsky (1978) famously identified the zone of proximal development as the difference between a learner's ability to perform a task independently versus with assistance. If the task presented to a student is too easy, then little learning will occur because the student may be bored and feel unchallenged. Conversely, if a task is too difficult, then limited learning will occur because the student may feel overwhelmed, become discouraged, and stop trying. The fundamental premise underlying differentiated instruction is that learning will flourish in classrooms where teachers provide opportunities for all students that are challenging, yet achievable—not too easy but not too hard.

Educators who truly differentiate instruction pay close attention to aligning the difficulty level of a task, resources, and support to each student's current level of learning, understanding, and competence.

Wood et al. (1976) is widely credited with describing "scaffolding" as the activities provided by a teacher to guide students through their zones of proximal development. Scaffolding occurs when a teacher supports student learning in a planned, progressive fashion. In this instructional model, supports to students are the most intense when they are first learning or are struggling to master skills. Supports are gradually withdrawn as competence increases; they are eventually removed altogether as students become independent and fluent in the skills they were taught. A teacher who makes a concerted effort to scaffold their classroom instruction to align with different student zones of proximal development is fully embracing the philosophy of differentiated instruction.

Perhaps the most widely cited proponent of differentiated instruction is Carol Ann Tomlinson (2017), whose book, *How to Differentiate Instruction in Academically Diverse Classrooms*, is in its third edition. She advocates differentiation by content (the curriculum, including standards, knowledge, and ideas that students are supposed to acquire as a result of the instruction), process (the ways in which students take in and make sense of the content), and product (the ways in which student show what they understand and what they can do). Table 5.1 provides an example of

TABLE 5.1 Differentiating Instruction for Kali Using Tomlinson's Framework

Subject: Math **Focus of instruction:** Concepts and computations associated with addition
Common Core standard: CCSS.MATH.CONTENT.1.OA.A.1 Use addition and subtraction within 20 to solve word problems involving situations of adding to, taking from, putting together, taking apart, and comparing, with unknowns in all positions (e.g., by using objects, drawings, and equations with a symbol for the unknown number to represent the problem).
Student's present level of performance and strengths: Kali is a first-grade student. She can identify numbers from 1 to 100, and rote count to 13 on a consistent basis. She has an emerging sense that numbers represent quantities and understands the meaning of mathematical symbols associated with addition and subtraction (i.e., +, -, =). She can attend to desk work (e.g., practice worksheets) as well as small- and large-group learning activities for up to 30 minutes with intermittent verbal reminders. After 30 minutes, she is exhausted and needs a break. Kali talks very quietly and is difficult to understand.

	CONTENT: knowledge, understanding, and skills that students use to learn	**PROCESS:** how students come to understand and make sense of content	**PRODUCTS:** demonstrate what they have come to know, understand, and be able to do after an extended period of learning
What is Kali's class (as a whole) doing?	Creating illustrations and writing equations to solve addition or subtraction word problems.	Students will (a) attend to teacher demonstrations, (b) produce mathematical representations, select correct strategies to solve problems, and correctly arrive at solutions through whole-group practice and small-group practice.	Students will independently (a) complete a worksheet with five addition or subtraction word problems, and (b) for each problem, will draw a representation of the problem, write an equation, and solve the problem correctly.

What is Kali doing?	Kali will use manipulatives to solve addition problems with sums up to 13.	Kali will (a) attend to teacher demonstrations with prompting from a peer and/or paraprofessional, (b) produce a mathematical representation using manipulatives and a graphic organizer with visual supports, (c) count the number of objects to correspond with each number, and count the total number of objects, and (d) identify the numbers by pointing to them in the word problem or on a number line, and vocally communicate the numbers she identifies with her peer.	Given two addition word problems, manipulatives, and a graphic organizer, Kali will (a) identify the numbers in the word problem, (b) write the numbers in the equation, and (c) count manipulatives to match each number. Kali will solve the word problems with sums up to 13 by counting manipulatives.

Note. Tomlinson, C. A. (2017). How to differentiate instruction in academically diverse classrooms (3rd ed.). ASCD.

how Tomlinson's content, process, and product framework may serve as a foundation for differentiating instruction for an individual learner. Notice how closely the ideas generated in the content column are aligned with the curricular adaptations of the SSPP, and how well the ideas generated under process are aligned with the instructional supports and participation support of the SSPP.

Differentiated Instruction in Action: Teaching Academic Content to Students With IEPs

General education classrooms are busy settings, with a multitude of learning activities taking place to provide a quality education for all students. For instance, during math instruction across the grade levels, it is common to find students attending to demonstrations, investigating concepts, engaging in discussions, interpreting representations, and doing computations. In the area of literacy, reading instruction in the early grades traditionally involves learning activities that develop skills in decoding and vocabulary, which include teaching the skills needed to make meaning from words and sentences, learning new words, and developing phonemic awareness. Literacy instruction also involves writing activities, such as journaling, outlining, and drafting. Science instruction often includes students reading texts, engaging in discussions, developing hypotheses, and analyzing data. Researchers at the College of William and

TABLE 5.2 Examples of Research-Based Practices in Relation to Core Academic Subjects

CORE ACADEMIC SUBJECT	RESEARCH-BASED INSTRUCTIONAL PRACTICE EXAMPLE
Literacy	**Shared reading** Ruppar et al. used shared reading within a high school general education cotaught English class to increase vocabulary use, engagement, and comprehension.
	Phonics instruction Ehri and Flugman (2018) taught general educators to implement daily phonics instruction, which resulted in increased reading and spelling scores for all students, including those with disabilities.
	Written expression Pennington et al. (2018) taught students with intellectual disability to select words to construct sentences.
Science	**Inquiry-based instruction** Jimenez et al. (2012) taught peers to implement constant time delay to teach students with intellectual disability to use a KWHL chart [a graphic organizer specifying what a student knows (K), what a student wants to know (W), how (H) a student will find the information, and what a student has learned (L) about a topic] during an inclusive middle school science inquiry lesson.
Math	**Problem-solving** Bowman et al. (2020) taught general educators to teach students with intellectual disability to solve word problems within the context of the general education math class.

Mary have developed a taxonomy of learning activities that are found in general education classrooms (Harris & Hofer, n.d.). Their work reveals an expansive array of learning experiences that are offered to students across multiple subjects over various grade levels (see https://activitytypes.wm.edu/).

Providing the Instructional Supports Students Need

The many learning activities within general education classrooms afford students a diverse set of experiences, but these are often not designed for students with disabilities in mind. However, researchers have found that the instructional activities and topics within the general education classroom can provide a quality education for all students, including those with the most significant support needs (see McDonnell & Hunt, 2014). The provision of meaningful instructional supports are key to making general education classroom learning activities useful to all students. A comprehensive review of all the instructional resources and strategies (instructional supports) for which research findings have shown to be effective for students with IEPs is beyond the scope of this chapter; but Table 5.2 provides a small sample

---

Note. Bowman, J. A., McDonnell, J., Ryan, J., Coleman, O. F., Conradi, L. A., & Eichelberger, C. (2020). Effects of general education teacher-delivered embedded instruction to teach students with intellectual disability to solve word problems. *Education and Training in Autism and Developmental Disabilities*, *55*(3), 318–331.

Ehri, L .C., & Flugman, B. (2018). Mentoring teachers in systematic phonics instruction: Effectiveness of an intensive year-long program for kindergarten through 3rd grade teachers and their students. *Reading and Writing*, *31*(2), 425–456. https://doi.org/10.1007/s11145-017-9792-7

Jimenez, B., A., Browder, D. M., Spooner, F., & Dibiase, W. (2012). Inclusive inquiry science using peer-mediated embedded instruction for students with moderate intellectual disability. *Exceptional Children*, *78*(3), 301–17. https://doi.org/10.1177/001440291207800303

Pennington, R., Flick, A., & Smith-Wehr, K. (2018). The use of response prompting and frames for teaching sentence writing to students with moderate intellectual disability. *Focus on Autism and Other Developmental Disabilities*, *33*(3), 142–149. https://doi.org/10.1177/1088357616673568

Ruppar, A., Afacan, K., Yang, Y., & Pickett, K. (2017). Embedded shared reading to increase literacy in an inclusive english/language arts class: Preliminary efficacy and ecological validity. *Education and Training in Autism and Developmental Disabilities*, *52*(1), 51–63. https://doi.org/10.2307/26420375

of research-based instructional practices in relation to content areas that are associated with general education instruction.

Instructional practices and learning activities such as those in Table 5.2 show how students with IEPs can profit from the same general education instructional activities provided to their peers without disabilities. Failure to use general education instructional activities as the foundation for instructional supports planning runs the risk of students with IEPs learning something different than their peers without IEPs for most of the school day, even though both groups are in the same physical space and have curricula aligned with the same content standards.

The infamous classroom within a classroom is created when students with IEPs get segregated into separate spaces within a classroom, even going so far as having a student spend time in a one-on-one teaching situation with an adult in a far corner of the classroom to reduce the distractions of the general education classroom instruction. When students with IEPs are partitioned from the other students in the classroom over a large swath of the school day, parallel learning displaces inclusive learning. A parallel education classroom where students are learning in close physical proximity to one another must not be confused with an inclusive education classroom where students are learning together.

The ongoing instructional activities in the general education classroom should always serve as the starting point for planning instructional supports for students with IEPs. Instructional support planning begins by carefully considering general education instructional activities. From there, teachers must use creative problem-solving and collaboration to identify instructional supports that promote the engagement and learning of all students (such as those listed in Table 5.2). Educators can implement the many available evidence-based instructional practices that are applicable to multiple subject areas. Two of the most important are explicit, systematic instruction and embedded instruction. Following are examples of how they can be applied in combination in the general education context.

Explicit, Systematic Instruction: The Teaching Strategies With the Strongest Evidence

To promote meaningful access and participation for students with IEPs, educators need to use evidence-based instructional methods. In this section, a short overview of explicit, systematic instruction will be presented. This class of interventions is multifaceted, and the numerous approaches to teaching that can be subsumed under this broad category have an exceptionally strong tradition in the special education research literature (see Spooner et al., 2012).

Principles of applied behavior analysis (ABA) provided the intellectual foundation for explicit, systematic instruction. ABA emerged from the field of psychology in the 1950s, and refers to a set of principles, such as positive and negative reinforcement, which focus on how behaviors change and learning occurs. For the layperson, it is important to acknowledge that ABA has its own nomenclature, and many words used in the ABA field do not have the same meaning as they do when used conversationally. For instance, to a behaviorist the word "punishment" means delivering a consequence that reduces the probability that behavior will occur in the future. Thus, a teacher saying, "No, that is the wrong answer, try again," is a punishment to a behaviorist if it results in a student not providing the same wrong answer to the question a second time. To the average person on the street, the word "punishment" implies a disciplinary consequence in response to some sort of misbehavior. Much misunderstanding can result when one educator is using ABA terms technically and another is interpreting them based on their everyday usage. For these reasons, this book avoids technical ABA terms that are easily misconstrued.

Although explicit, systematic instruction emerged from ABA principles, it has matured over time into its own set of instructional practices. A teacher can implement explicit, systematic instruction without claiming to be an ABA therapist. Scholars in the area of more-severe disabilities are likely to refer to these instructional practices simply as systematic instruction (see Collins, 2012), whereas scholars coming from a background focused on the direct instruction of academic skills are more likely to refer to them as explicit instruction (see Hott et al., 2017). Although there are differences in the historical use of the terms "explicit" and "systematic," and some authors continue to distinguish the two (see Udvari-Solner et al., 2017), the contemporary use of these terms is muddled. Hearing that educators are approaching their instruction systematically or explicitly is meaningless without additional information regarding their actual instructional practices. For the purposes of this book, explicit, systematic instruction should be thought of as a set of diverse instructional techniques that fall under a big umbrella. Features included are: (a) a straightforward, clearly defined, and logical sequence and scope for instruction, which builds on previously learned skills; and (b) a preplanned structure for delivering instruction that requires data collection to monitor student progress. Table 5.3 provides a sample of evidence-based teaching practices that are aligned with explicit, systematic instruction.

Although instructional practices associated with explicit, systematic instruction are among the most effective teaching methods for students with IEPs, implementing them within the context of general education classroom instruction has been an ongoing challenge. Explicit, systematic instruction can be multifaceted, and fidelity of implementation is reliant on observing students closely and following procedures to make certain that reinforcement and prompting are delivered as planned. Although some have suggested that the challenges in implementing teaching methods in general education classrooms that have been shown to be effective in special education settings provides a rationale for maintaining classrooms consisting entirely of students with IEPs (Kauffman et al., 2018), it is not necessary for educators to take such a defeatist attitude. Establishing successful inclusive education classrooms that infuse explicit, systematic instruction into general education classroom learning activities can be accomplished by teachers who engage in the types of creative problem-solving that are advocated in this book. A key to infusing any type of evidence-based intervention for an individual student into classroom-wide instruction is the thoughtful application of embedded instruction.

Embedded Instruction

When teachers make intentional efforts to include instruction on student individualized learning goals during general education instruction, classroom routines, and transitions, embedded instruction has occurred. "This approach to instruction is distinguished by an emphasis on providing learning opportunities that are naturally or logically embedded in activities, rather than decontextualized" (Snyder et al., 2018, p. 214–215). There are multiple examples of explicit, systematic instructional methods that have been embedded into learning activities within the general education setting. For instance, Jameson and colleagues (2007) taught a peer to implement constant time delay with a student with extensive support needs to help her learn content taught in junior high school general education health class. Constant time delay is a teaching approach where there is no delay between the instruction and prompt when a student is first learning a skill. However, as the student becomes increasingly proficient a

TABLE 5.3 Examples of Explicit, Systematic Instruction

Evidence-based practice associated with explicit, systematic instruction	Example
Time delay procedure allows a student a set amount of time (e.g., 3 seconds) to respond before being offered assistance	The teacher provides a partial physical prompt after a 3 second delay to help the student learn to raise their hand to answer a question during whole-group instruction.
System of least prompts delivers a prompt hierarchy starting with the least intrusive and moving to the most intrusive prompt until the student displays the desired response	To assist a student to identify the correct synonym for "X" from a choice of three, a peer first provides a verbal prompt by saying, "the synonym of X is X." If the student does not respond, the peer provides a gestural prompt of pointing to the correct choice. If the student does not respond to this prompt, the peer provides a physical prompt to assist the student to touch the correct choice.
Task analysis delineates each step involved in completing a larger task (i.e., a behavioral chain) to structure instruction	The student follows a list of every step in the editing process to complete a peer edit of a writing sample during language arts class.
Direct instruction directs the student through carefully structured and sequenced lessons that include demonstration, supported practice, and independent practice with feedback	First, the educator models how to solve the addition problem. Second, the student solves the addition problem with the educator. Third, the student independently attempts to solve the addition problem.
Graduated guidance delivers the minimal amount of physical prompting necessary to assist the student to perform the desired skill	The educator provides maximum physical assistance for a student to put on their goggles for a science experiment. During the subsequent science experiments, the educator provides minimal physical assistance to help the student put on their goggles.

continued

TABLE 5.3 ***continued***

Evidence-based practice associated with explicit, systematic instruction	Example
Shaping reinforces successive approximations of a desired skill until skill is performed with proper quality/accuracy	Student prints name from a model using lined writing paper. In the beginning, letters that either exceed or fall short of the target space for each letter by 1 inch or less are counted correct and reinforced. As student meets criteria consistently, the amount of distance that letters can exceed or fall short of the target space is reduced (the criteria for correctness and reinforcement is changed) up until all letters are consistently printed one-quarter inch or less outside or inside the target space.

fixed amount of time is inserted between the instruction and the prompt. Reyes et al. (2021) taught a paraprofessional to implement video self-monitoring using a system of least prompts to instruct a student with intellectual disability to make independent transitions within ongoing routines in his inclusive elementary classroom. Cohen and Demchak (2018) taught two elementary students with extensive support needs to complete writing and reading tasks using a visual task analysis during a general education language arts class.

Embedded instruction circumvents the need to remove students from the general education classroom because learning opportunities are provided naturally or logically over the course of the school day. Instruction in learning goals that are directly related to the general education curriculum but are different in scope can be embedded. An example of this might be learning to write short sentences while most other students are learning to write personal narrative essays. Also, embedded instruction can be used to teach learning goals outside the general education curriculum, such as teaching conversational communication skills as a part of a morning routine with teachers and peers. Although instruction on alternative learning goals may not be relevant to the majority of a student's classmates, it is often best to deliver such instruction in the context of the general education classroom because of the opportunities that are available for generalizing learned skills. For instance, it makes little sense for a student to learn and practice skills related to a goal focused on initiating communication with others in a setting void of peers and adults beyond the student's instructor. If working on this goal with a speech therapist in a private speech room, it is likely that the student will be taught to initiate communication with an adult who is providing them with undivided attention—which is quite different than the goal of learning how to initiate communication with others in everyday situations.

Proponents of embedded instruction emphasize that much of its value lies in something it *doesn't* do; namely, it doesn't disrupt the ongoing routines and instruction in the general education classroom (Johnson et al., 2004). Take, for example, the case of a third-grade student with a learning goal of identifying numbers. The instructional support plan may call for a paraprofessional to disperse constant time-delay trials for number identification during a third-grade, class-wide lesson on fractions. By embedding learning opportunities into general education classroom lessons, students with IEPs are able to gain exposure to general education content while also working on their individual goals.

Both discrete skills (those that target a single behavior, such as identifying a number or raising the hand to be called on in class) and chained tasks (ones that require many steps to complete, like solving a math problem) can be embedded during ongoing classroom instruction. For instance, discrete skills can be taught within ongoing instruction using a prompting system. When the opportunity to demonstrate the skills arises, educators might elect to use a system of least to most prompts to teach the discrete skill. If the learning target is a chained task, a task analysis can be created and used in combination with a prompting procedure for each step of the chain. For chained tasks, only part of the chain might be embedded (e.g., turning on the water, as part of a chain to learn handwashing during a science lab) or completion of the entire chain may be required (e.g., putting away materials for the activity that has ended and gathering materials for next activity).

It is possible to use embedded instruction to employ either distributed practice (practicing emerging skills over relatively short, frequent sessions) or massed practice (practicing emerging or newly learned skills in relatively lengthy, infrequent sessions). However, distributed practice is far more compatible with embedded instruction due to the fact that embedded learning opportunities are intended to allow the student to remain engaged in class-wide learning activities. If a student remains focused on the embedded learning opportunity for too long, they will lose track of what the rest of their class is doing. Fortunately, distributed practice within natural contexts has been shown to be the most effective way to teach (see Jameson et al., 2007) and it should be chosen over massed practice whenever possible.

Figure 5.1 shows an example of embedded instruction in a fifth-grade social studies class focusing on civics. The PowerPoint slide in the figure is one the teacher uses to facilitate a class-wide discussion on the meaning and role of government. The word "Vote" in the bottom, left-hand corner of the slide is a sight word for a student with an IEP in the class. This student has a goal of reading and explaining the meaning of several sight words associated with the civics unit. Each PowerPoint slide has one of the student's sight words on it. In this case, before this teacher transitions to a new slide, the student will be asked, "What word is this?" and then the teacher will proceed to ask the student to explain the meaning of the word. The teacher may also choose to ask other students to comment on the word on the slide, and make additional attempts to highlight the relationship of the sight word to the rest of the discussion.

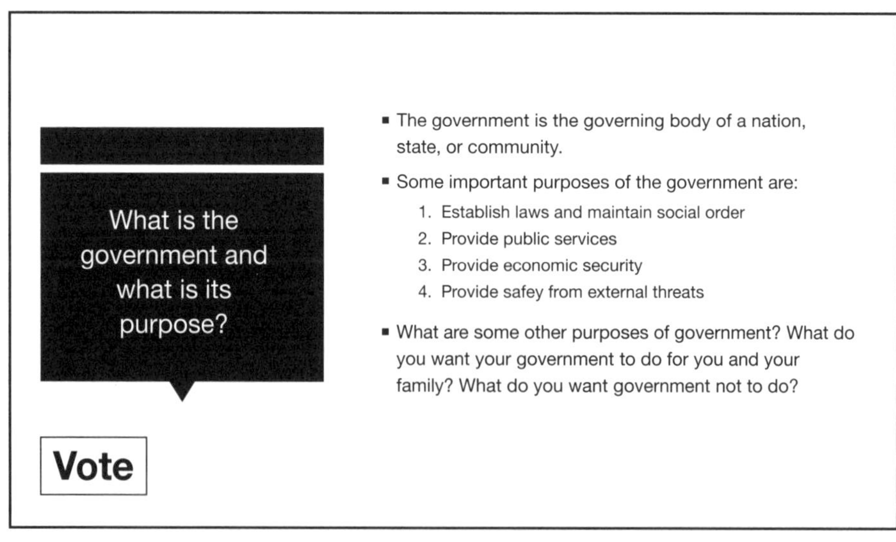

FIGURE 5.1: PowerPoint Slide Used in 5th-Grade Lesson with Sight Word Embedded in Left, Lower Corner

Formative Assessment: When Is a Support Really a Support?

By definition, instructional supports are teaching methods, strategies, and materials that maximize student learning in the general education classroom. Therefore, evidence of student learning is essential to make the claim that an instructional support has been put into place. Instructional supports are not efforts *intended* to maximize learning, but rather are teaching methods, strategies, and materials that *succeed* in maximizing learning. Information in this section is provided to guide educators on ways to efficiently collect formative data to document student learning and guide the delivery of supports.

Formative assessment occurs at the same time that instruction is delivered, and data are collected regularly over time. The purpose of formative assessment is to enable teachers to assess the effectiveness of instructional supports and to guide instructional changes. This contrasts with summative assessment, which is administered after instruction has been provided and is conducted to get an indication of the extent to which a student has mastered a body of content or skills (Rodrigues & Oliveira, 2014).

Instructional supports are not efforts intended *to maximize learning, but rather are teaching methods, strategies, and materials that* succeed *in maximizing learning.*

Multiple approaches to formative assessment are available to educators, and the relative usefulness of each will depend on the purpose for which they are used as well as on teacher preferences and information needs. Although educators want to select formative measures that provide the information they seek, selecting ways to collect formative data can be overthought. Sometimes the simplest, low-tech solution is the best option. For example, the paper-and-pencil entry and exit slips shown in Figure 5.2 may be perfect for a teacher who wants to take a "quick pulse" regarding whether or not students learned the most critical information from a particular lesson. As the figure shows, students are provided a "ticket" when entering the classroom where they take a few minutes to answer a question (or two). At the end of the class, they are given another ticket with the same questions. Teachers can compare the two sets of responses to determine if the instruction was effective. Entry and exit slips are also useful to sort students into instructional groups by splitting those who are

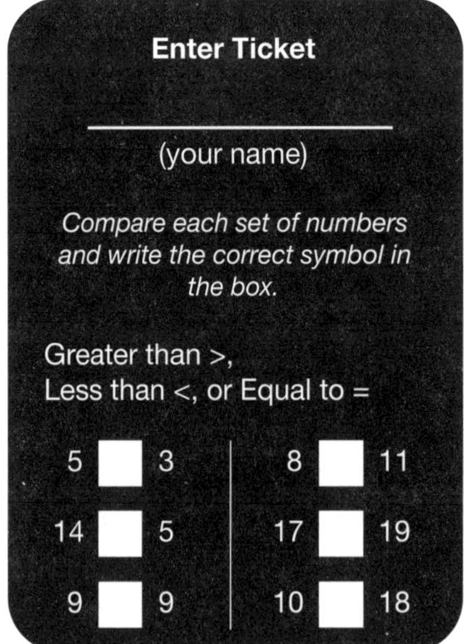

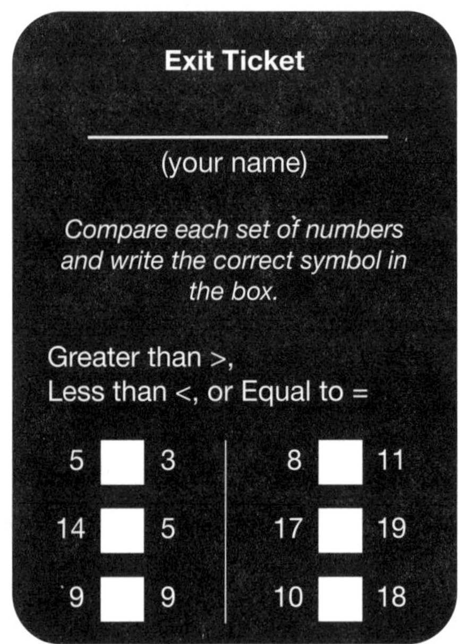

FIGURE 5.2: Entry and Exit Slips as a Means of Formative Assessment

understanding the concept being taught and are ready to learn advanced material from those who need additional instruction to absorb the basic information on a topic.

Fortunately, today's technology has expanded teacher options in regard to ways of quickly assessing student learning for the purpose of formative assessment. Google Forms (https://www.google.com/forms/about/) provides readily available software that can be used to get a quick read on student attitudes and competencies within a classroom. Responses to closed-ended questions can immediately be displayed as graphs using the "Responses" tab in the form. Padlet (https://padlet.com/), Plickers (https://get.plickers.com/), Poll Everywhere (https://www.polleverywhere.com/), Kahoot (https://kahoot.com/what-is-kahoot/), Socrative (https://www.socrative.com/), and Quizlet (https://quizlet.com/) are other apps that offer efficient options for teachers to obtain a snapshot of what students know prior to instruction and what they retain after instruction.

Student self-assessment is another efficient way to gauge how well students are understanding content in the classroom. Figure 5.3 shows a paper form that allows the student to respond using emojis. The form takes students only a

Rating Scale Self-Assessment

This is how I rate my understanding of the ______________________________ activity. (circle one)

I think I got this!	I need a little bit more practice.	I'll get there, but I need help!

FIGURE 5.3: Student Self-Assessment as a Means of Formative Assessment

few seconds to fill out and provides them with a means to communicate a self-evaluation of their own learning without having to share it aloud with others.

The student interview is an exceptionally straightforward option. Although scheduling a private interview with every student in the class every day would be impractical, interviewing students is something that teachers should consider doing on occasion. Simply asking a student a series of questions about how they are performing academically—or in other goal areas, such as those related to behavior—allows them opportunities to orally communicate what they have learned about a topic and where they feel they need help. This can provide educators with a wealth of information that is germane to planning and implementing instructional supports (e.g., see Puckett et al., 2017). For students who may dread a teacher interview, technology resources such as Flipgrid (https://info.flipgrid.com/) or Explain Everything (https://explaineverything.com/) can provide good alternatives for students to express what they know and offer teachers a permanent product that can be accessed at a later date.

Remember, formative assessment is only useful to the extent that it provides a clear representation of what a student is comprehending and how they may benefit from different types and intensities of instructional supports. Providing students with choices and opportunities to show what they know is a good strategy to obtain a sample of a student's best work, and therefore provide the information teachers need to monitor student growth and development. It is essential that formative assessment not be treated as an afterthought. Determining how student learning will be assessed should be an integral part of planning instructional supports. Tracking student progress is vital to determining that an instructional support is actually operating as an instructional support—not purely as an artifact of an educator's good intentions or wishful thinking.

Data-Based Decision-Making

If formative assessment data show that instructional supports are not working (i.e., the student is not making adequate progress), then it is incumbent upon educators to try out new types and intensities of supports. Conversely, if data show that the instructional supports are efficacious, then the supports need to be kept in place and documented so that future educators are aware of the nature of the supports a student needs. Educators who routinely use formative assessment data to guide instructional decisions for their students have taken a huge step toward becoming the type of systematic, creative problem-solvers that students with IEPs deserve.

Curriculum-based measurement (CBM) provides a more detailed and sophisticated means to measure student progress than the approaches to formative assessment discussed earlier. CBM is a method used to inform teachers of how their students are developing in academic areas. Advantages of CBM are that they are quick to administer, can be given often, and are explicitly aligned with content that is being taught in the classroom. Figure 5.4 shows six components of CBM that, according to Van den Bosch et al. (2017), need to be present in a student's progress-monitoring graph. The components are: (1) baseline data that shows where the student is currently performing; (2) peer data that displays the difference in performance between the student who is the focus of progress monitoring and a comparison peer group; (3) a goal line that signifies the expected performance by the end of the designated learning period; (4) data points that showcase the incorrect and correct student responses on each probe; (5) rate of growth line over time; and (6) intervention lines that show when changes occurred in instruction.

CBMs are typically collected through weekly administration of short, simple measures or probes that sample student performance in an academic area. The most common CBM is words read correctly per minute (WCPM). The number of WCPM by a student has proved to be highly correlated with every type of standardized achievement test of reading (see Stage, 2001). Obviously, the reading material must be controlled for reading-level difficulty during the

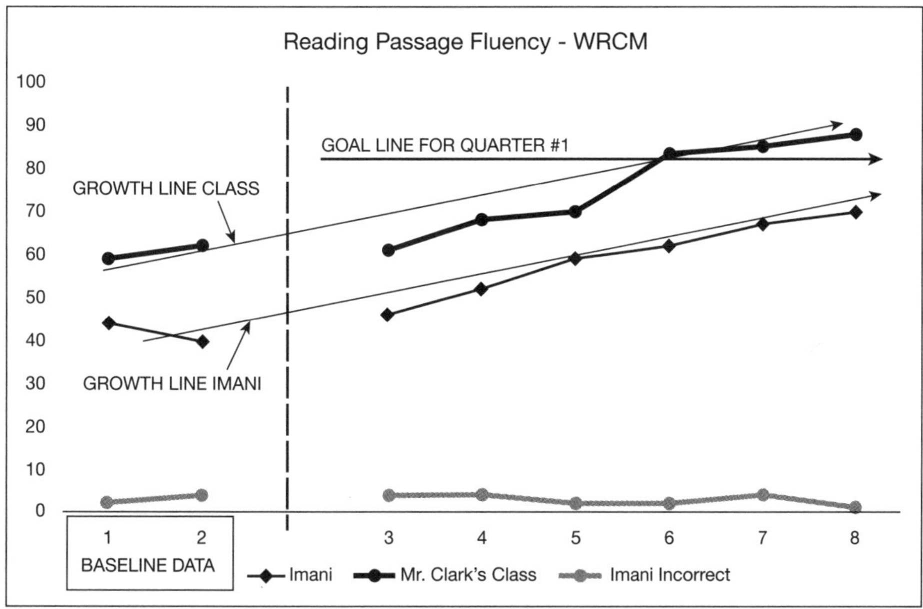

FIGURE 5.4: CBM Graph Documenting Imani's WRCM

CBM assessments over time. But the fact is that for most students, the number of words they can orally read correctly in a minute provides an exceptionally accurate screening of their reading achievement or their present level of performance. This is a remarkable research finding because it offers a very efficient means to measure student progress in reading on a regular basis.

Hasbrouck and Tindal (2017) published a compilation of norms based on three widely used and commercially available oral reading fluency assessments. Therefore, anyone can consult Hasbrouck and Tindale's work to identify how many WCPM is typical of readers at any age. Understanding a student's relative standing in regard to a representative sample is helpful when screening for the possibility of delays in achievement. If delays are evident, early intervention can prevent or reduce poor outcomes down the road (see Bakken et al., 2017).

Teachers can find free resources to help with the weekly probes that are utilized for CBM data collection. The website easyCBM (https://www.easycbm.com/), provides teachers with free CBMs in reading and math. Intervention Central (https://www.interventioncentral.org/curriculum-based-measurement-reading-math-assesment-tests) provides free and accessible probes in reading, math, and writing.

CBM probes are designed to match curriculum objectives, and are administered under timed, standardized conditions. When used to monitor an instructional intervention, CBMs provide instructors well-timed feedback about the efficacy of an intervention. Teachers are able to see what gains or deficits characterize a student's performance in a particular curricular area. Numerous research studies (see Foegen et al., 2007; McMaster & Espin, 2007; Wayman et al., 2007, for reviews) have shown the utility of CBMs for educators who want to monitor the academic growth of students in basic academic skills and use the information to inform their instructional approach.

The Wrong Way to Differentiate Instruction

By definition, supports are resources and strategies that reduce the mismatch between student competencies and environmental demands. If a teaching resource or strategy does not improve the alignment between classroom instruction and a student's learning needs, then it isn't operating as an instructional support. Because students and the classroom/school context are dynamic and complex, no type of instructional support is going be entirely successful for every student all of the time. As was pointed out in a prior section, collecting progress-monitoring data is fundamental to determining whether an instructional support is working as intended. Or in other words, whether the resources and strategies are truly functioning as an instructional support.

Although there is not a magic solution that is guaranteed to work perfectly for every student with an IEP all of the time, there are instructional supports that research shows have a strong track record of success for students with IEPs. Some of the most important supports were reviewed in an earlier section of this chapter. Conversely, there are instructional approaches that will not work according to all of the available evidence. Unfortunately, over the years there has been no shortage of bogus instructional, medical, and social interventions targeted toward children with disabilities. Some of the most infamous interventions over the past 50 years include the Feingold diet, which claimed restricting and ingesting certain foods could improve or eliminate symptoms of ADHD and other

If a teaching resource or strategy does not improve the alignment between classroom instruction and a student's learning needs, then it isn't operating as an instructional support.

learning problems (Smith, 2007), dyslexia glasses that promulgated the use of colored lenses as the solution for children with reading difficulties (American Academy of Pediatrics, 2009), and the Doman–Delecato technique (psychomotor patterning) involving a sequence of physical exercises that purported to reprogram the brain and boost general intelligence (Zigler, 1981). Educators have a particular responsibility to spot and reject treatments that have been discredited. Differentiated instruction based on poorly studied or ineffective interventions is a waste of time and energy and embedding such instruction into classroom learning activities may well do more harm than good.

A Word of Caution

Rejecting misguided interventions is not the same as becoming obsessed with justifying every action through the framework of evidence-based practice. Occasionally, one will encounter a teacher who emphatically announces, "Nothing happens in my classroom that is not evidence-based!" This, of course, is a bunch of bunk. Any teacher who would monitor their every interaction with students in relation to its relative degree of scientific evidence would collapse from their own self-consciousness by the end of a school day. Schools not only provide a multitude of teachable moments that are not planned in advance, but educators must allow for times to simply have fun and enjoy their student's company without weighing every action relative to the degree of supporting evidence. Although it could be argued that teachable moments have support in the research literature related to inquiry-based learning (Haug, 2014; Lazonder & Harmsen, 2016) and that evidence shows that positive teacher–student relationships are strongly associated with learning outcomes (Sparks, 2019), there is no reason to feel a burden to provide post hoc rationalizations for every moment of the school day. An obsession with evidence-based practices in granular interactions can distract from the importance of applying evidence-based practices as the foundation for selecting the major instructional strategies and resources that are going to be used to promote student learning. If a colleague should question whether a Valentine's Day party is evidence-based, it is a sign that they have gone overboard.

Educators should also be careful about criticizing interventions that parents have embraced, even when the practice may have limited research evidence in support of it, as long as the practice is benign and doesn't divert school resources from legitimate interventions. For instance, Hyman et al., (2016) pointed out that there is no evidence that gluten-free/casein-free (GFCF) diets ameliorate autism spectrum disorder (ASD), but they also noted that children with ASD often experience gastrointestinal (GI) problems and that GFCF diets have been shown to relieve discomfort from GI symptoms for many people. Thus, although a parent may overstate the benefits of GFCF diets in terms of alleviating their child's symptoms of ASD, suggesting to parents that they are misinformed and that any improvement in their child's communication and behavioral skills an artifact of reduced GI symptoms may come across as pedantic and closed-minded. More importantly, dismissing a parent's ideas may pose a barrier to establishing trust and communication between the school and home, and positive home–school collaboration is one of the most robust evidence-based practices in the field of special education (Turnbull et al., 2015).

Why Single Out Learning Styles?

Just as space limitations in this book prevent a comprehensive review of effective instructional methods, space does not allow detailed descriptions and critiques of all of the questionable teaching strategies and resources that have appeared in the educational landscape over time. There is, however, a class of instructional approaches that ha[s] become so widespread in relation to the concept of differentiated instruction that it merits special mention. Namely, designing instruction based on types of learners according to their learning styles. At first blush, the logic underlying these practices appears compelling. It is reasoned that because students differ in the ways that they learn, teachers should tailor their instruction to each student's natural learning style in order to increase their ability to educate different kinds of learners.

The premise underlying learning styles as the basis for instructional planning falls completely apart, however, upon considering a basic fact: Learning occurs through mental processing within the brain, specifically, neuronal connections at synapses. As Willingham et al. (2015) pointed out, the brain absorbs information from multiple sources and builds on prior learning. Planning and delivering instruction that engages all of the senses and taps into student prior knowledge, emotions, and interests will be a far better use of time and effort than attempting to isolate and align instruction with a student's preferred learning style.

Learning is not enhanced by presenting information in a manner that strictly aligns with a hypothetical, discrete style of learning. Mental processing is enhanced when receiving information through multiple modalities (auditory, visual, kinesthetic, reading/writing). Artificially focusing instruction so that it is heavily slanted toward one modality in every learning situation is bad teaching, and this is especially true for certain subjects in certain grades. For example, trying to teach advanced algebra through a sequence of dance activities is probably not going to work very well. This does not mean that students won't have learning preferences; they most certainly will, and their preferences should be respected. For some students, a visual aid will be critical to learning a certain concept, whereas for others it will be the auditory explanation that makes the concept click. However, both self-identified visual and auditory learners will benefit from a combination of visual and auditory information, and they may not be able to learn unless provided with both types (Farmer-Dougan & Alferink, 2013). Is Johnny a visual *or* an auditory learner? The answer is "no" because Johnny is a visual *and* an auditory learner.

For example, teaching content about the solar system should incorporate not only visual and auditory information during class presentations; most students would also benefit from a kinesthetic activity, such as model building. In addition, so-called reflective learners will not be the only students who profit from opportunities to engage in discussions about the solar system in small groups, and students who are perceived to be active learners are not the only ones who might benefit from independent study activities. All students are visual learners, auditory learners, kinesthetic learners, reflective learners, active learners, and whatever other real or imagined category of learner type that people wish to propose (Kirschner, 2017) with very few exceptions. Certainly, a student who is totally blind due to optic nerve damage will not be a visual learner. Sorting students into learning types and developing instruction that corresponds to different types of learners is not differentiated instruction, it is misguided, lousy instruction.

Students may get sorted into learning types based on self-reports of their learning preferences. Unfortunately, the learning style inventories that are relied upon to identify types of learners are invalid based on standard psychometric indices of reliability and validity (Kirschner, 2017). The real trouble arises when student-learning preferences (based on invalid assessments) become conflated with learning styles in the minds of educators. Educators then assume that students won't benefit from instruction outside their preferred learning style (Willingham et al., 2015). Although learning-styles instruction has permeated teacher education programs and professional development workshops in recent years, research from multiple reviews have confirmed that matching instruction to learning styles doesn't work (Nancekivell et al., 2020; Newton & Atharva, 2020).

It is a bad idea for students to develop learning strategies only through their preferred modalities. Students need to learn how to be lifelong learners, and sometimes this means pushing oneself to learn in ways that may not be entirely comfortable at first. As Alferink and Farmer-Dougan (2010) pointed out, "The larger the child's inventory of learning strategies, the more likely the child is to learn across environmental settings" (p. 47). A teacher's planning time is finite, and using it to plan learning activities that are going to motivate students to learn and differentiating instruction using the strategies discussed earlier in this chapter (e.g., embedding explicit, systematic instruction in lessons) will yield far better outcomes than vesting time in attempts to tailor instruction to student learning styles.

Key Ideas From This Chapter

- The premise underlying differentiated instruction is that students differ in many ways, including the rate and depth at which they learn material. Therefore, all students should not be taught in exactly the same way. Educators who differentiate instruction pay close attention to aligning the difficulty level of a task, resources, and support to each student's current level of learning, understanding, and competence. Learning will be maximized when instruction is aligned with each student's zone of proximal development.
- The ongoing instructional activities in the general education classroom should always serve as the starting point for planning instruction supports for students with IEPs. This will give students with IEPs the opportunity to learn the same content as their peers without IEPs. Fortunately, there are many evidence-based instructional practices available to educators that are applicable to multiple subject areas.

- Explicit, systematic instruction is a set of diverse instructional techniques whose defining features are: (a) a straightforward, clearly defined, and logical sequence and scope for instruction that builds on previously learned skills, and (b) a preplanned structure for delivering instruction that requires data collection to monitor student progress. Although instructional practices associated with explicit, systematic instruction are among the most effective teaching methods for students with IEPs, implementing them within the context of general education classroom instruction has been an ongoing challenge. To meet this challenge, teachers must use creative problem-solving and collaboration.
- Embedded instruction occurs when educators make intentional efforts to include instruction on student individualized learning goals over the course of the school day within the general education context. Because learning opportunities are provided naturally or logically during classroom activities during general education instruction, classroom routines, transitions, and so forth, the need to pull children with IEPs out of the general education classroom for purposes of working on individualized goals is diminished.
- Formative assessments provide evidence that student learning has or has not progressed. Therefore they must be completed on a regular basis to document that an instructional support has been put into place. There are multiple approaches to formative assessment; their relative usefulness will depend on the purpose for which they are used and on teacher preferences and information needs. Some formative assessments, like entry and exit slips, are low-tech and uncomplicated. Others, like curriculum-based measurements (CBM), are more complex and require a substantial investment of time and expertise to arrange. Formative assessment data are absolutely essential to decision-making regarding whether to maintain or change instructional approaches.
- Unfortunately, there has been no shortage of misguided instructional, medical, and social interventions targeted at students with disabilities. Relatively recently, differentiating instruction based on student learning styles has gained favor despite a lack of evidence for its efficacy.

Questions for Discussion

1. Mr. Clark monitors his 25 third-grade students' progress in reading using weekly reading probes. Every day, time is set aside for him or the classroom paraprofessional to spend time individually with five students. Each student reads third-grade level reading material aloud for 1 minute. He (or the paraprofessional) reads along silently with them, striking through every word a student gets incorrect. When a minute is up, the number of words read correctly and incorrectly are counted and recorded. At the end of the second week of reading probes, Mr. Clark was not satisfied with Imani's reading progress. Imani had been receiving the same reading instruction (guided-reading groups) as the other students in his class during the first 2 weeks of school, and Mr. Clark made a change in Week 3 in Imani's instruction. The change included: (a) incorporating a direct instruction reading program to supplement the guided reading that characterizes the class-wide instruction, and (b) extra practice reading at home each evening with his parents. Refer back to Figure 5.4, which shows Imani's progress during the first 8 weeks of school.

    - What does the Baseline (i.e., the data collected during the first 2 weeks, before the extra reading interventions were introduced) show about Imani's achievement compared to the achievement of the class as a whole?
    - How does Imani's growth line compare to the growth line of the class as a whole? Is the discrepancy between Imani's achievement and the achievement of other students in the class narrowing as a result of the extra reading interventions? Are the trajectories of Imani's progress and the progress of other students in the class the same or different?
    - Mr. Clark set the goal line for Quarter 1 as 83 words read correctly per minute, based on the Hasbrouck and Tindal (2017) norms for third-grade readers. This source states that by the middle of the fall semester, half of the third-grade students in a national norm group could read 83 words or more words correctly per minute, and half could read 82 words or less. If you were Mr. Clark, what conclusions would you draw about the

progress of the class as a whole as well as Imani's individual progress in relationship to the goal line?
- Words read incorrectly were also counted, and are show on their own line graph. Should the number of words that Imani is reading incorrectly be of concern?

2. Ms. Winkerton teaches language arts to seventh-grade students. She attended a workshop on learning styles last summer and left the course determined to do great things with her newfound knowledge. In an effort to differentiate instruction in her classroom, she devoted considerable time reformatting her lessons to align with student learning styles so that all her students would be able to use their preferred style of learning to master the material that she was teaching. Ms. Winkerton also is the coach of the seventh-grade girls' basketball team. One of the best players on the team, Jordan, is almost unstoppable when she has the basketball on the right side of court. She is an exceptional dribbler when controlling the ball with her right hand, has an especially quick step when pushing out from her right foot, and she is very accurate with her shot at the hoop when shooting from the right side. Conversely, Jordan is only average from the left side of the court, and she knows it. She only tries to score from the left side when she is uncontested. Coach Winkerton spotted Jordan's left-side weakness right away, and she has inserted drills into the practices that will develop Jordan's ball handling and shooting skills on the left side. Jordan has bought into her coach's philosophy, and she is trying her best to become a better basketball player by working on a part of her game that is more difficult for her.

   Does Ms. Winkerton, the teacher, have the same philosophy toward teaching as Ms. Winkerton the coach? Why or why not? If not, is Ms. Winkerton being a better educator in the classroom or on the basketball court?

6

Participation Supports

Engaging Students to Be Full Members of the Classroom

The Systematic Supports Planning Process (SSPP) focuses planning on three broad categories of supports that students with IEPs need to be successful in general education classrooms. The categories are curricular adaptations, instructional supports, and participation supports. Curricular adaptations were reviewed in Chapter 4 and involve adjustments to the general education curriculum to make it more accessible to students with IEPs and/or incorporate additional content that students need to learn. Chapter 5 focused on instructional supports that are teaching methods, strategies, and materials needed to maximize student learning in the general education context. This chapter centers on the third category, participation supports, which function to promote the full engagement of a student in classroom learning activities as well as in other school settings.

Being Included Without Belonging

A student with an IEP can be listed on a classroom roster, be physically present in a classroom, and have targeted learning goals on which teachers focus their instruction, yet the student may still only be tangentially involved in classroom activities. Physical presence in a classroom is a necessary but insufficient condition for active engagement in a classroom. In the preceding sentence, try replacing "classroom" with any social group or any community of people. For instance, someone could be on the roster of a sports team, but if they habitually missed practices and never played in the games, they would be perceived to be less a part of the team than teammates who were regularly engaged in all of the team's activities. The experience of being assigned to a committee at a workplace is universal, as is the corresponding experience of realizing that there are committee members who willingly contribute their time and effort to their committee's charge, just as there are other members who make conscious effort to do as little as possible. Being listed on a roster of any group provides no guarantees that someone is anything more than nominally engaged in a group's activities.

The extent of participation a person has in any type of group is on a continuum. People can be full participants or they can be so inactive that they are members in name only. Stepping back and being a passive member is not necessarily the wrong choice for someone in a given situation. The multitude of groups within society have many different purposes, and people bring different motivations to their affiliations. For instance, one person may wish to be wholeheartedly involved in their faith community and would feel a gaping hole in their spiritual life if they were not. In contrast, another person may want to continue an association with a faith community for variety of good reasons, but may feel that their spiritual needs are rarely met through organized religious activities. This person may not find it meaningful to vest considerable time and energy into participating in group activities within their faith community.

Because school communities occupy a distinct place in modern society, an overly passive membership in a classroom or school should not be an option for any student, let alone an option that is encouraged by the school. Unless a family opts for homeschooling, compulsory education laws require children and adolescents to attend schools for 13 years. For the vast majority of today's children, the amount of time they will spend in a school setting during their childhood is only surpassed by the amount of time they spend in their family home. Therefore, all students enrolled in a school need to feel a sense of belongingness while attending school, and a sense of connectedness with their fellow students and the staff. This does not mean that every student must strive to be totally enmeshed in every aspect of school life, or that something is wrong with a student who prefers to step back from organized school activities more so than most. However, it does mean that all students should feel that they are part of school community and that their presence is valued.

Research findings have confirmed the importance of students perceiving that they belong as valued members of their school community. For instance, Christenson et al. (2012) reported that students who lack a sense of belongingness at school or feel alienated will not only be more prone to drop out but will also likely experience low achievement, engage in riskier health and sexual behaviors, experience depressed social-emotional well-being, and experience negative long-term adult outcomes such as chronic unemployment. Few would disagree that schools should strive to ensure that every student is welcomed at school, or that schools be perceived by students to be safe and nurturing places. Moreover, all students enrolled in a school should be engaged in activities, alongside adults and classmates, that foster their personal growth and development. This chapter is focused on how participation supports can be identified and arranged to promote the full participation of students with IEPs in schools.

From Participation to Engagement to Belongingness

In their seminal writings in field of psychology, both Carl Rogers (1951) and Abraham Maslow (1943) stressed the importance of a sense of belongingness to people's mental health and well-being. Of course, "belonging" is a subjective experience contingent on an individual's perceptions. It is within the realm of possibility that someone could feel socially rejected and alienated from a group, when in actuality they are welcomed, valued, and accepted. Conversely, a person could perceive that they belonged in a group although an outside observer might conclude that the person was mistreated and rejected. Because belongingness is a subjective, personal experience, the individual's perception is paramount. If a student perceives that a school is hostile to them and that they don't belong there, it is problematic for the student—whether or not their perceptions are fair or are even based in reality.

Engagement is related to the construct of belongingness. Engagement is still reliant on people's perceptions, but efforts have been undertaken to measure it and therefore it is a more operationalized construct than is belongingness. After surveying scholars who were active in research related to school engagement, Christenson et al. (2012) concluded that school engagement was "multidimensional, comprised of observable behavior, internal cognition, and emotion" (p. 814). Behavioral engagement is evidenced through actions such as good attendance, compliance with school rules, assignment completion, and participation in class; it is also indicated by involvement in cocurricular activities like theatre productions, sports teams, and music groups. Students demonstrate their emotional engagement through actions and words that show they like school, are interested in learning, and identify as being a part of the school. Cognitive engagement is signified by students putting forth efforts to achieve in school; it is further evidenced by self-regulation, a strong academic self-concept, and articulation of goals for academic success.

Participation, the act of taking part in something, is a more concrete concept than either belongingness or engagement. Whereas belongingness is based on an individual's perceptions on the extent to which they fit in and are welcomed in a setting, and engagement requires consideration of numerous components (some of which may overlap and/or not be well defined), identifying a student's degree or level of participation is comparatively straightforward. A student is either taking part in an activity or is not a part of it. The adjective proceeding any report of a participant or participation is important, as a student might be a full participant (taking part in every aspect), unwilling participant (taking part in something the student doesn't want to be involved in), unlikely participant (someone whom others did not expect to participate), or some other qualifier.

Figure 6.1 shows that participation can be conceptualized as the foundation for engagement and belongingness in schools. Indicators for engagement, such as those proposed by various authors contributing to the Christenson et al. (2012) *Handbook of Student Engagement*, are all contingent on a student participating in the activities of a classroom and school. Moreover, it is hard to imagine how a student could perceive they truly belonged in a school without

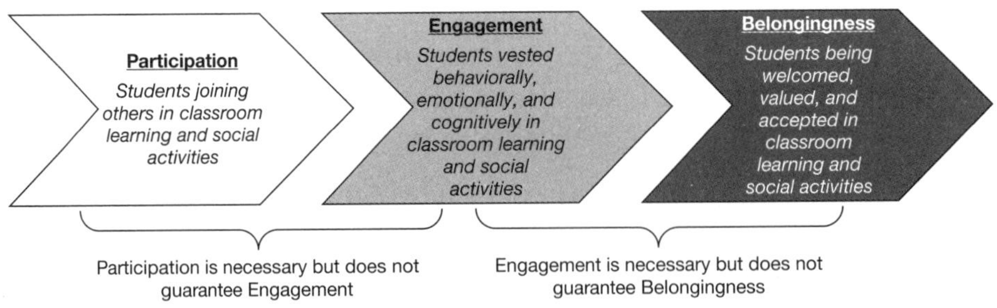

FIGURE 6.1: Participation Provides the Foundation for Engagement and Belongingness

opportunities to regularly participate or if they were only occasionally engaged in classroom activities. Because participation is necessary for engagement, and engagement is necessary for belongingness, participation provides the foundation for both concepts. Therefore, educators must be vigilant about supporting their students to participate in classroom and school activities to the greatest extent possible. School-wide policies and frameworks in conjunction with individualized supports are needed to promote the full participation of students with IEPs in general education classrooms and schools.

School-Wide Participation Supports

The SSPP is focused on supports planning at the individual student level, or the micro level as proponents of ecological system theory would call it (Bronfenbrenner, 1979). Although going into detail on how factors at the macro level (e.g., policies at the state and national levels) and meso level (within a school district or school building) influence student supports and inclusive education is beyond the scope of this book, macro- and meso-level influences must be acknowledged. Even the most creative and dedicated educators will be severely challenged to plan individualized supports in school contexts where structural barriers to participation dominate.

As mentioned in Chapter 1, IDEA emphasizes providing supplementary aids and services as the means to support a student's education in the least restrictive environment and for them to be educated alongside same-age peers to the maximum extent. This is an example of a macro-level support because it is a legal mandate at the jurisdictional/system level. This law compels local schools, as well as individual teachers, to make genuine efforts to provide supports that enable students with IEPs to receive a high-quality education within general education classrooms.

In Chapter 5, which centered on planning instructional supports, the value of using differentiated instruction as a guiding framework/philosophy within a school building to promote inclusive education across classrooms provided an example of meso-level support. In terms of the focus of this chapter, participation supports, there are two other meso-level approaches that deserve special mention because they provide a strong foundation on which to develop more-intense individualized (micro-level) participation supports. Specifically, the school-wide positive behavioral interventions and supports (SWPBIS) framework and Check & Connect (C&C) program have acquired a considerable amount of research evidence supporting their efficacy since being introduced in the 1990s.

School-Wide Positive Behavioral Interventions and Supports (SWPBIS)

Multitiered system of support (MTSS) frameworks are intended to promote positive academic, behavioral, social, and emotional outcomes among all students within a school. As a preventative model, they offer support on a continuum where support intensity increases across multiple levels or tiers. Several MTSS models have been adopted by schools, including response to intervention ([RTI]; see Fuchs & Fuchs, 2006) to address academic outcomes; SWPBIS to address behavioral outcomes (Sugai & Horner, 2006); and comprehensive integrated three-tiered model of prevention ([Ci3T]; Lane et al., 2014) to address a range of student outcomes. Here, special attention is given to SWPBIS because student behavior in a classroom and the supports educators provide to promote positive behavior are critical influences on participation in a classroom. SWPBIS focuses on preventing challenging behavior and promoting a positive and safe school climate. It has been used to produce positive behavioral outcomes across a range of students, and recent research suggests that positive academic outcomes often accompany improvements in classroom behavior (Lee & Gage, 2020).

Figure 6.2 illustrates how a SWPBIS framework directs schools to deliver behavioral supports based on the MTSS logic of increasing supports by intensity as needed (Lewis et al., 2016). Tier 1 universal supports are provided to all students in a school. In this case, "all" really does mean all. Tier 1 supports are intended to prevent challenging behavior across the entire student population. At this level, students are explicitly taught the school-wide behavioral expectations and receive public acknowledgment for engaging in schools and classrooms in a manner where they are meeting those expectations. For example, a school might identify three positively stated expectations (e.g., be safe, be respectful, be responsible) that are unambiguously defined and directly taught by staff across different school settings. Students who exhibit these established behaviors might be acknowledged by receiving tokens that can be accumulated and exchanged for a reward at a later time.

For students who require additional support beyond Tier 1, secondary supports at Tier 2 are provided in conjunction with Tier 1 supports. At this

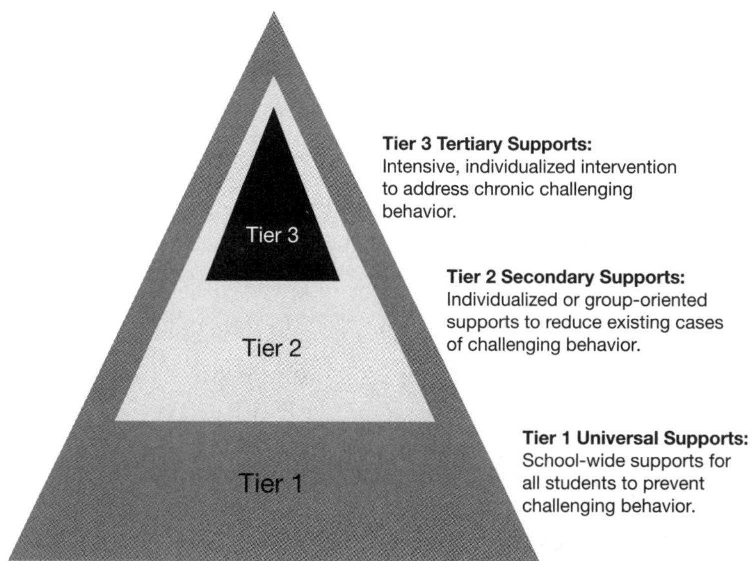

FIGURE 6.2: SWPBIS Framework

level, more focused, frequent support is provided to reduce instances of challenging behavior. Tier 2 supports can be individualized or group focused and often include self-management strategies and social-skills instruction (Sugai & Horner, 2006). One example of a Tier 2 support, check-in check-out (CICO), is discussed later in detail. The tertiary level (Tier 3) is characterized by intensive and individualized supports to address persistent challenging behaviors that are not adequately addressed at Tiers 1 and 2. Only a small number of students will require Tier 3 supports, which are highly individualized interventions. These include interventions that are based on a functional behavior assessment (FBA). As discussed in Chapter 3, FBA is a technique to determine the probable cause of a challenging behavior and/or what is maintaining the behavior. FBAs are conducted by a classroom teacher and/or the school psychologist, behavior specialist, or other school members who are qualified to do so. At this level, students may require other wraparound supports including mental health services, depending on their specific needs (Sugai & Horner, 2006).

Across all three tiers, a SWPBIS team that is composed of general education teachers, special education teachers, school administration, counselors, or other service providers, will carefully monitor data to make informed decisions about the supports that are offered. For example, if data suggest that office discipline referrals are being delivered most often at the playground during recess, the SWPBIS team may wish to focus on how supports within the playground setting could be adjusted. Likewise, the SWPBIS team also will need to consider the effectiveness of the public acknowledgment system being used to reinforce expected behaviors at the playground.

Students are more likely to achieve their prioritized learning goals when they can access and fully participate in SWPBIS. Therefore it is important that students with IEPs not be excluded from SWPBIS data collection and intervention efforts. Although it is intended to be a fully inclusive framework available to all students in a school, some students with IEPs have not fully accessed supports offered through their school's SWPBIS framework. Specifically, students with IEPs have received Tier 3 supports without having first participated in Tiers 1 and 2 (Shuster et al., 2017; Walker et al., 2018). To ensure that students with IEPs fully participate and benefit from the behavioral supports available through SWPBIS, educators will need to consider whether and how to adapt existing supports to meet the unique needs of these students. Walker and Loman (2021) recommend following universal design for learning (UDL) guidelines (see Chapter 7) in planning efforts to consider how to:

a. present the school-wide expectations in different ways (e.g., visual supports to teach school-wide expectations; more frequent, systematic instruction),
b. provide opportunities for students to demonstrate understanding of the school-wide expectations in different ways (e.g., student uses augmentative and alternative communication or draws a picture to answer questions about school-wide expectations), and
c. utilize materials and instructional strategies that are meaningful (e.g., deliver rewards when acknowledging expected behaviors that are motivating and reinforcing to a student).

Check & Connect

Check & Connect (C&C) was originally developed as a drop out prevention program. However, as opposed to focusing on preventing something, it was actually designed to promote engagement and success at school, both of which are antithetical to dropping out. The premise underlying C&C is that the best way to prevent students from dropping out of school is to make sure they have good reasons to persist in attending school. Students who perceive their school to be a welcoming place where they can prosper are not going choose to remove it from their lives (Christenson et al., 2012).

Literature reviews of research studies investigating students who drop out of K–12 schools reveal that there are many factors or combinations of factors that influence students to stop attending (see McDermott, 2019). It is abundantly clear, however, that dropping out is nearly always a process and almost never happens out of the blue. Students who are doing well in school don't simply wake up one morning and decide to stop going. Rather, it is students with a history of unsuccessful and unhappy experiences in school over a prolonged time, those with failing grades, disciplinary problems, or repeated truancies, who are most at risk for dropping out. It is common for students to drop out and return to school several times before they reach the point of deciding that they will never come back again. Although often characterized as a monumental event (depicted as "the day I decided to never step foot in that school again"), longitudinal studies have established that dropping out is most often a process that occurs over time (Jimerson et al., 2000).

The goal of C&C is to catch students early in the drop out process and provide them with extra support to reverse it before they reach the point of no return. C&C is a structured program that requires ongoing school resources, mostly in the form of educator time and training. When implementing C&C, schools regularly screen for students who are at risk for dropping out and select them for the program when warning signs first emerge. C&C matches students with a mentor for a minimum of 2 years. The mentor's charge is to develop a close and significant relationship with the student. The mentor checks in weekly with their student and develops plans with the student to encourage the development of competencies related to success in school such as sticking with their goals and maintaining positive relationships with adults and peers.

The "Check" component refers to the systematic monitoring of alterable disengagement indicators, including school attendance, tardiness, participation, and homework completion, which can be modified through interventions. The "Connect" component refers to individualized interventions put in place for targeted students based on their "Check" data (Goulet et al., 2018). There is also an important parent component in C&C to assure that both the school and home are working in concert to promote a student's engagement and perseverance (Christenson, 2012).

Distinguishing Check-In/Check-Out (CICO) From C&C

Check-in/check-out (CICO) is an intervention similar to C&C, but there are some important differences (Qian & Klemm, 2016). CICO is the most common Tier 2 intervention used by schools adopting a SWPBIS framework (Bruhn et al., 2014), and it is focused on addressing challenging behaviors that impede a student's success in school. This is related to, but in contrast with C&C, where the focus is on preventing a student from dropping out (Qian & Klemm, 2016). CICO involves using a daily point card to monitor student engagement in the school-wide expectations (established in Tier 1) during the school day at predetermined intervals, such as every class period. Teachers rate the student's behavior across each expectation at each interval using a numerical rating system. For example, 0 = did not meet expectation, 1 = somewhat met expectation, 2 = fully met expectation. CICO requires that a mentor meet with the student at the beginning of the school day to review expectations and the student's daily point goal, and at the end of the school day to discuss progress toward the daily goal. Typically, the point card is sent home for a family member to review.

Both CICO and C&C are data driven (Qian & Klemm, 2016). In this sense they are similar to the progress monitoring data discussed in Chapter 5. Data on school engagement and behavior are used to drive decisions regarding the intensity of the interventions and supports that are being provided. Dosage, or the intensity of support, is adjusted based on student progress. Best practice is to use the least intrusive and least intensive interventions necessary to promote progress and achievement in social and behavioral curriculum.

School Leadership and School-Level Supports

SWPBIS, C&C, CICO, RTI, and Ci3T—the various frameworks and interventions that have been introduced in the section can begin to blur together like letters in a bowl of alphabet soup. These are only the tip of the iceberg in terms of processes and practices for school-wide implementation that have been proposed over time. Despite the expansive array of options, establishing comprehensive approaches that the entire school staff embraces is clearly the most effective way to address student behavior and engagement at the building level. Fullan and Quinn (2016) indicated that degree of coherence with a school staff, which they defined as a shared depth of understanding about the nature of the work accomplished within a school, is possibly the most critical feature distinguishing high-performing schools from low-performing schools. Although SWPBIS, C&C, and the other approaches mentioned in this chapter have a wealth of research evidence supporting their effectiveness, which approach is used will likely matter less than whether or not there is widespread agreement and commitment among a school's educators in regard to their school's approach. The most critical elements are the extent that the entire school staff understands what to do and the assurance that implementation is consistently applied across adults and school settings.

School leadership must have a clear vision in regard to inclusive education. District- and building-level administrators need to communicate that teaching students with a wide diversity of learning needs in the general education classroom is a priority. Without proper commitment to inclusive education from school leadership, educators will be inclined to rely on past practices which involve establishing separate classrooms for students with IEPs. School administrators also need to have a positive vision for behavioral and learning outcomes for all students, and be able to communicate this vision. Teaching staff, parents, and students should all be well aware of what behaviors are encouraged and nurtured at school, what behaviors cannot be tolerated, and how student progress is going to be measured and evaluated. Moreover, classroom management procedures that are standard across all grade levels and classrooms should be instituted, and teachers need to be supported by administrators in their classroom management efforts. Principals and other school leaders who communicate a clear vision of these areas can establish a basis to productively work with their staff toward developing the types of meso-level, school-wide routines and procedures that provide the students, parents, and teachers with a sense of consistency as well as communicate high expectations to students and parents (Hallinger, 2018). Fullan and Quinn (2016) stress the need for school leaders to develop a culture of ongoing and cumulative coherence, where educator expertise is cultivated and is focused on a collective purpose.

Although it is possible for teacher teams to develop good individual supports for students with IEPs in the absence of good school leadership, a lack of administrative support makes it far more difficult. Teacher teams that know that their school leadership is committed to assuring students with IEPs have access to the high-quality supports that are needed to be successful in general education classrooms will approach supports planning differently than do educators who perceive their building or district leadership lacks a commitment to changing the status quo. York-Barr and colleagues (2016) stressed the need for school- and district-level leaders to grow ownership for inclusive education, and not simply provide lip service. They caution, "Just telling them to do it doesn't work" (p. 101). What works is committing to implementing school-wide practices with fidelity for which there is a substantive amount of research support, such as SWPBIS and C&C.

Committing to school-wide practices comes with a cost. Namely, precious time, resources, and effort must be expended when establishing a school-wide culture of proactive planning and implementation of supports. However, meso-level investments make planning and implementing supports at the micro level a far more workable and efficient undertaking. In contrast, a failure to invest in comprehensive, school-wide approaches will cost excessive amounts of time, energy, and resources in the long run. Frameworks, such as SWPBIS, and interventions, such as C&C, provide the means to build capacity to address the complexities that are inherent in a school—an enterprise that requires the cooperation of a diverse population of children and adults to succeed. The alternative to a comprehensive approach is to invest time, energy, and resources dealing with a host of concerns and issues as they arise—to spend time putting out fires all day long. In such schools, energy devoted to resolving the short-term crisis of the moment will regularly displace energy devoted to achieving the long-term goal of developing a school community that maximizes each student's learning and growth.

Planning and Implementing Individual Participation Supports

In Chapter 3, the taxonomy of learning activities found in general education classrooms (Harris & Hofer, n.d.) was introduced (https://activitytypes.wm.edu/). This taxonomy offers a useful starting point for special educators and general education teachers to plan individual participation supports. A special education teacher's global request along the lines of "Tell me about the learning activities that occur in your seventh-grade earth science class," may be greeted with puzzlement by a general education teacher who doesn't know where to begin to describe the array of planned and unplanned learning activities that will occur over the course of a quarter, semester, or year of instruction. However, going through the list of 40 science learning activity types identified by Blanchard et al. (2011) displayed in Table 6.1 and identifying how often (in general) various learning activities are likely to be used offers educators an efficient way to identify the most common types of learning activities. Insights gained from Table 6.1 can be used to proactively plan and arrange participation supports for students with IEPs.

Targeting Classroom Learning Activities

For example, consider a class where Learning Activity 6, participating in simulations, was going to be regularly used during a semester. If a student who was the focus of the supports planning had traditionally experienced difficulties with assignments requiring abstract reasoning but had done well in cooperative learning scenarios, identifying different types of peer supports to use during simulations could be a useful participation support.

The table shows the learning activities commonly used in science instruction. Harris & Hofer (n.d.) have provided equivalent taxonomies for eight other instructional areas, namely, K–6 literacy, mathematics, music, physical education, secondary English and language arts, social studies, visual arts, and world languages (https://activitytypes.wm.edu/). It bears repeating that participation supports are intended to promote the participation, engagement, and belongingness of students with IEPs in general education classrooms. Participation supports are different than instructional supports (Chapter 5), which are targeted toward promoting the achievement of specific learning goals and outcomes. Instructional supports directly affect student achievement, but participation supports will have a secondary effect. Students receiving supports to participate in any of the learning activities more fully in Table 6.1 will reap benefits in regard to their achievement. But participation supports should not be fully focused on, nor judged by, their potential value to improve student achievement outcomes. Participation supports function to promote engagement in learning activities, and engagement criteria should be used to assess their value.

Table 6.2 provides a means to measure student engagement through periodic observations. Fifteen minutes of observing a student in a classroom once every couple of weeks can provide ongoing data to assess the effectiveness of

TABLE 6.1 Frequency of Learning Activity Types Associated With Science Instruction

SCIENCE INSTRUCTION: LEARNING ACTIVITY TYPES FOR CONCEPTUAL KNOWLEDGE BUILDING	**How often will it be used this semester?**				
	Not sure X	**Never 1**	**Seldom 2**	**Some of the time 3**	**Often 4**
1. *Reading text* (extracting information from print-based and digital formats)	X	1	2	3	**4**
2. *Attending to presentation/demonstration* (attending to information via video, oral, or multimedia)	X	1	2	3	**4**
3. *Taking notes* (recording information from presentations, group work, etc.)	X	1	2	**3**	4
4. *Viewing images/objects* (examining still and moving images/objects in print-based or digital formats)	X	1	2	**3**	4
5. *Discussing* (engaging in dialogue with peers; synchronous/asynchronous)	X	1	2	**3**	4
6. *Participating in simulations* (interacting with live/digital simulations)	X	1	**2**	3	4
7. *Exploring a topic/conducting background research* (gathering information using print-based and digital sources)	X	1	2	**3**	4
8. *Studying* (studying terminology, classifications, test review, etc.)	X	1	2	**3**	4
9. *Observing phenomena* (observing phenomena that raise scientific questions from physical objects, organisms, or digital media)	X	**1**	2	3	4
10. *Distinguishing observations from inferences* (differentiating directly observed sensory input from inferences requiring background knowledge)	X	**1**	2	3	4
11. *Developing predictions, hypotheses, questions, variables* (developing predictions, selecting hypothesis, generating questions, and identifying variables to study)	X	1	**2**	3	4

12. *Selecting procedures* (selecting procedures and instruments to test hypotheses and/or answer questions)	X	**(1)**	2	3	4
13. *Sequencing procedures* (sequencing the order of procedures to collect data)	X	**(1)**	2	3	4
14. *Organizing/classifying data* (creating a structure to organize data)	X	1	**(2)**	3	4
15. *Analyzing data* (recognizing patterns, describing relationships, prioritizing evidence, determining possible sources of error/discrepancies, etc.)	X	1	**(2)**	3	4
16. *Comparing findings with predictions/hypotheses* (evaluating findings in relationship to hypotheses)	X	1	**(2)**	3	4
17. *Making connections between findings & scientific concepts/knowledge* (linking findings to concepts from textbook/research publications)	X	1	**(2)**	3	4
SCIENCE INSTRUCTION: LEARNING ACTIVITY TYPES FOR PROCEDURAL KNOWLEDGE BUILDING					
18. *Learning and practicing safety procedures* (learning how to safely and appropriately handle equipment)	X	1	2	**(3)**	4
19. *Measuring* (learning how to make measurements using specific tools)	X	1	2	**(3)**	4
20. *Practicing* (practicing using equipment, software, measurement tools, etc.)	X	1	2	**(3)**	4
21. *Preparing/cleaning up* (organizing equipment or information for the laboratory)	X	1	2	3	**(4)**
22. *Carrying out procedures* (running trials or otherwise carrying out steps to investigations)	X	1	2	**(3)**	4
23. *Observing* (making observations from physical or digital experiences)	X	1	2	**(3)**	4
24. *Recording data* (recording observational and previously recorded data in tables, graphs, images, lab notes)	X	1	**(2)**	3	4
25. *Generating data* (manipulating equipment or animations to generate data such as heart rate, cooling water temperatures)	X	1	**(2)**	3	4

continued

TABLE 6.1 ***continued***

26. *Collecting data* (collecting data with physical objects or simulations)	X	1	(2)	3	4
27. *Collecting samples* (obtaining sample items to study such as bird songs, soil, video footage, etc.)	X	1	(2)	3	4
28. *Computing* (calculating results from data)	X	1	(2)	3	4
SCIENCE INSTRUCTION: LEARNING ACTIVITY TYPES FOR KNOWLEDGE EXPRESSION					
29. *Respond to questions* (responding to teacher-supplied, peer-written, published, or digitally posed questions that require short answers, explanations, or elaborations)	X	1	2	3	(4)
30. *Write a report* (writing a laboratory or research report)	X	1	2	(3)	4
31. *Create an image* (creating an image to demonstrate their knowledge of a science concept and/or process)	X	1	(2)	3	4
32. *Present or demonstrate* (presenting/demonstrating laboratory or research findings, or other learning	X	1	(2)	3	4
33. *Take a quiz or test* (responding to questions on an exam)	X	1	2	(3)	4

the participation supports that are put into place. Just like other progress monitoring data discussed in Chapter 5, if several observations reveal that a student is not satisfactorily engaged in classroom learning activities or that engagement is decreasing over time, it would be essential to adjust participation supports accordingly. Educators could provide more intense supports and/or different types of supports. Students who are not engaged in classroom learning activities are at risk of being "bored out of their minds" and they learn very little. Also, asking general education teachers to simply include students physically in their classrooms with little attention paid to whether students are thriving is a recipe for disaster. Teachers who are asked to simply manage students with IEPs in their classrooms will likely feel that their skills are being devalued, because they are not babysitters, they are teachers (York-Barr et al., 2016). A culture

34. *Debate* (discussing opposing viewpoints linked to ethics, nature of science, personal preferences, politics, etc.)	X	(1)	2	3	4
35. *Develop or build a model* (physically or digitally creating models to demonstrate content knowledge or conduct experiments)	X	1	2	(3)	4
36. *Draw/create images* (physically or digitally drawing or creating images from labs, observations, etc.)	(X)	1	2	3	4
37. *Develop a concept map* (developing graphic organizers, semantic maps, etc.)	X	(1)	2	3	4
38. *Play a game* (participating in group or individual games to review or learn content)	X	1	(2)	3	4
39. *Develop a game* (developing a physical or digital interactive game)	X	(1)	2	3	4
40. *Create/perform* (creating/performing a skit, song, poem, poster, exhibit, etc.)	X	(1)	2	3	4

Note. The learning activity types in this table are adapted from the Science Learning Activity Types taxonomy developed by Blanchard et al. (2011). More comprehensives descriptions of each learning activity type, along with possible technologies that may be applicable to instruction, are available online (https://activitytypes.wm.edu/ScienceLearningATs-Feb2011.pdf).

for inclusive education within a school building is established through special educators and general education teachers acknowledging and respecting one another's expertise and roles.

Full and Partial Participation

Earlier, the case was made that without participation the chances to experience higher-order inclusion constructs like engagement and belongingness were unlikely, if not impossible. Not participating in the activities of a group clearly diminishes any chance of becoming a valued member of that group. Yet, it was also pointed out that within any type of community, level of participation will vary among members due to circumstances and by choice. Some people may not fully participate in all aspects of a group's activities for a variety of reasons, including time constraints, personal preferences, and level of competence. For

TABLE 6.2 Class Session Observation Form to Monitor Student Engagement

	Never	A little bit of the time	Some of the time	A lot of the time	Almost all of the time
	0	**1**	**2**	**3**	**4**
1. The student's body, face, and/or eyes were in the direction of the teacher and/or instructional materials during the class session.	0	1	2	3	4
2. The student was using instructional materials in a way that corresponded to the class session's learning activities	0	1	2	3	4
3. The student followed teacher instructions/directions or the natural sequence of the instructional activities during the class session.	0	1	2	3	4
4. The student commented, asked/responded to question(s), and/or used other modes of responding (e.g., noises, gestures) that corresponded to the class session.	0	1	2	3	4
Additional Comments/Observations:					

instance, local running clubs will typically advertise that they strive to be a community that is open to all type of runners; all that is needed to belong is an interest in running. Members include advance runners who race competitively in marathons, as well as "weekend athletes" whose motivation for belonging is primarily social and largely limit their participation to jogging and walking in relatively short fun runs. The point is, participation in a group is usually not an all-or-nothing proposition. There are degrees of participation.

Recognizing the validity of different degrees of participation was the underlying premise of the Baumgart et al. (1982) principle of partial participation. The fundamental idea here is that students with IEPs should be allowed to "function, at least in part, in a wide variety of least restrictive school and non-school environments and activities" (p. 19). It makes more sense to identify the portions of a classroom activity in which a student can meaningfully participate and to work with those opportunities and experiences than it does to discard an activity altogether because of aspects that are not well suited to a student. Yet, like many other good ideas, the principle of partial participation can be misused. When it was first introduced in 1982, Baumgart and colleagues provided several cautions, including the importance of not selecting activities only because a means to partially participate can be identified. Rather, activities should be selected because of their saliency to the student's education and life. Ten years later, Ferguson and Baumgart (1991) further identified ways the partial participation had been misapplied, including inadvertently promoting (a) passive participation, when the student hardly does much of anything, and mostly just watches others; (b) myopic participation, or narrow participation that does not take the student's or family's preferences into consideration; (c) piecemeal participation, which is participation that is so unique to a situation that it doesn't build on a repertoire of skills or experiences; and (d) missed participation, or overemphasizing completing a step or activity independently versus looking for opportunities to participate interdependently in collaboration with others.

Unfortunately, there is no secret checklist that can be provided to assure partial participation is not misapplied. Educators must take a step back from the learning activity, classroom routine, or whatever it is that is happening in the school to identify where a student's participation could be more meaningful. Consider the activity holistically, focus attention on the ways the student could meaningfully take part in it, and introduce the supports that are needed to increase meaningful participation. These could be in the form of extra instruction, assistance from another person, adapted materials, or it could be a combination of several things. Finally, build on successes. Once a student begins to partially participate, look for ways to expand their participation both in terms of quality and quantity.

Partial participation assumes that students with IEPs need not be excluded from activities because they cannot complete a task fully or independently.

Finding ways for students to meaningfully participate is not overly complicated. It does, however, require thoughtful observations of students, consideration of the demands of the activities and settings, and a willingness to think creatively.

Ecological Inventories

In Chapter 3, ecological inventories were briefly mentioned as a useful tool to help educators plan supports for students with IEPs in general education environments. The purpose of an ecological inventory is to identify the knowledge and skills a student will need to be successful in the environments in which they participate. Generally, an ecological inventory is conducted by identifying (a) relevant current and future environments and sub-environments in which the student participates (or will participate), (b) activities or routines that take place in those environments, and (c) the knowledge and skills required to participate in those environments.

Within the context of the general education classroom, ecological inventories should be completed for each general education class or setting that a student attends (or will attend) and the activities or routines within those settings. For example, an educator who conducts an ecological inventory for a student in ninth grade will need to consider the activities and routines (including the learning activity types noted previously in the chapter) across the classes in which the student is enrolled. (e.g., English 1, geometry, world history, biology, Spanish 1). Gathering this information can be particularly helpful to educators for identifying appropriate learning priorities based on the content delivered and expectations across settings and informing instructional supports planning. Gathering this information also can assist educators in determining when and how to provide participation supports across settings. For example, technology-aided instruction, such as text-to-speech, might be an appropriate participation support for a student who reads significantly below grade level during independent reading time in English 1. Likewise, peer support provided during a small-group book report project in world history might be an appropriate participation support for a student who requires additional prompting to maintain engagement during less structured classroom time. Educators can create an ecological assessment tool to meet their needs, where information is collected from direct observations of the general education environments and in consultation with general education teachers.

Accommodations and Modifications

In Chapter 4, it was mentioned that the concepts of accommodations and modifications are often included under the umbrella of curricular adaptations (e.g., Janney & Snell, 2013) because of their relevance to altering either the (a) standards of performance associated with a curriculum or the (b) process for teaching/evaluation of the curriculum. Although this is not an incorrect way to consider accommodations and modifications, it is also useful to consider these concepts in relation to participation supports. Although accommodations and modifications alter the curriculum for the student receiving them, their overarching purpose is to enhance and encourage meaningful participation in the general education curriculum and classroom. A common expression used in the field of special education over the years has been that accommodations level the playing field for students, whereas modification changes the playing field (e.g., see Vanderbilt University, 2021). In terms of participation supports, the critical point is they move the students onto the field participating instead of sitting on the sidelines.

The key feature of accommodations is that the learning outcomes and performance standards for students who receive them are not altered from those established in the general education curriculum. Accommodations can be so slight that they hardly require any formal documentation or discussion. For example, a student with relatively poor fine motor muscle development and control might prefer to write their paper using a pencil grip. The pencil grip is technically an accommodation because (a) the student's difficulties in producing quality writing due to fine motor strength, fatigue, and control are being compensated by providing a pencil grip, but (b) the expectations for quality writing (both in terms of content and penmanship) are not any different for this student than for others. Why on earth any educator would object to a student using a pencil grip is a mystery, although there are undoubtedly some inflexible teachers who could come up with any number of misguided reasons such as "He will never ever learn to write without one." Of course, this argument is not true. Providing a pencil grip encourages perseverance in writing tasks, which will likely lead to strengthening a student's fine motor muscles, which combined with the practice will increase control, and in the vast majority of cases will lead to the student eventually not needing the grip to produce legible work. Some may claim, "It's not fair to the others!" (Huh? What is not fair is excluding a student from meaningful learning opportunities.) If someone becomes obsessed with the notion of treating all students the same, then perhaps the path of least resistance may be to suggest allowing every student to use a pencil grip who wants to, whether they actually need it or not. It is amazing how often discussions about the fairness of certain accommodations can be quickly resolved by suggesting that they be available to anyone who wants to use them. When accommodations become readily available to all, the classroom has actually become more universally designed. (More about this in Chapter 8.)

Not all accommodations are as simple as a pencil grip, and many of these can require significant efforts to implement. For instance, a teacher who highlights key information in a textbook or research materials to support a student in identifying the main ideas—but requires the student to achieve the same learning outcomes as other students—is making an accommodation. Preparing materials in this way is an ongoing responsibility and requires an investment of educator time that goes far beyond what is required by allowing a student to use a pencil grip. Accommodations requiring a substantial investment of people's time and preplanning need to be documented in a support plan and listed on an IEP.

In contrast to accommodations, modifications include adjusting learning outcomes and performance standards. Most likely, the difficulty level of the content being taught and learned is clearly different from that which is specified in the general education curriculum. Some examples of modifications might be: requiring a student to research and prepare a PowerPoint presentation on life of a US president instead of writing a report, asking a student in a class discussion about only the "big ideas" in a science unit instead of the more detailed information the other students are responsible for learning, providing a student with a less demanding reading assignment (using text that is written at a lower grade level, provides less details, but whose content aligns with the grade level the rest of the class is reading), and providing a student with a word bank for fill-in-blank items on a classroom test.

From a participation support perspective, making clear distinctions between accommodations and modifications is not nearly as important as figuring out what adjustments make sense for a student in terms of enabling them to fully participate in class-wide learning activities. Actually, trying to brainstorm the answer to the broad question, "What accommodations or modifications does the student need?" is probably not as useful as asking a simpler question: "In regard to the core instructional and evaluation activities of the class, what changes can be made to help assure that this student will meaningfully participate in classroom learning activities and therefore be a part of the intellectual life of this classroom?"

A sample of some the most common accommodations and modifications used in today's schools is listed in Table 6.3. There are far more expansive lists available to those who find scrolling through different ideas to be helpful. For instance, Lighter (2018) offers a free download of a 90-page "Ultimate List of IEP Accommodations, Modifications, and Strategies" at (https://adayinourshoes.com/wp-content/uploads/IEP-Accommodations-and-Strategies-printable.pdf). Despite the appeal of these lists, the planning team that (a) obtains a clear understanding of what the teachers and students will be doing during a unit of instruction, and (b) closely observes a student in classroom learning activities will be in a good position to problem-solve ways in which student participation and learning can be enhanced. Specific accommodations and modifications needed by students will eventually become apparent. Planning accommodations and modifications should be a dynamic and ongoing process; what might be a perfectly reasonable accommodation at one point, may not be an ideal solution at another. As is discussed in Chapter 8, as students get older it is especially important that they understand what accommodations and modifications they need, and how to advocate for these.

From a participation support perspective, making clear distinctions between accommodations and modifications is not nearly as important as figuring out what adjustments make sense for a student in terms of enabling them to fully participate in class-wide learning activities.

Providing Personalized Supports and Assistance

Some students with IEPs will require personalized supports and assistance beyond that offered to other students in the classroom. Delivery of personalized supports and assistance can be shared across adults in the classroom (e.g., teachers, paraprofessionals, related services providers, student teachers) as well as peers. Planning for the supports falls to the entire educational team, with leadership from the special education teacher. For example, a special education teacher and general education teacher who meet during their planning time might develop a lesson on conducting an experiment related to plant growth for a sixth-grade class. During this time, they identify any

TABLE 6.3 Sample Accommodations and Modifications in the General Education Classroom

MODIFICATIONS	ACCOMMODATIONS
Modifying assignments (e.g., reducing the number of assigned items on a worksheet; providing assignments with less difficult materials/questions/prompts to be better aligned with the student's achievement level; creating parallel assignments such as creating a collage or outline instead of writing a multipage report/essay)	**Preferential seating in a classroom or school building** (e.g., allowing student to be in space in their classroom where potential distractions are minimalized; allowing students to take quizzes and tests outside of the classroom)
Modifying student evaluations (e.g., providing alternative ways to demonstrate knowledge gained at the end of unit, such as preparing a PowerPoint presentation or providing a word bank for fill-in-the-blank quiz items)	**Accommodated student evaluations** (e.g., allowing students have test questions read to them or to answer them orally; allowing extra time on tests)
Modifying social/behavioral expectations (e.g., allowing a student a certain number of opportunities each day/week to leave the class and go a designated area when they sense a negative behavior coming on)	**Social/behavioral accommodations** (e.g., graphic organizers or a written schedule to keep track of time and space in school; social narratives to prepare students for potentially difficult or anxiety-provoking situations)
Modifying learning materials (e.g., providing reading material that is at a lower reading and comprehension level; providing speech to text devices to compose and submit assignments that other students submit through word processing software)	**Accommodated materials** (e.g., large print or braille text; writing essays with speech-to-text software; reading text with grade-level material using text-to-speech software; providing access to online textbooks or allowing students to have two sets of books, one for school and one for home; earplugs or headphones to remove distractions)

curricular adaptations and instructional supports needed for students with IEPs and decide that, although the general education teacher will deliver a majority of the lesson, the classroom paraprofessional will support students by encouraging peer cooperation and engagement during the practical application portion of the lesson.

Paraprofessionals (also referred to as paraeducators, teacher assistants, and classrooms aides—and from henceforth in the book will be called simply "paras") often support one or more students with IEPs in general education classrooms (Carter et al., 2009). By definition, paras work in school settings to assist special education teachers and other professionals in the provision of special education and related services (IDEA, 2004). In this role, paras work under the supervision and guidance of highly qualified professionals (e.g., general education teacher, special education teacher) in a number of ways. These include supporting students in different instructional arrangements (i.e., one to one, small group, whole group), delivering academic instruction as designed by general and special education teachers, and supporting students' behavioral and social needs. Paras often have little preparation for their roles and responsibilities, and will benefit from training and direct support from supervising teachers to develop the knowledge and skills necessary to be successful (see, for example, the 2015 CEC paraprofessional standards, https://exceptionalchildren.org/sites/default/files/2020-07/Specialty_Set_Special_Education_Paraeducator.pdf).

It is important for educators to carefully consider how to best utilize and support paraprofessionals in general education classrooms to promote student participation. Yates et al. (2020) recommended the following three-step process: (1) write a comprehensive lesson plan, (2) communicate the lesson plan to the paraprofessional, and (3) provide feedback on the paraprofessional's effectiveness in delivering supports outlined in the lesson plan. As illustrated in the sample lesson plan in Figure 6.3, a comprehensive lesson plan includes the purpose and goals of the lesson; specific information about the strengths, needs, and required supports of students with IEPs who will participate in the lesson; the sequence of lesson activities; and the specific roles and expectations for all adults who will implement the lesson, including the paraprofessional. Once the lesson plan has been developed, the paraprofessional and others implementing the lesson need to set aside time to review the plan and expectations. During this time, the teacher may find it helpful to model and practice certain aspects of the lesson plan with the paraprofessional as additional guidance. To encourage growth in paraprofessional implementation, the teacher should observe and provide feedback on how well the paraprofessional implemented the lesson plan. This can occur during implementation or after implementation in a post-observation meeting. Yates et al. (2020) also noted the importance of providing coaching to paras when additional training is necessary.

FIGURE 6.3: Sample Paraprofessional Lesson Plan for the General Education Classroom

PARAPROFESSIONAL LESSON PLAN	
GENERAL INFORMATION	
Grade: 3 **Standard(s) addressed:** CCSS.MATH. CONTENT.3.NF.A.3.D **Lesson objective:** Compare two fractions with the same denominator or same numerator	**Lesson purpose:** Students will create a visual representation of two fractions with the same numerator or denominator and then compare the fractions. **Student goals (long and short term):** Short-term goal: Create a visual representation of fractions. Long-term goal: Compare two fractions with the same denominator or numerator.

INFORMATION FOR INDIVIDUAL STUDENTS		
Strengths	**Needs**	**Supports (including accommodations/ modifications)**
Cammie: grade-level academic work in math and reading	• Requires support to effectively communicate with peers, attend to instruction, and follow adult directions	• Token board • Sentence starters for communication with peers • Tasks broken into smaller chunks (e.g., complete ½ of worksheet, break, complete second ½)
Ramone: counting up to 20, works well with peers, follows 1–2 step directions, reads at the Grade 1 level	• Requires support to complete grade-level work and fine motor activities (e.g., drawing, writing, cutting) • Requires support to vocally communicate	• Precut fraction bars and pieces • Adapted writing tools • Visual supports for directions • Sentence starters and visual supports for communication

Lesson sequence	Two-person instructional team responsibilities	
	General education teacher	**Paraprofessional**
Introduce topic (full class)	• Review of prior content • Review homework • Go over an example • Turn and talk about example	• Monitor all students for on-task behavior, redirect with gesture/visual prompts • Give Cammie a token every 3 min to earn a break every 15 min • Remind peer to present visually supported choices to Cammie during Turn and Talk • Ensure Cammie has correct sentence starters for topic of conversation
Main lesson (full class)	• Introduce vocabulary and day's objective • Demonstrate how to create a model of the fractions, as students follow along and do the same • Demonstrate how to compare the fractions, as students follow along and do the same • Provide communication supports for Ramone and Cammie during whole group discussion	• Ensure Ramone takes out his precut fraction bars and uses his adapted writing tools • Monitor all students to remain on task • Answer students' questions • Give Cammie a token every 3 min to earn a break every 15 min

continued

FIGURE 6.3 *continued*

Lesson sequence	Two-person instructional team responsibilities	
	General education teacher	**Paraprofessional**
Small-group practice	• Teacher writes two fractions to compare on the board • Students draw and compare fractions • Teacher reviews during whole-group discussion • Give Cammie a token every 3 min to earn a break every 15 min	• Ensure Ramone's peer buddy has visual reminders to help keep him on task • Ensure Ramone takes out his precut fraction bars and uses his adapted writing tools • Remind peer to present visually supported choices to Ramone during turn and talk • Monitor Ramone's peer buddies to ensure they are prompting him to participate • Monitor Cammie's peer buddies to ensure they are helping him her communicate about the lesson • Remind Cammie to use sentence starters
Independent practice	• Have adapted worksheets ready for Cammie (fewer problems) and Ramone • Monitor and answer questions • Remind all students to remain on task • Give Cammie a token every 3 min to earn a break every 15 min	• Pass out worksheets to all students, including adapted worksheets for Cammie and Ramone • Monitor student behavior • Assist all students who have questions

Note. Adapted with permission. Based on Yates et al. (2021). Yates, P., Chopra, R., Sobeck, E., Douglas, S., Morano, S., Walker, V. L., & Schulze, R. (2020). Working with paraeducators: Tools and strategies for planning, performance feedback, and evaluation. *Intervention in School and Clinic*, *56*(1), 43–50. https://doi.org/10.1177/1053451220910740

Although teachers and other professionals can provide effective paraprofessional oversight and training (Brock & Anderson, 2021), educators must be responsive to the potential issues concerning the overreliance and misuse of paras in general education classrooms (Giangreco, 2021). As noted earlier, paras, who typically are the least qualified adults in the classroom, often are assigned to support students with the highest support needs, with many assuming primary instructional responsibilities despite having limited training and qualifications to do so. Giangreco further documented the numerous ways in which overreliance on paras can (a) interfere with student relationships and interactions with peers and teachers and (b) result in poor-quality instruction, separation within the general education classroom, and increased levels of dependency on adults.

To address these concerns, educators, with support from administration, will need to ensure that paras are adequately trained and supported and that their responsibilities do not extend beyond the scope of their assigned position. In other words, teachers must assume the primary role of instructor by designing supports and delivering the bulk of instruction to students with disabilities.

Peer support strategies have also been recommended as a support for students with disabilities and as a potential alternative to one-to-one paraprofessional support. Peers offer a natural support in the general education classroom and can increase opportunities for participation and classroom membership for students with disabilities. These relationships can also offer benefits to peers without disabilities, including improved academic engagement (Brock & Huber, 2017). These strategies involve peers without disabilities supporting students with disabilities in a range of skill areas (e.g., academics, social/communication) using models such as focused peer tutoring or less formal peer support programs that promote friendship and classroom membership. However, peers should only provide personalized assistance when it is appropriate. For instance, one would not expect (nor would it be appropriate), for example, a peer to assist in a gastronomy tube (G-tube) feeding.

The Supports Schedule: Putting It All Together and Getting Everyone on the Same Page

The saying "No budget = No mission" refers to the reality that the most wonderfully written, spot-on mission statement will be ineffectual in bringing about any actionable change in absence of financial support. For example, a mission statement calling for an astronaut to walk on Mars is one thing, but it won't happen until the rocket ship is paid for and there has been sufficient investment to figure out how to do everything that is needed to get an astronaut to Mars and back. Without a budget, the mission to Mars is words on paper versus an actual mission.

A parallel logic is applicable to a new saying that was created just for this book: "No schedule = No supports." One can talk about supports until blue in the face, but until a schedule is agreed upon that specifies what, when, and how supports will be delivered, educators may find it challenging to accomplish goals related to supports implementation. Table 6.4 shows a supports schedule that is structured around four matter-of-fact questions:

One can talk about supports until blue in the face, but until a schedule is agreed upon that specifies what, when, and how supports will be delivered, educators may find it challenging to accomplish goals related to supports implementation.

1. What time of day are we planning for?
2. What is the rest of the class doing during this time?
3. What should the student with the IEP be doing and how will they be supported doing it?
4. Who is responsible for providing support, and what are they doing to provide it?

The schedule in Table 6.4 does not provide the level of detail discussed in other sections of this book; for instance, the para lesson plan is not included and progress monitoring forms are not provided. This plan is descriptive. The lack of detail in Table 6.4 is a strength, as incorporating detailed planning documents into a master schedule would make it impossible to see the forest (namely, the basic plan to support the student) for the trees (the planning documents).

Although detailed planning forms are not part of Table 6.4, this scheduling form is not a superficial set of notes of vague references to classroom staff providing supports as needed. Rather, it is a transparent and straightforward documentation of the supports a student needs and the people responsible for providing them. School administrators, parents, teachers, and paras can all read the information in this schedule and gain an unambiguous picture of what supports are going to be provided to a student and what a student will be doing throughout their school day. Of course, it can be updated at any time as new supports are added or activities change. Its purpose is to make sure all educators are on the same page and working from the same playbook. In this way it is invaluable to fostering collaboration and cooperation among members of the school team.

Questions for Discussion

1. Researchers have reported that educators often have widely different views on student discipline, including what are and are not good school rules and how student problem behavior should be handled (Rimm-Kaufman et al., 2006). Experts on SWPBIS like Sugai and Horner (2006) contend that at least 80% of a school's educators need to supportive of implementing SWPBIS, which requires agreement on how to reinforce students' positive behavior as well as the consequences for problem behavior. Coming to consensus often requires considerable time devoted to discussions and a willingness for practically all teachers to change their daily classroom management practices to some extent. What do you suspect are some points of contention and disagreement among educators regarding how student behavior (both good and problematic) should be handled by teaching staff? Why is it so important to get educators in a school to come to agreement?
2. Accommodations, modifications, and other supports should always be based on what a student needs at the current time. A student may not have needed a certain support last year but does need it this year. Another student may have needed a certain support last year but does not need it this year. How does an educational team determine when a new support is needed or when a current support is no longer needed? Why would it be important to include the student in this discussion?
3. Table 6.4 provides a daily schedule for Robert that lists all the supports he receives and the people who provide him supports. In the text, it was mentioned that this provides a significant degree of transparency for the teachers, parents, and school administrators. Why is transparency important? How does it serve the interests of the teachers, parents, and school administrators involved?

TABLE 6.4 Planning Supports to Align With the Class Schedule

DAILY SCHEDULE FOR ROBERT IN MR. WEBSTER'S SECOND-GRADE CLASS AT PARKVIEW ELEMENTARY SCHOOL		
Time of day	**What the class is doing**	
Breakfast **7:15 to 8:00**	Breakfast is available to students who want it.	
Arrival at school **7:45 to 8:00**	Students are arriving to the school by walking/bike riding, family cars, & school busses; school doors open at 7:45 and students have options of going to their classrooms or going to a common area (e.g., playground, gym, cafeteria).	
Arrival at class-room **8:00 to 8:15**	A bell rings at 8:00 indicating students are expected to come inside the school building and go to their classrooms. When students arrive in Mr. Webster's class, they put their coats and backpacks in their cubbies. School-wide announcements occur at 8:10, at which time students should be in their desks (and are counted as tardy if they are not). Classroom activities begin following announcements.	

	What the student (Robert) is doing & how student will be supported to participate in class/school	Who is responsible for providing the support and what they are doing
	Robert doesn't participate in breakfast program as he eats breakfast at home.	Nonapplicable
	Robert lives a couple blocks from school and walks to school with his siblings and neighborhood friends. He always chooses to go to the playground when the weather is nice, and to the gym when it is not. He hangs around his classmates and neighborhood friends before school, and reports he is content with his before-school activities.	Robert's older brother and his neighborhood friends are conscientious about watching out for and including him. The natural supports work well during this time of the day, and there is no need for more formal, adult-directed supports.
	Robert knows exactly what to do when the bell rings at 8:00. Social narratives were used to teach him the classroom arrival routine last year, and he generalized these to this year's class without difficulty. He occasionally needs help locating his backpack on the playground, but peers assist him and he always locates it quickly. He has learned the routine of going to his classroom, putting his coat and backpack in his cubby, finding his desk and sitting down. In fact, he does this more quickly and efficiently than the vast majority of his peers. He likes a "connect the dots/numbers" coloring book, and has one stored in his desk. He immediately gets this out and proceeds to work on it until school announcements. He does, however, pause to interact with others (greet his fellow students or check in with a teacher). When the school announcements are over and the teacher begins the classroom activity instruction, Robert benefits from further explanation about what is going to happen in the language arts lesson.	The para in the room waits until Robert gets settled in his desk, and then comes over and greets him so that he knows she is available. Once the teacher is done introducing the lesson, the paraprofessional unobtrusively checks in with Robert, and to confirm that he understands what is going to happen next, especially in terms of the learning activities that have been mentioned/introduced.

continued

TABLE 6.4 *continued*

Time of day	What the class is doing
Language arts **8:15 to 9:00**	This period involves teacher-directed learning activities that alternate between whole-class teaching and small-group work. The session ends with a worksheet that reviews the concepts taught in the lesson material and checks for student understanding. The worksheet typically is set up as a game. When students finish, they raise their hand and an adult in the classroom (e.g., teachers, para, parent volunteer) checks the work. Students either move to the next activity or are provided assistance/feedback on work that was not completed correctly.
Super quiet reading time (SQRT) **9:00 to 9:15**	Students transition into SQRT when they are done with the concluding assignment for the language arts lesson. All students have a book (or other reading material) in their desks, and students who don't can raise their hands and are given a "short read" from the Scholastic guided-reading packets available in print in the classroom and on the multiple Chromebooks in the classroom.
Snack & vocabulary **9:15-9:30**	Students are told to put away their SQRT books and are instructed to share what they read today with their partner (assigned by teacher and seated in close proximity). While students are talking, snacks are distributed. The session, ends with a teacher-directed vocabulary activity that is more intended for fun and transition to the next activity than as a targeted learning goal. A classroom procedure, involving cleaning up one's space after snack and lining up to exit the classroom, is used to transition to the next activity (recess).

What the student (Robert) is doing & how student will be supported to participate in class/school	Who is responsible for providing the support and what they are doing
Robert attends to the whole-class instruction with "check-ins" for confirmation from the para. The teacher is careful not to call on the most eager students during large-group instruction, and makes a point to periodically offer all students the opportunity to contribute to large-group learning activities. This includes having Robert respond to a question, or require a response that includes Robert and a peer. During the small-group instruction, the para will support Robert based on lesson plans that the special education teacher prepares in advance and provides at the start of the school day. Robert's small-group and individual work are aligned with the general education curriculum and with his achievement level (which is lower than that of most students in the class).	The para is monitoring Robert's participation and supporting him through "checks-ins" during whole-class instruction, and delivering instruction on individualized learning goals during the small-group and individual-work times (based on the lesson plans in a packet provided by the special educator). The para makes efforts to not be overly intrusive so that Robert is truly a part of the small-group work. The special educator and general educators collaborate to assure Robert's learning activities are aligned to the instruction provided to the class as a whole but also relevant to his achievement level.
Robert has a strong preference for reading "Scholastic Short Reads" on a Chromebook. He can successfully read the KRB, KA, and KB level stories silently, and follows along well when text-to-speech is activated for higher-level stories. He is able to put on earphones, highlight text, and activate the text-to-speech feature without assistance.	There is a Chromebook in the classroom that is somewhat dedicated to Robert. The Chromebook is set up to allow easy access to the "Scholastic Short Read" library and has other apps that Robert likes to use. The para observes what Robert is reading in order to support him in the next activity.
Robert quickly complies with the teacher's signal to end SQRT. He always requests that his student partner go first in telling him about their reading. Expressive communication is more difficult for him, and although he struggles with vocalizing a summary of his reading for the day, he doesn't become frustrated but rather soldiers through it. The para can assist by suggesting a question that his student peer may want to ask him and that typically is enough to engage Robert and his peer in a meaningful conversational exchange. Robert follows the snack routine without any prompting or assistance.	The para may need to gently support Robert in communicating the short summary of his reading for the day, and suggesting a question for a peer to ask is helpful. Some peers are better at listening and sharing information with Robert than others, and thoughtful selection of partners for Robert can also provide him a useful support.

continued

TABLE 6.4 *continued*

Time of day	What the class is doing
Recess **9:30 to 9:45**	Students stop by the restrooms on the way to recess and engage in free play either on the playground or in the gym. A classroom procedure is used to return to the classroom, and students also have the option to use the restroom on their return.
Word study **9:45 to 10:00**	On Monday–Wednesday, a whole group lesson is provided that focuses on the vocabulary words for the week to educate students on regularities, patterns, and derivations in the week's vocabulary words. During the whole-group lesson students write words in their word study notebook. Every Thursday, students practice in small groups for the vocabulary/spelling quiz on Friday.
Math **10:00 to 11:00**	Teacher-directed learning activities that alternate between whole-class teaching and small-group work characterize math instruction. Throughout each session there is independent work to assure the concept or operation is being understood—this includes visiting websites (either commercial or teacher generated) to reinforce skills taught. The session always ends with 3 problems and the teacher's "friendly warning." The students may see one of these problems on their next math test. When students finish, they raise their hand and an adult in the classroom (e.g., teachers, para, parent volunteer) checks the work; students are provided assistance as needed. Students who finish are allowed to read their book, write in their journal, color, or do additional math problems that are provided in their math textbook.

	What the student (Robert) is doing & how student will be supported to participate in class/school	Who is responsible for providing the support and what they are doing
	Robert needs no assistance in the restroom. He does not choose to participate in organized games, and seeks to use playgroup equipment or play with whatever was laid out for the students in the gym. Although he engages in mostly parallel play, he enjoys the break that free play provides to him from task-focused learning activities.	Robert needs no formal supports or adult-focused assistance when transitioning to and from recess. He needs no more monitoring than other students during recess time.
	The para provides Robert additional information/explanation about what's happening in whole-group lesson, and assists as needed in gluing words (typeed in advance on strips of paper) in his word study notebook. While other students try to recall how to spell words from memory during the Thursday practice sessions, Robert finds the word and reads the letters from his notebook. For the quiz, Robert is provided the vocabulary words on strips of paper and glues them on his quiz sheet as they are called out.	The special educator prepares the vocabulary words on strips of paper in advance, and these are included in the packet provided to the para before the start of the day. The para closely attends to the instructor, making sure to allow Robert to try (and possibly fail) to find the correct vocabulary word during the whole-group lesson before intervening. The alternative quiz materials (i.e., strips of paper with vocabulary word and glue stick) are provided to Robert prior to the quiz, but he is not provided any assistance on the quiz. The grade he earns for the quiz is based on his responses.
	Robert participates in all whole-class, small-group, and individual-work activities with support, as needed, from the special educator. Because Robert's math skills are well behind that of the vast majority of his peers, he has alternative learning/achievement targets. The skills Robert works on are taught within the large- and small-group math instruction. His special educator prepares his learning materials in advance. For this particular period, the special educator joins the class and supports Robert during the whole-group and individual-work activities. The special educator also leads a small group and always takes the one that Robert is a part of.	For this period, the para takes a step back from Robert and assists other students in the classroom. The special education teacher joins the class and provides direct support to Robert in whole-group and individual-work activities, and also leads the small group in which Robert participates. The special educator prepares lessons and materials for Robert in advance, which often include manipulatives for Robert to use to complete his math assignments.

continued

TABLE 6.4 *continued*

Time of day	What the class is doing	
Music or art **11:00 to 11:30**	On Monday, Wednesday, and Friday, the students go to the music room for music class, and on Tuesday and Thursday, they go to the art room. The classroom volunteers and paras go with the students. The teachers (general ed and special ed) have a common planning time. There are classroom procedures in place to transition to and from the classroom to the art/music rooms. The art and music teachers are both whole-group and activity oriented in their instruction. There is typically an opening activity, next comes instructions and a preview of the day's lessons/activities, and the activity then follows with students receiving assistance as needed.	
Individual work **11:30 to 12:00**	When students return to the classroom, they find on their desk a "lunch ticket folder" with instructions from the teacher. Often, the instructions will call for students to join a small-group activity (e.g., carefully take your chair to the back of the class and sit by Mrs. Bell. She will give you your next instructions!). Sometimes the instructions will call for independent work, or work with just one other student (e.g., You and Marie need to keep writing the story you started last week about a dog named Jake. Meet Mr. Webster at the front of the room and he will get you started!). Under the guise of "this is your lunch ticket," upon completion of their activities, students submit the folders and earn their ticket to lunch. This is also a time for the progress monitoring assessments used by the school (e.g., DIBELS).	
Lunch **12:00 to 12:45**	Classroom procedures are in place for transitioning to and from the cafeteria. Students choose where to sit, and cafeteria restrooms enable students to use the facilities as needed. Cafeteria staff and multiple other adults (e.g., school resource officer, clerical staff) are present in cafeteria to provide supervision, and classroom staff (e.g., teachers, paras) eat lunch in the teacher's lounge.	

What the student (Robert) is doing & how student will be supported to participate in class/school	**Who is responsible for providing the support and what they are doing**
Robert successfully transitions to music or art class without any more support than other students require. He participates in all whole-group learning activities with supports as needed from the para.	As with other whole-group learning activities, the para unobtrusively checks in with Robert to confirm that he understands what is going to happen next and what is expected of him—especially in terms of the learning activities that have been mentioned/introduced. For the most part, he only needs gentle guidance in the form of monitoring and verbal prompting.
Robert receives his own assignments tailored to his needs and interests, just like other students. Progress-monitoring data are collected during his time. Also, Robert may receive 1:1 instruction in a learning area of particular emphasis. One of Robert's communication goals is focused on expressive communication in a social situation with a peer or small group of peers, and a cooperative activity where these skills can be addressed is often set up during these times.	Robert is provided with direct assistance from the special educator or the para during this time period, and the nature of the support is determined by the nature of the assignment/task/activity in which Robert is participating.
Robert transitions to and from lunch without difficulties. He always gets to the cafeteria, and he eats as much of his meal as other students. He sits with his classmates and is content to be a passive observer during lunchtime—just happy to hang out with others. He is able to dispose of his lunch tray and use the restroom without additional supports.	Robert needs no formal supports or adult-focused assistance when transitioning to and from lunch. He needs no more monitoring than other students during recess time.

continued

TABLE 6.4 *continued*

Time of day	What the class is doing	
Writing **12:45 to 1:45**	Teacher-directed learning activities that alternate between whole-class teaching, small-group work, and individual work characterize the instructional period. Instruction focuses on the writing process (e.g., strategies from prewriting to drafting, to revising, etc.), how to write for different purposes (e.g., communicating with different audiences, writing fiction versus nonfiction), using and refining basic writing conventions (e.g., sentence structure and grammar), and evaluating one's own writing. The session always includes a writing prompt and short writing assignment, and ends with students writing in their journals.	
Science or social studies **1:45 to 2:30**	Instruction in science and social studies topics are alternated throughout the year. As with other academic subjects, teacher-directed learning activities that alternate between whole-class teaching, small-group work, and individual work characterize the instructional period. Class sessions typically begin with the instructor informing students of the most important ideas for the lesson and end with students expressing (orally, through writing, or through short-answer worksheets) the main ideas.	
Physical education **2:30 to 3:00**	There are classroom procedures in place to transition students to and from the classroom to the school gym, where the class always begins. The classroom volunteers and paras go to class with the students. Teachers have an independent planning time. The gym class combines two second-grade classrooms. The PE teacher always begins class with a series of exercises, and then students are engaged in gross motor activity, often in the form of a game. Socialization (e.g., cooperation with others) and sportsmanship are heavily emphasized throughout the PE class.	

	What the student (Robert) is doing & how student will be supported to participate in class/school	Who is responsible for providing the support and what they are doing
	Robert participates in all whole-class, small-group, and individual-work activities with support, as needed, from the para. Robert uses a Chromebook with the Writing with Symbols software program. Writing prompts are often modified for him. He writes in an e-journal which only he and his teachers can access from the school's cloud drive. Although all students have an e-journal, about half of them prefer to write in a paper journal.	As with other whole-group learning activities, the para unobtrusively checks in with Robert to confirm that he understands what is going to happen next and what is expected of him. The para follows instructions from the special education teacher's lesson packet in regard to directions that differ (or are in some way adapted) from those given to the class as a whole (e.g., Robert's writing prompts are usually different). The Writing with Symbols software is useful to Robert in constructing grammatically correct content and speeds up the process of writing for him so that he can complete learning activities and assignments with fluency.
	Robert participates in all whole-class, small-group, and individual-work activities with support, as needed, from the para. The special educator identifies the main concepts and the para cues Robert during the times the key concepts are being highlighted/discussed in the teacher's lesson. Usually, the closing assignment is adapted for Robert, and he completes it alongside his fellow students.	As with other whole-group learning activities, the para unobtrusively checks in with Robert to confirm that he understands what is going to happen next and what is expected of him. The special educator prepares the notes regarding the key concepts that Robert should focus on and prepares an adapted closing assignment based on these main ideas.
	Robert has no difficulties making the transition to PE, and Robert participates in all activities with support, as needed, from the para or from peers. Robert's gross motor skills are below average compared to his peers, but he is able to fully participate in most of the games and activities that are planned. If there is an activity where partial participation makes the most sense for a variety of reasons (e.g., risk of injury), there are other students in his class who are partially participating as well.	As with other whole-group learning activities, the para unobtrusively checks in with Robert to confirm that he understands what is going to happen next and what is expected of him. For activities that are especially complicated or novel, occasionally a peer who works well with Robert will be recruited to support him, and only very general instructions (e.g., Give Robert a hand in this activity when he needs it, OK?) are necessary.

continued

TABLE 6.4 *continued*

Time of day	What the class is doing	
Wrap-up **3:00 to 3:15**	Mr. Webster uses this time period to review the school day and support students in getting their materials organized for the next day's learning. There is usually some type of fun, whole-group activity to end the day (e.g., a class-wide vote on who is the best superhero between three choices).	
Depart from school **3:15 to 3:40**	A bell signals that students are dismissed from school and they either go to the gym to attend an afterschool program, or go home (via bus, walk/bike, or parent pick up). School staff provides supervision and monitoring of students, but efforts are made to clear the school grounds starting at 3:30.	

	What the student (Robert) is doing & how student will be supported to participate in class/school	Who is responsible for providing the support and what they are doing
	Robert participates in all whole-class, small-group, and individual-work activities with support, as needed, from the para. Other than the occasional clarification or explanation, he typically is able to fully participate in the closing-day activity as few demands are placed on the students. He uses a checklist to gather his belongings for school exit.	As with other whole-group learning activities, the para unobtrusively checks in with Robert to confirm that he understands what is going to happen next and what is expected of him. The para reviews his checklist with him, but unless there is something unusual happening, Robert doesn't need much support in preparing to leave school.
	Robert gathers up the things he needs to take home using his checklist, and waits in the classroom for his older brother and neighborhood friends to pick him up to walk home. They don't waste time coming to the classroom, and meeting in Robert's classroom was the most efficient way to gather everyone together to head home.	The natural supports work well during this time of the day, and there is no need for more formal, adult-directed supports.

Key Ideas From This Chapter

- Because participation in school does not guarantee engagement and belongingness, it is essential to provide supports to students with IEPs so that they are active members of their classroom and school communities. They must be supported sufficiently to share meaningful learning and social experiences with their classmates and teachers.
- Identifying learning activity types used in classroom lessons in conjunction with classroom ecological inventories provides insights for educators regarding opportunities for student participation.
- Applying the concepts of accommodations, modifications, personalized supports, and partial participation can facilitate meaningful participation in practically all school learning activities for student with IEPs.
- A schedule aligning student support needs with the classroom daily activities provides a practical and transparent approach for planning participation supports.

7

Universal Design for Learning

Designing Classrooms for All Students

The origin of the term "universal design for learning" (UDL) is generally attributed to David Rose, Anne Myer, and their colleagues at the Center for Applied Special Technology (CAST). The UDL framework emerged during a period in the late 1990s when inclusion efforts provided students with disabilities physical access to the general education classroom but limited or no access to the one-size-fits-all format of the general education curriculum. Here is a link to a short video (just 2 minutes long!) of David Rose talking about the origins of CAST and UDL (http://www.youtube.com/watch?v=MbGkL06EU90). The close alignment of UDL principles and the social–ecological conceptualization of disability discussed in Chapter 1 of this book is apparent in this video. Dr. Rose relates how he and his team abandoned their notions of using technology to "fix a student" and focused their efforts on fixing the classroom context instead. It was the mismatch between the student and the classroom setting and learning activities that needed to be the focus for repair. He recalls, "We saw the kids as highly diverse and the curriculum as fixed and the same for everybody . . . somehow we needed to change the materials rather than change the students."

UDL was derived from concepts of universal design developed in the field of architecture and based on the insight that it was more effective to design accessibility features into buildings at the outset of planning and construction rather than retrofitting needed revisions. For example, consider the need for doorways that are wheelchair accessible. In existing buildings, doorways are commonly 23 to 27 inches wide. However, wheelchairs are typically 30 inches wide. Hence, buildings designed to anticipate wheelchairs will make doorways 32–34 inches wide. Consider the cost of including this feature when a building is being designed—the added cost is near zero. However, if you need to remodel an existing home to make it wheelchair accessible, the cost is likely to be in the tens of thousands of dollars, or hundreds of thousands of dollars for a school or office building. This example underscores the economics of addressing accessibility at the outset rather than trying to retrofit for unanticipated needs later. There are myriad other benefits to universal design, including but not limited to equitable access and unanticipated beneficiaries—for instance large deliveries can now be made more easily through the wider door.

The promise of UDL was presented as a design intervention that would improve opportunities for students with disabilities to access and engage with grade-level standards-based curricula (Rose & Meyer, 2002). Rather than waiting for students to fail and educators to respond reactively, UDL challenged instructional designers to think about how to embed supports within instructional technologies, curricula, and learning materials that could be accessed by any student as needed. As a result, there is an urgent need to expand curriculum design to meet the diverse instructional needs of learners by improving the design and delivery of instruction.

Rather than waiting for students to fail and educators to respond reactively, UDL challenged instructional designers to think about how to embed supports within instructional technologies, curricula, and learning materials that could be accessed by any student as needed.

The purpose of this chapter is to describe the conceptual foundations of UDL and its application for students with IEPs. Despite the fact that UDL was first recognized in the 1990s, the practical benefits of UDL have been isolated. One critic has compared the problems associated with finding the essential elements for UDL implementation as elusive as searching for "Bigfoot" (Diedrich, 2021). Yet, the potential of UDL is so great, the work goes on. This chapter highlights practical suggestions for inclusive educators as they explore the potentials of UDL for all students.

Foundations of UDL

In 2002, Rose and Meyer published a book called *Teaching Every Student in the Digital Age*, which focused widespread attention toward UDL. The authors described the UDL conceptual framework as grounded in emerging insights about brain development, learning, and digital media. They challenged educators to think of the curriculum—rather than the students—as disabled. The authors' conversion of the principles of universal design from architecture to education were nothing short of a major paradigm shift in understanding how to address learner differences.

CAST is the nonprofit organization where Rose, Meyer, and their colleagues advanced the concept of UDL as a means of focusing research, development, and educational practice on understanding diversity and applying technology to facilitate learning. CAST's philosophy of UDL is embodied in a series of principles that serve as the core components of UDL:

- Multiple means of representation to give learners various ways of acquiring information and knowledge;
- Multiple means of expression to provide learners multiple options for demonstrating what they know; and
- Multiple means of engagement to tap into learners' interests, challenge them appropriately, and motivate them to learn.

Multiple means of representation may be understood as providing students with a variety of options for learning information beyond solely using a textbook. Teachers today have many choices when it comes to presenting instructional content to students: Watch a YouTube video; listen to a podcast; read text on a webpage—or have text-to-speech read the webpage aloud; use Wikipedia to learn more about a topic, and so on. The key idea is to encourage educational publishers and teachers to try to reach diverse students by breaking out of the one-size-fits-all model that assumes that all students learn in the same way, at the same rate, and need the same learning materials to achieve the desired learning outcomes.

Multiple means of expression draws attention to the need to provide students with multiple options for demonstrating what they know. Some teachers recognize the value of this principle as they allow students a choice of writing a paper, preparing a slideshow presentation, recording a video, and so on. The key notion is to provide students with choices in how they demonstrate what they have learned and the media they use to express themselves. This component of UDL can be implemented when publishers and educators design instructional practices to place students in the role of Goldilocks. That is, allowing students to sample multiple options to determine which option is "just right" for providing them with the best opportunities to reach high levels of achievement.

The key notion is to provide students with choices in how they demonstrate what they have learned and the media they use to express themselves.

Of the three principles of UDL, perhaps the most important is multiple means of engagement. The research on learning indicates that deep learning is only accomplished through sustained engagement. Hence, access to the curriculum is a prerequisite for engagement. However, sustained engagement is achieved by activities that are interesting, motivating, and at the right challenge level. As was discussed in Chapter 1, educators should strive to calibrate instruction to what Vygotsky (1978) called the zone of proximal development.

CAST (2018) has elaborated on the core principles through the development of nine UDL guidelines and 31 checkpoints (udlguidelines.cast.org). Because UDL has been written into both the Higher Education Opportunity Act (2008) and the Every Student Succeeds Act (2015), UDL has become particularly relevant to teacher education, accreditation agencies, and state departments of education as a policy intervention for inclusive education. As a result, educators are expected to apply the principles of UDL in their classrooms.

Challenges to Achieving the Vision of UDL

Despite its relatively short history, the potential of UDL has captured the imagination of federal policy makers, administrators, teachers, and parents. However, a number of authors have critiqued elements of the UDL vision and identified components that have limited the impact of UDL to date. Four issues are at the core of these critiques: (a) how to operationally define UDL, (b) who is responsible for the design of UDL applications, (c) how the needs of all students are considered when designing UDL applications, and (d) how to measure claims of UDL's effectiveness.

Operationally Defining UDL

A number of scholars have called attention to problems associated with defining UDL and how many components must be present to constitute a true application of UDL (Edyburn, 2010; Rao et al., 2014). For example, if a teacher simply allows students to choose the type of assignment they work on, can she claim she is implementing UDL in the form of multiple means of expression? Similarly, can a teacher claim he is implementing UDL when he simply points to computers in the classroom with text-to-speech software that is available to students? Howery (2021) argued that the language CAST has used to describe and implement UDL has changed over time. She suggested five different time periods where the meaning of UDL shifted away from the original conceptualization of accessibility. The foundational problem of defining UDL has critical implications for evaluating anyone claiming to implement UDL (Diedrich, 2021; Moore, 2021).

Designing UDL Applications

The literature also documents a debate about whether UDL is a design practice, and therefore the responsibility of instructional designers and publishers, or an instructional practice that is the responsibility of the individual teacher. Those arguing that UDL is best applied to instructional design suggest that one does not need to know the individual students in the classroom in order to provide supports that can be used by diverse students. Yet, others argue that UDL is the domain of teachers because they know what students need. The problem obscures who has the primary responsibility for creating UDL interventions and whether the problem is a design challenge or a new requirement for teacher lesson planning—or both.

Considering the Needs of All Students

A third issue concerning the challenges associated with implementing UDL focuses on the word "all." Lowrey (2021) and Howery (2021) argued that CAST has shown little interest in understanding the unique needs of individuals with intellectual disability, and when they say all students, they really mean "most" students. Despite a small literature advocating for the application of UDL for fostering inclusion in general education classrooms (see Hartmann, 2015;

Wehmeyer, 2006), a significant number of logistical challenges must still be addressed. They include: (a) additional preservice and in-service teacher education concerning how to support learner differences, (b) increased use of flexible digital learning materials, and (c) determining what meaningful access looks like for students who need cognitive access to complex concepts (Coyne et al., 2012; Lowrey & Smith, 2018).

Measuring UDL Effectiveness

A final issue permeating the UDL literature is related to the problem of defining the framework's effects. That is, how does one measure claims that UDL interventions are benefitting students? If UDL cannot be precisely defined, then it is unlikely that various researchers claiming to measure UDL are measuring the same construct (Edyburn, 2010; Rao & Cook, 2021).

Time will tell whether or not UDL revolutionizes education or becomes the latest in a sequence of educational bandwagons that come and go (Edyburn, 2020). However, the problem UDL seeks to address is a real one: *How to help the general education curriculum evolve in ways that permit meaningful engagement and yield measurable gains in academic achievement for all students, including students with disabilities.* As a result, work continues in an effort to operationalize the vision of UDL into practical classroom applications. To this end, the remainder of this chapter provides descriptions of several practical strategies that educators might explore to use principles of UDL to enhance accessibility, engagement, and outcomes for their students.

Translating UDL Theory Into Practice

One way of thinking about UDL is that any design intervention has the potential to improve the user experience for everyone, and the impact of a design intervention on both primary and secondary beneficiaries must be considered. The primary beneficiaries are the people for whom the design intervention is directly targeted. For example, a home that has been designed to be wheelchair accessible can be directly measured by the safety, independence, and satisfaction of the resident who uses a wheelchair. Secondary beneficiaries include everyone else who gains from the design feature. Although there is no known downside to having wider doorframes in a home, all the residents of a household could be considered secondary beneficiaries of accessible doorways. This is especially true when they are carrying an armload of groceries and the baby in a car seat. As a result, instructional designers and educators can find it useful to think about UDL as a means of embedding supports in the environment *before* they are needed—and then observing their use by both primary and secondary beneficiaries and documenting the outcomes.

Designing for All: Platform Tools

In the context of the classroom, one way to think about UDL is to consider the academic expectations students will be asked to meet. Often much of the curriculum is text-based and it is reasonable to consider how many students will enter the classroom without grade-level reading skills. This is an ideal context to think about UDL because it demonstrates a mismatch between the environment (e.g., academic expectations to read text) and the learners (e.g., those without grade-level reading skills, some of whom may have a disability). How does an educator prepare the classroom learning environment to support learners who are at many different reading levels?

One foundational UDL strategy that educators can employ in every inclusive classroom is to become familiar with accessibility control panels. As illustrated in Table 7.1, every technology platform (e.g., computer, tablet, mobile) has universal accessibility features that support reading by allowing users to gain access to text-based information by listening as the text is read aloud by the computer. Text-to-speech is one universal design application that also affords advantages to secondary beneficiaries such as learners interested in reading complex texts, people who have misplaced their reading glasses, and more. Hence, educators interested in UDL need to become familiar with these accessibility tools and teach all students when and how to activate them to support their performance.

A second characteristic common to many students with intellectual and development disabilities involves difficulty in writing that may be attributed to poor handwriting and/or difficulty spelling. These types of problems limit written communication and often contribute to negative attitudes toward writing. Dictation (also known as voice typing) is an application that allows users to dictate their thoughts and have their device convert speech into text. As illustrated in Table 7.2, every technology platform has universal

TABLE 7.1 Text-to-Speech Tools by Operating System

PLATFORM	HOW TO ACTIVATE	LEARN MORE
Computer		
Chrome OS	• Open Settings • Select Advanced • Select Manage Accessibility Features • Select Text-to-Speech • Activate ChromeVox (spoken feedback)	Hear text read aloud https://support.google.com/chromebook/answer/9032490?hl=en
Mac OS	• Open System Preferences • Select Speech • Select the Text to Speech • Select a voice • Check the box next to Speak Selected Text—when the key is pressed, click on "Set Key"	How to activate text to speech in Mac OS X www.wikihow.com/Activate-Text-to-Speech-in-Mac-OS-X
Windows OS	• Narrator is a screen-reading app that's built into Windows 10, so there's nothing you need to download or install. To read from where your cursor is, press "Narrator + R"	Complete guide to Narrator https://support.microsoft.com/en-us/windows/complete-guide-to-narrator-e4397a0d-ef4f-b386-d8ae-c172f109bdb1 Hear text read aloud with Narrator https://support.microsoft.com/en-us/windows/hear-text-read-aloud-with-narrator-040f16c1-4632-b64e-110a-da4a0ac56917

accessibility features that support the writing composition process by allowing users to speak their thoughts and have the device type out the words they dictate.

Designing for All: Creating Accessible Documents

Text-to-speech features depend on accessible files or documents that screen reader technology can identify as text and read aloud. They must also contain

PLATFORM	HOW TO ACTIVATE	LEARN MORE
Mobile		
Android	• Open Settings • Select Accessibility • Select Text-to-Speech Output	Android accessibility help: Text-to-speech output https://support.google.com/accessibility/android/answer/6006983?hl=en
iOS	• Opening Settings app • Select General • Select Accessibility • Select Speech • Select Speak Selection	How to enable text to speech on iOS devices https://www.wikihow.com/Enable-Text-To-Speech-on-iOS-Devices www.wikihow.com/Enable-Text-To-Speech-on-iOS-Device
Windows 10 Mobile	• Use the search box to type "speech" • Select the Speech Recognition Control Panel • Select Set Up Microphone • Use the search box to type "speech" • Select Start Speech Recognition	How to set up speech-to-text in Windows 10 www.digitaltrends.com/computing/how-to-set-up-speech-to-text-in-windows-10/

the appropriate digital markers to indicate to the listener the type of text being read, such as to differentiate when bold text signifies a heading versus representing a spoken emphasis. Thus, checking the existing electronic documents used in classrooms for accessibility is important. It is also prudent to ensure that all new electronic documents that teachers create are accessible. This requires a little up-front effort to learn how to execute these things using the software available to school staff, but once learned, requires little to no additional effort when creating electronic files. The US Department of Health and Human Services (2020) offers easy-to-use fact sheets for creating accessible Microsoft Word, PowerPoint, and Excel files, as well as accessible PDFs (www.hhs.gov/web/section-508/additional-resources/index.html). On this same webpage, there are links to additional resources for creating accessible electronic materials and determining the accessibility of other online platforms.

TABLE 7.2 Speech-to-Text Tools by Operating System

Platform	How to Activate	Learn More
Computer		
Chrome OS	• Open Settings • Select Advanced • Select Manage Accessibility Features • Select Keyboard and Text Input • Activate Enable Dictation (speak to type)	Enter text using your voice on Chrome OS/Chromebook—Speech recognition https://mcmw.abilitynet.org.uk/chrome-os-chromebook-speech-recognition-2
Mac OS	• Open System Preferences • Select Accessibility • Select Voice Control • Activate Voice Control	Use voice control on your Mac https://support.apple.com/en-us/HT210539
Windows OS	• Open Start • Select All Programs • Select Accessories • Select Ease of Access • Activate Windows Speech Recognition	Dictate text using speech recognition https://support.microsoft.com/en-us/windows/dictate-text-using-speech-recognition-854ef1de-7041-9482-d755-8fdf2126ef27
Mobile		
Android	• Open Settings app • Select System > Languages & Input • Select Virtual keyboard • Select Google Voice Typing	Free up your hands with speech-to-text on Android https://www.makeuseof.com/tag/free-hands-speechtotext-android/
iOS	• Open Settings app • Select General • Select Accessibility	Use dictation on your iPhone, iPad, or iPod touch https://support.apple.com/en-us/HT208343
Windows 10 Mobile	• Open Settings • Activate Speech Services • Press "Windows key + H"	How to use speech recognition and dictate text on Windows 10 https://www.pcmag.com/how-to/how-to-use-speech-recognition-and-dictate-text-on-windows-10

Designing for Choice

Educators can use a third UDL design intervention that involves the creation of choice boards or tic-tac-toe grids. These learning guides can be created in a word processor or PowerPoint by inserting a 3 × 3 table. This tic-tac-toe format requires educators to identify relevant learning activities for a topic to populate each of the nine cells. Ideally, the choices teachers offer are informed by their knowledge of the students as well as their understanding of high-quality learning activities. Students are then expected to select three in a row (using the traditional rules of tic-tac-toe) to complete the assignment. An excellent example is the Texas Computer Education Association's *My First Choice Board* at https://docs.google.com/presentation/d/1KfnAK_KWi5YH_5-z_32JW9HoncA1VayuM98gfjf098M/edit#slide=id.p. Once these activities become routine, there are many variations on the concept, such as allowing students to select any three activities or to create their own choice boards for use in subsequent units of instruction.

Designing for Challenge

Learning occurs best when the challenge level is "just right" for the learner. As a result, learners in a UDL environment should operate like Goldilocks, exploring options to find what is just right for them. The promise of UDL suggests that instructional materials can be designed to provide adjustable instructional design controls. One way to think about these controls is to consider a volume-control slider that is adjustable to be off or at some level between low and high. Tomlinson (1999), whose work on differentiated instruction was discussed in Chapter 5, speaks of this concept as the equalizer. This concept can be observed in word processing programs where users can change the size of the font by dragging a slider to increase or decrease the size of the text. Each user can adjust the slider to obtain text that is just the right size for their needs.

Because it may be difficult to visualize what universally designed curricula might look like, Table 7.3 identifies digital resources that illustrate the potential of UDL. It is important for educators to consider how each of the resources listed was designed to support the success of all learners by embedding supports that can be used by any learner as needed. Also consider the following questions:

- Would these instructional materials be helpful to a single student? (If so, it might be considered assistive technology, which by definition increases, maintains, or improves the functional capabilities of persons with disabilities) (Assistive Technology Industry Association, 2021).
- Would these instructional materials be helpful to a small group of students? (If so, it might be useful as a multitiered system of support [MTSS] Tier 2 intervention as discussed in Chapter 6.)
- Would these instructional materials be of value to the entire class in order to reach those who we anticipate will struggle plus many other students whom we cannot identify in advance? (If so, it might be considered UDL.)

UDL Outcomes and Benefits

In schools and classrooms that claim to implement UDL, all students would be introduced to the universal usability features of their technology devices. All students would know how to activate speech-to-text tools and text-to-speech tools on all common devices, even on those devices they do not personally own or use, so that they can assist others. Classroom observation would reveal that ubiquitous tools, like text-to-speech and speech-to-text, have secondary beneficiaries because they are used routinely by many general education students in addition to those students whose disability characteristics necessitate the use of these tools.

When trying to calculate the return on investment of universal usability tools, a foundational measure should be the number of minutes the devices are used. This simple metric of usage (versus non-usage) will reveal patterns that offer insight about the value and use of ubiquitous tools. Examining use by secondary beneficiaries—that is, by students you did not expect would use the tool—can also be an important indicator of the value of the tool. Subjective self-report measures of students' confidence in using the tools, perceived efficacy, and decreased frustration can also be valuable in understanding the application of universal usability among primary and secondary beneficiaries. Finally, educators and researchers are encouraged to use quantitative measures to assess increased productivity and enhanced academic outcomes as another persuasive argument of the value of the UDL interventions. Finally, educators and researchers are encouraged to use quantitative measures to assess ways in which UDL practices increase productivity and enhanced academic outcomes. Additional

TABLE 7.3 Instructional Designs That Proactively Value Learner Differences

Instructional challenge	Strategy	Technology options
Design instructional materials that support diverse learners before they fail.	Create multilingual instructional materials that include a variety of levels to engage students at different skill levels.	ReadToday https://readtoday.net/#pgOnline
	Create instructional text at multiple levels to account for different interest and reading levels.	Tween Tribune www.tweentribune.com
Students' independent reading skills make it extremely difficult and tedious to complete grade-level reading assignments.	Copy the desired text and paste it into Text Compactor. Use the slider to create a summary. Continue moving the slider until you get the right level of text length/difficulty. If further support is needed, copy the summarized text into a text-to-speech tool or a language translation tool.	Text Compactor www.textcompactor.com
Students often struggle with grade-level texts because of the advanced vocabulary.	Copy the desired text or website URL and paste it into Rewordify. The tool replaces advanced vocabulary with easier words.	Rewordify rewordify.com

resources for assessing UDL practices are available through the Implementation Research Network (a professional organization devoted to the implementation of UDL at udl-irn.org) and the National Center on UDL, an authoritative resource concerning UDL research, policy, and practice (udlcenter.org).

The UDL Revolution Starts–Now!

There is a story of school principal who attended a full-day workshop sponsored by the state department of education on professional development for teachers. Upon returning to the school district, a colleague asked the principal "What did you learn at the workshop?" The principal replied "They really

TABLE 7.4 10 Things Busy Educators Can Do to Design and Implement Universal Design for Learning (UDL) Principles in Their Classroom—Now!

TARGET	ACTION STEPS	RESOURCES
Teacher professional development	1. Learn more about the principles of UDL.	What is universal design for learning (UDL)? www.understood.org/en/learning-thinking-differences/treatments-approaches/educational-strategies/universal-design-for-learning-what-it-is-and-how-it-works Universal design for learning: Creating a learning environment that challenges and engages all students https://iris.peabody.vanderbilt.edu/module/udl/
Environmental audit	2. Explore the accessibility features on all classroom technologies and configurations.	See Tables 7.1 and 7.2 in this chapter
Curriculum review	3. Review your curriculum and think about expectations and how UDL can be applied to improve access and engagement.	CAST UDL curriculum self-check http://udlselfcheck.cast.org/
Digital supports	4. Identify a short list of web resources to provide the teachers with a toolkit to support choice during lesson planning.	Two thousand categorized "best" lists from Larry Ferlazzo's blog https://larryferlazzo.edublogs.org/%20about/my-best-of-series/ Educational technology and mobile learning https://www.educatorstechnology.com/ AlternativeTo https://alternativeto.net/ Capterra https://www.capterra.com/
Design for diversity	5. Create learning activities using choice boards to support diversity students in exercising choice and challenge.	My first choice board (PPT template) https://docs.google.com/presentation/d/1KfnAK_KWi5YH_5-z_32JW9HoncA1VayuM98gfjf098M/edit#slide=id.p

TARGET	ACTION STEPS	RESOURCES
Support learner efficacy	6. Help students understand the learner expectations in your classroom.	In the UDL-designed classroom, students operate as Goldilocks to make meaningful choices about what is the "just right" challenge level and format they need to be successful.
Student skills in universal accessibility tools	7. Teach students how to adjust font size in their word processor and web browser using the Zoom feature to allow them to view text at the "just right" size. Then, ask them to teach a parent or grandparent how to use these features and report back to the class what they learned.	Zoom in or out of a document, presentation, or worksheet https://support.microsoft.com/en-us/office/zoom-in-or-out-of-a-document-presentation-or-worksheet-0a0ebbed-10e7-444b-b16b-6f0c090f8ec7 Change text, image, and video sizes (zoom) https://support.google.com/chrome/answer/96810
Help students master a variety of tools that support performance	8. Introduce students to a variety of software tools that alter how traditional academic tasks might be completed.	NaturalReader www.naturalreaders.com/ Text Compactor www.textcompactor.com Newsela https://newsela.com/ Wolfram alpha www.wolframalpha.com/ Photomath https://photomath.com/en/ How to use voice typing in Google Docs www.howtogeek.com/399757/how-to-use-voice-typing-in-google-docs/
Monitor barriers to engagement	9. Routinely ask students where they get stuck in order to discover the need for new UDL interventions.	Enhance capacity for monitoring progress https://udlguidelines.cast.org/action-expression/executive-functions/monitoring-progress/monitoring-progress

continued

TABLE 7.4 *continued*

TARGET	ACTION STEPS	RESOURCES
Outcomes and benefits of UDL	10. Assess the impact of your UDL work.	To understand the outcomes and benefits of UDL, consider both the primary and secondary beneficiaries. For example, if you provide text-to-speech on each of your computers, the primary beneficiaries should be students with below grade-level reading skills and English-language learners. Assess to see if they are using these tools and if their academic performance is better when the tools are used than when they are not. Then, consider which other students are routinely using the speech-to-text tools and what types of benefits they are deriving. The UDL classroom will be characterized by supports that are embedded in the environment to explicitly support the primary beneficiaries, but also have significant impact for secondary beneficiaries who could not have been identified in advance.

stressed the fact that lecture-based, sage on the stage, one-shot workshops are a very ineffective way to provide professional development for educators. Turns out that these one-day workshops have very little impact on educator practices." The colleague replied, "Well, that is very interesting to know. What do you plan to do differently for your teacher's professional development in the future?" The principal replied, "Nothing. Like they said, these one-shot workshops don't have much of an effect on people's behavior!"

Unfortunately, the same critique of the one-shot teacher workshop could be leveled at educational book chapters as well. It is easy for an educator to read information about UDL and say, "Well, that is interesting, and it makes sense, and it seems useful. One of these days I ought to try these ideas out." Only to never quite get around to doing anything about it. In this spirit, Table 7.4 is offered as a way for teachers to get cracking on implementing UDL in their classrooms. Completing all 10 of the action steps in Table 7.4 will not create a model UDL classroom, but completing any one of them it will move a teacher forward in terms of UDL implementation. Collectively, the 10 actions can yield big benefits in terms of creating classrooms and content that recognize students with all kinds of different abilities. So, to begin, chose one of the action steps in Table 7.4 and start the UDL revolution in your classroom and school! Then, choose another one, and keep going.

Conclusion

Perhaps the most important contribution of UDL is that it makes explicit the diverse ways children learn. This is not a new concept to general education classrooms, but efforts to give students with disabilities equitable access to the general education curriculum drew attention to how detrimental a one-size-fits-all ways of teaching and learning was to all students, not just those with IEPs. In a universally designed classroom, all students benefit from the more flexible, "just right" approach to learning, even if some students still need additional, individualized supports such as those that are identified through the Systematic Supports Planning Process (SSPP). Thus, efforts continue to specify and clarify UDL should not distract teachers from taking action. Increasing the number of teachers who make conscious efforts to consistently expand the ways they teach in order to close the gap with the many ways that students learn is the most important factor to bridging the gap between today's status quo and the UDL vision of what classrooms would be if the framework were fully applied.

Key Ideas From This Chapter

- The foundations of UDL were created during a period when there was a need to move inclusion beyond physical access to the general education classroom to an environment that offered access, engagement, and improved outcomes of learning by students with disabilities within the general curriculum.
- Applying the principles of UDL in the classroom can start with and build upon the accessibility control panels and tools already available in every technology device.
- One practical way to think about UDL is as a volume-control slider. It could be set to off, low, or high. The student is the one who manipulates the slider to provide more or less support as needed.

Questions for Discussion

1. Why is choice—or multiple means of teaching and learning—such an important concept in UDL?
2. Look again at Table 7.1. Turn on the text-to-speech feature on whatever device you have in your vicinity. How long did it take to turn on text-to-speech? How do ubiquitous accessibility features in today's technologies affect how we can apply UDL principles in our classrooms?
3. Why is UDL an important first step in thinking about supporting access to the general education curriculum for students with IEPs?

8

Personal Agency

Teaching Self-Determination to Learners

In Chapter 1, great special educators were described as expert problem-solvers. If a student is having difficulty learning, the onus is on the teacher to identify the supports needed for success. The outstanding special educator consistently devises effective supports, including supports that include different types or intensities of instruction or use technologies in innovative ways. It is important, however, not to overlook a critical source of support—the students themselves. Great teachers encourage and prepare their students to solve their own problems. Or, to put it another way, great teachers teach their students the skills needed to become self-determined learners. Self-determination and its importance to the education of learners with disabilities will be discussed, along with what it means to be a self-determined learner. The chapter will conclude with a consideration of strategies that support self-determined learning.

Self-Determination

In Chapter 1, it was mentioned that The Education for All Handicapped Children Act (PL 94-142) was passed in 1975, and this landmark legislation was the first national law guaranteeing students with disabilities access to a free, appropriate public education. By the early 1990s, the first generation of youth with disabilities whose rights to an education had been protected under PL 92-142 throughout their schooling had started graduating from high school. Considerable resources had been invested in this new generation's education, and their postschool outcomes were of considerable interest. Unfortunately, a large number of research studies revealed that most students with IEPs experienced dismal outcomes as young adults. Most were unemployed or underemployed, socially isolated, and lacked residential independence (see Levine & Nourse, 1998). A concern with the transition of youth with disabilities from school to adult life prompted the initial interest in promoting the self-determination for students with IEPs (Wehmeyer, 1992).

Great teachers encourage and prepare their students to solve their own problems. Or, to put it another way, great teachers teach their students the skills needed to become self-determined learners.

In the early 1990s, this was evidence that the student was clearly missing from the transition planning process. Students were passive recipients of transition planning, as opposed to being active participants. Poor postschool outcomes were connected to lack of student engagement in planning for their futures. Thus, the US Department of Education Office of Special Education Programs (OSEP) launched an initiative to increase student involvement in transition planning and to develop methods, materials, and strategies to promote self-determination (Wehmeyer, 1999).

In the 30 years since this initiative was launched, promoting the self-determination of young people with disabilities has become best practice in the fields of transition and special education (Shogren, Wehmeyer, & Singh, 2017). So, what is self-determination and why is promoting the self-determination of youth, or people of any age for that matter, an important support? Causal agency theory (Shogren, Wehmeyer, Palmer, Forber-Pratt et al., 2015) provides a theoretical framework within which to understand self-determination and its development, and to design and evaluate interventions to promote self-determination. Within causal agency theory, self-determination is defined as:

> a dispositional characteristic manifested as acting as the causal agent in one's life. Self-determined people (i.e., causal agents) act in service to freely chosen goals. Self-determined actions function to enable a person to be the causal agent in his or her life. (Shogren, Wehmeyer, Palmer, Forber-Pratt et al., 2015, p. 258)

The theory of causal agency is central to understanding self-determination. The term "self-determined" is derived from the philosophical doctrine of determinism, which posits that all action is in some way caused (Wehmeyer, 1992). Self-determined action, then, is self-caused action. By definition, people who are self-determined have agency in regard to what happens in their lives, in contrast to someone or something else causing them to act in other ways. Self-determined action is goal-oriented and volitional, where volitional refers to acting based upon conscious choice (Shogren, Wehmeyer, Palmer, Forber-Pratt et al., 2015).

Teaching someone to become a causal agent is not the same thing as promoting independence. Causal agents make or cause things to happen in their lives, at times doing these things themselves, and at other times relying on someone or something else for assistance. The key is that the action, whether self-directed or other-directed, is in service of goals of a person's choosing. Every student can become more self-determined to some degree, and it should be an important aim for all students. When we focus on promoting the self-determination of students, the intention is not solely or even primarily to promote personal independence in a task or activity. The objective is to develop skills (including problem-solving, goal setting and attainment, self-management) that a student can utilize to pursue goals that they themselves deem to be important. By enabling students to be more self-determined, educators empower them to become their own support. Further, becoming self-determined is a noteworthy developmental milestone for all students (Wehmeyer et al., 2017).

Efforts to promote self-determination can be implemented for all students using class-wide and school-wide approaches, thus supporting inclusive education (Raley et al., 2018). For example, Shogren et al. (2016) discussed the role of embedding interventions to promote self-determination within multitiered systems of support (MTSS). MTSS was introduced briefly in Chapter 2 in the context of supplemental instruction. MTSS refers to efforts within schools to support students' academic and

When we focus on promoting the self-determination of students, the intention is not solely or even primarily to promote personal independence in a task or activity. The objective is to develop skills (including problem-solving, goal setting and attainment, self-management) that a student can utilize to pursue goals that they themselves deem to be important.

behavioral challenges by increasing intervention intensity in response to student intensity of needs. Tier 1 interventions involve implementing high-quality instruction to all students in a school. Tier 2 interventions are intended to support students who need more-intensive supports than most students receive. Tier 3 interventions provide the most intensive supports for a relatively small group of students who need them. The critical focus of MTSS is that when a student struggles either academically or behaviorally, it is the supports that are changed rather than the place where the student receives supports. Implementing MTSS provides a means to systematize the delivery of supports to enable students to succeed in inclusive settings . . . as its name suggests! And, as Shogren et al. (2016) noted, promoting self-determination can be a support that is implemented at all three MTSS tiers.

Importance of Promoting Self-Determination to Students With Disabilities

In the 30-plus years since the OSEP self-determination initiative, research and practice have established the value of students becoming more self-determined. Over this time, evidence has shown that

- Young people with disabilities, across disability categories, are often less self-determined than their peers without disabilities and benefit from instruction to promote self-determination (Carter et al., 2006; Shogren et al., 2018; Wehmeyer & Metzler, 1995).
- When provided interventions and opportunities to promote self-determination, students with disabilities become more self-determined (Wehmeyer et al., 2011; Wehmeyer, Palmer, et al., 2012; Wehmeyer, Shogren, et al., 2012).
- Promoting the self-determination of youth with disabilities improves academic performance and student access to the general education curriculum (Konrad et al., 2007; Lee et al., 2010; Shogren et al., 2012).
- Teaching students to become more self-determined raises teachers' expectations of the performance of students with disabilities (Shogren et al., 2014).
- Promoting self-determination has been causally linked to more positive postgraduation outcomes, including more positive employment

and community inclusion outcomes for youth with disabilities (Shogren, Wehmeyer, Palmer, Rifenbark, et al., 2015).
- Promoting student self-determination has been linked to more positive quality of life and life satisfaction (Lachapelle et al., 2005; Nota et al., 2007; Shogren et al., 2006; Wehmeyer & Schwartz, 1998).

This list of evidence is not exhaustive; it is included here to emphasize that promoting self-determination as a means of support has well-documented positive impacts on the school and postschool lives of students with disabilities. Enabling young people to become self-determined empowers them, in essence, to become their own best support and to pursue goals that are important to them.

Self-Determined Learning

This chapter began by confirming the statement presented at the onset of this book that great special educators are expert problem-solvers. At this point, though, it is time to refine that sentiment just a bit. In 1981, Buckminster Fuller created a "knowledge doubling curve" intended to chart the rate that knowledge was generated over time. According to Fuller, until 1900, the amount of knowledge doubled approximately every 100 years. By 1945, the amount of knowledge doubled about every 25 years, but by the time Fuller published the curve, the estimate was that knowledge was doubling every 12 to 13 months. Based upon Fuller's estimations, an IBM report in 2013 estimated that by 2020, worldwide knowledge would double every 12 minutes (Chamberlain, 2020). Literally, by the time you finish teaching something, it could be obsolete.

Relatedly, consider this statement, repeated by then US Secretary of Education Richard Riley in 2006: "We are currently preparing students for jobs that don't yet exist . . . using technologies that haven't been invented . . . in order to solve problems we don't even know are problems yet" (Gunderson et al., 2004, p. 57). Of course, the specifics of these statements may be difficult to prove with empirical data. The important idea, however, is that knowledge is being generated at a rate unparalleled in history and therefore it is no longer sufficient to teach students a discrete set of skills if they are to be successful. Great special educators (and great teachers in general) not only need to be expert problem-solvers in terms of coming up with solutions and supports to address students' learning challenges, but great teachers are the ones who teach students to be expert problem-solvers in regard to their own lives. Great teachers teach students to be self-determined learners. Students who are self-determined learners set goals and make decisions as the hero and the expert of their own lives.

Pedagogy, Andragogy, Heutagogy—Oh My!

So, how do educators prepare students to be self-determined learners? In part, it requires rethinking the fundamental mission of education and how teachers work with students. It requires moving from teacher-directed learning to students using self-directed learning. All teachers are familiar with the word "pedagogy," referring to methods used by educators to promote learning in students. The word is derived from the Greek words *pais* (παῖς)—meaning child—and *ágō* (ἄγω) meaning leader. Together they form *paidagōgía* (παιδαγωγία), or, as it came to mean in ancient Greece, "the office of a child's tutor." A pedagogue is a person who "leads" children. It is a one-way relationship; pedagogy refers to teachers teaching students or teacher-directed learning. This is consistent with the vocabulary for what happens in schools: synonyms for educate include "train," "instruct," "lecture," "discipline," "drill," "direct," "tutor," and "edify." Even the less authoritative synonyms—"coach," "develop," "enlighten," "foster"—imply that it is the adult who does something to the child.

But there are other ways of thinking about instruction. For decades, the field of adult education has based its practices on the idea of andragogy rather than pedagogy. The Greek ἀνδρ (*andr-*) means "man" or "person," and andragogy refers to the idea of a man or person leading their own education: self-directed learning. Knowles (1975), a pioneer in adult education and the originator of the term "andragogy," observed that "[i]ndividuals who take the initiative in learning, learn more things, and learn better, than do people who sit at the feet of teachers possibly waiting to be taught" (p. 14).

Self-directed learning has a fundamental set of beliefs holding that adults learn better when their intrinsic curiosity and their life experiences are harnessed to make them more responsible for their own learning. Here the idea of responsibility is used not as an obligation or requirement to adhere to a rule, but instead to refer to the idea of learner autonomy. Responsibility as autonomy means that:

> one can and does set one's own rules, and can choose for oneself the norms one will respect. In other words, autonomy refers to one's ability

> to choose what has value, that is to say, to make choices in harmony with self-realization . . . to be free from all exterior regulations and constraints. (Chene, 1983, p. 39)

According to Candy (1991, p. 125), an autonomous learner, in self-directed learning, is someone who

- conceives of goals and plans,
- exercises freedom of choice,
- uses the capacity for rational reflection,
- has willpower to follow through,
- exercises self-restraint and self-discipline, and
- views himself or herself as autonomous.

However, the trend previously mentioned regarding the rapid increase in knowledge and the need to continue to learn to meet the changing demands in the workplace have impacted adult learning just as they have K–12 education. In response, the field of adult education has shifted to another approach to learning: heutagogy. Blaschke (2012) observed that

> [p]edagogical, even andragogical, educational methods are no longer fully sufficient in preparing learners for thriving in the workplace, and a more self-directed and self-determined approach is needed, one in which the learner reflects upon what is learned and how it is learned and in which educators teach learners how to teach themselves. (p. 57)

"Heutagogy"—from the Greek εὕρημα, which means "discovered"—is discovered learning, or, more commonly, self-determined learning. Blaschke indicated that "in a heutagogical approach to teaching and learning, learners are highly autonomous and self-determined and emphasis is placed on development of learner capacity and capability with the goal of producing learners who are well-prepared for the complexities of today's workplace" (p. 56). Practices in self-directed learning encourage instructors to relinquish "ownership of the learning path and process to the learner, who negotiates learning and determines what will be learned and how it will be learned" (p. 59).

Although these "-gogy" terms may seem overly academic, it is crucial that teachers understand how the transition from teacher-directed learning to self-directed learning to self-determined learning has proceeded. Historically, the educational models used by special educators were teacher directed. With the emphasis on self-determination in the field, over the past two decades there has been a shift to a focus on student-directed learning. The next frontier in shifting more fully to a supports mindset is to promote young people, both with and without disabilities, to become self-determined learners. This empowers students to become their own best support. Wehmeyer and Zhao (2020, p. 35) indicated that self-determined learning occurs with the following strategies:

- Teachers teach students to teach themselves.
- Students learn how to set and achieve goals and make plans.
- Teachers relinquish ownership for learning to students, not by abdicating all roles in teaching, but by creating learning communities and using teaching methods that emphasize students' curiosity and experiences; that are autonomy-supportive and ensure that learning is tied to activities that are intrinsically motivating or lead to the attainment of goals that are valued and based upon student preferences, interests, and values.
- Teachers provide competence supports by emphasizing mastery experiences, using assessment (both teacher-directed and student-directed) to provide supportive feedback, and aligning instruction with students' strengths and abilities.
- Teachers provide relatedness supports by providing choice opportunities, supporting volition, and emphasizing the goal process and not just goal outcomes.
- Students take initiative in learning because learning is meaningful and of personal value to them. They act volitionally because they are provided choices that are meaningful, meaningfully different, and autonomy-supportive.

Fortunately, there are strategies that enable educators to promote their students' self-determined learning. The final section of this chapter overviews these elements.

Promoting Self-Determined Learning

Creating classroom environments that promote autonomy and student agency is the first step to promote self-determined learning. Within such environments, teachers can employ strategies that promote student self-regulation in problem-solving, goal setting and attainment, and self-determination.

Autonomy-Supportive Educators and Classrooms

Johnmarshall Reeve and his colleagues conducted extensive research in how to promote autonomy and autonomous-functioning in classrooms (Reeve, 2002; Reeve et al., 2021). This line of research has investigated teacher–student interactions that promote the intrinsic motivation of students. Chang et al. (2017) synthesized the important characteristics of autonomy-supportive teachers as

- communicating frequently to clarify expectations and acknowledge students' feelings and ensuring that students know what is expected of them so that they can self-determine learning,
- providing multiple opportunities to make choices by considering the linkages of instructional activities to students' interests and values, and not relying on controlling events and experiences such as competitions or evaluations,
- encouraging and supporting students to participate actively, rather than being passive observers or listeners, and emphasizing active involvement in generating, delivering, and consuming information and content,
- providing informational feedback that is constructive but positive, and not negative, and
- providing guidance that clearly states expectations and the student's role, and supports students to plan for learning and action.

Consider, in your viewpoint, the educational experiences of students with disabilities in today's schools. Would you say classrooms and instruction emphasize autonomy or control? Is instruction teacher-directed or self-determined? Years ago, Martin and colleagues (1993) made the following observation about the transition experiences of youth with disabilities, which likely reflects the reality for far too many students with disabilities:

> If students floated in life jackets for 12 years, would they be expected to swim if the jackets were suddenly jerked away? Probably not. The situation is similar for students receiving special education services. All too often these students are not taught how to self-manage their own lives before they are thrust into the cold water of post-school reality. (p. 53)

Special education has too often been a dependency-creating system emphasizing protection and control, instead of autonomy. One of the powers of inclusive education is that students may, in fact, experience greater opportunities for autonomy, choice, and self-direction. They may have the opportunity to become self-determined learners. But that will not happen without educators providing instruction that teaches students the skills they need to self-determine learning. The *Self-Determined Learning Model of Instruction* (SDLMI; Wehmeyer et al., 2000) was developed for just this purpose; to provide teachers with an instructional model that enables them to teach students to be self-determined learners.

The Self-Determined Learning Model of Instruction (SDLMI)

The SDLMI is a fully formed and empirically validated model of instruction to enable learners to become more self-determined and to set and attain goals that are important to them. A thorough teacher's guide to the SDLMI has been developed by Shogren, Raley, and colleagues (2019) (download for free at https://selfdetermination.ku.edu/homepage/intervention/#sdlmi). As such, this chapter will only provide a broad overview of the theoretical framework and process for the model.

The SDLMI is a *model of teaching*, and therefore it provides a plan or pattern that can be used to shape curricula, drive the selection of instructional materials, and guide instruction (Joyce & Weil, 1980). To some degree, models of teaching exist in the space between theories of human development and curricular materials and strategies. These teaching models take knowledge from human development and behavior and provide a framework with which teachers and researchers can create instructional methods and materials. The theoretical framework that undergirds the SDLMI is causal agency theory (Shogren, Wehmeyer, Palmer, Forber-Pratt et al., 2015), described previously. Based upon research driven by a previous iteration of causal agency theory, Mithaug and colleagues (2003, 2007) proposed several elements of instruction that would be critical to promoting self-determined learning. They suggest that educators teach students to self-regulate a problem-solving sequence so that students can set instructional goals based upon their current knowledge, preferences, and interests, and create action plans to achieve their goals. Additionally, students need instruction in self-monitoring and self-evaluation processes to track their progress. The ultimate goal is for students to act as *causal agents in their lives* to attain their goals.

Mithaug and colleagues (2003, 2007) recommendations are reflected in the three essential characteristics of self-determined action proposed by causal agency theory: volitional action, agentic action, and action-control beliefs. People who are self-determined act volitionally in that they consciously make choices about their actions based on their preferences and their goals. They act agentially by self-directing actions to achieve their self-set goals. Finally, self-determined people act with the belief that the actions they take will lead to success.

Based upon these principles, Mithaug et al. (1998) and Wehmeyer et al. (2000) developed and evaluated the SDLMI. The basic intent was to provide a model of teaching for use by teachers to teach students to, in essence, teach themselves. Although developed initially with students with disabilities, the model is applicable for use with students without disabilities; in more recent years has been used to support instruction across age ranges and disability status (Wehmeyer & Zhao, 2020).

Implementing the SDLMI involves a three-phase instructional process in which each phase presents a problem that the student must solve.

- What is my goal? (Phase 1 problem)
- What is my plan? (Phase 2 problem)
- What have I learned? (Phase 3 problem)

With teacher support, students solve these problems by answering a series of four student questions—which vary for each phase to suit the specific problem being solved—that comprise the same four steps in a problem-solving sequence.

1. Identify the problem.
2. Identify potential solutions to the problem.
3. Identify barriers to solving the problem.
4. Identify consequences of each solution.

Student questions are linked with teacher objectives and each teacher objective is linked to educational supports that educators can implement to teach or support students to answer the questions. Therefore, students are taught to self-regulate problem-solving to set and attain goals and to self-determine their learning.

Although the SDLMI is a model of teaching, it is structured such that the student is the causal agent for actions in their own learning, from solving the problem of what they want or need to learn and setting goals related to this learning need, to creating action plans to achieve the goal, to monitoring progress and evaluating progress. Students learn to revise their action plan or goal as necessary to achieve outcomes that are important to them. By repeated use of the SDLMI, teachers can enable students not just to self-direct learning, but to have greater agency over their learning.

Importantly, there is solid evidence supporting the efficacy of the SDLMI. In fact, the SDLMI was included in many of the studies mentioned previously as supporting the importance of promoting self-determination. Wehmeyer, Palmer et al. (2012) showed that implementing the SDLMI along with other interventions promoted student's self-determination, while Shogren, Wehmeyer, Palmer, Rifenbark, et al. (2015) determined that these same students achieved more positive postschool employment and community inclusion outcomes than did students in the control group. Wehmeyer and Shogren et al. (2012) found that implementing the SDLMI resulted in students becoming more self-determined and Shogren and Palmer et al. (2012) showed that implementing the SDLMI resulted in more positive academic and transition outcomes for students with disabilities. Shogren and Burke et al. (2019) studied the goal attainment of youth with cognitive disabilities who set goals using the SDLMI, and found that students attained educational and transition goals at higher than expected rates after receiving instruction with the SDLMI. Finally, Lee et al. (2015) conducted a meta-analysis of single-case design studies of the SDLMI, and concluded that evidence from multiple studies showed it benefitted students in academic and job training settings.

Assessment of Self-Determination

As in any educational intervention, assessment is important to promoting self-determined learning. To assess areas of instructional need and to evaluate progress in promoting self-determination, Shogren et al. (2020) developed a system of assessments, the Self-Determination Inventory (SDI) assessments, that align with causal agency theory (Shogren, Wehmeyer, Palmer, Forber-Pratt, et al., 2015). The SDI assessments include two parallel versions: a student self-report version and a parent/teacher-report version, both of which have been normed with students with and without disabilities. The SDI assessments measure the three essential characteristics of self-determined action (volitional action, agentic action, and action-control beliefs), as well as overall self-determination. The self-report version was normed with adolescents ages 13 to 22 with and without disabilities. The measures are fully available online (https://selfdetermination.ku.edu/homepage/assessments/).

Conclusions

When considering the types of supports for students with disabilities, it is important to not overlook one of the central supports: students themselves. Research and practice have established that promoting the self-determination of students with disabilities is critical for success in school as well as for life after school. Further, when considering whether to provide supports in inclusive settings, promoting self-determined learning is relevant to all students—not only to students with disabilities. As Wehmeyer and Zhao (2020) emphasized, all students need support to become self-determined learners, to take ownership over and agency in their education, and to be causal agents in their lives. Interventions like the SDLMI and assessments such as the SDI measures provide educators with the tools they need to be great educators . . . that is, educators who support students to learn to be their own best problem-solvers!

Key Ideas From This Chapter

- Students who learn the skills that they need to be self-determined learners can use those skills to become their own best source of support.

- When teaching students how to become self-determined learners, the focus is on developing skills that are necessary to take action to pursue goals that the student deems to be important, not to develop greater independence in a task or activity.
- Promoting self-determination can be included in all tiers of multi-tiered systems of support.
- In over 30 years of studies, educational researchers have documented the considerable benefits that can be gleaned from promoting self-determination as a means of support.
- The exponential knowledge growth of the recent decades provides an even greater rationale for students to learn how to be problem-solvers in regard to coming up with solutions (i.e., supports) to address any learning challenges they may encounter.
- Self-determined learning is synonymous with a heutagogical approach to teaching and learning; it is student-directed learning versus teacher-directed learning. The role of the teacher is to facilitate a student's learning path and process in regard to what will be learned and how it will be learned.
- The Self-Determined Learning Model of Instruction is a fully formed and empirically validated model of instruction designed to prepare students to become causal agents in the own lives. Self-determined learners display the skills that are needed to set and attain goals that are important to them.

Questions for Discussion

1. First, think of a time in your life when you were the furthest away from being a self-determined learner—when the whole impetus for instruction was on a learning something that others had said was important, but (at the time) you did not embrace it. That is, you either didn't understand its relevance or perhaps it was something that was not truly relevant or meaningful to your current or future life. Second, try to think of a time or episode in your life when you were the closest to being a self-determined learner. You had set your own goal/outcome for learning, determined how you were going to reach that goal/outcome, problem-solved when you encountered some difficulties, and were truly the

driving force behind you own learning. As you reflect back on these two experiences, which was the more meaningful experience in terms of how it affected your future learning and life? Compare what you could demonstrate today from the two learning experiences if asked to do so (e.g., if asked to write an essay explaining what you learned, or asked to demonstrate a competency stemming from the instruction). Finally, for the experience you had when you were the furthest away from being a self-determined learner, what could your teachers have done (if anything) to make you more invested in the learning experience?

2. An elementary school teacher expresses that he understands the importance of his students developing self-determination skills, but he isn't sure how to get started. He says, "They are so young, and some are very immature; I think putting them in charge of their own learning would be a disaster." After pointing out that educators who embrace self-determined learning are not suggesting that students be given carte blanche control over all aspects of their school day from the time they enter to the time they leave the building, what are some suggestions to give this teacher regarding how he might incorporate instruction of self-determination skills (such as problem-solving, goal setting and attainment, self-management) into his teaching?

9

Putting It All Together

Supports Planning with Students

The Individual with Disabilities Education Act (IDEA) of 2004 does not require that 100% of students with IEPs be educated in general education classrooms with their same-age peers 100% of the time. The law does require that every student with an IEP be afforded the maximum opportunity to learn alongside students without IEPs in academic, nonacademic, and extracurricular activities. The days of educating large percentages of students with IEPs in separate classrooms are fading away, and in some schools these practices have become a thing of the past. School districts that continue to use separate educational settings as their modus operandi are likely limiting students' opportunities for growth (Hehir et al., 2016). Additionally, these school districts are risking conflicts with families who understand IDEA requirements, recognize the benefits that students gain from inclusive educational opportunities, and are willing to fight for what is best for their child.

A piecemeal approach to inclusive education—where students are selected for inclusion in general education in an effort to appease those parents who complain loudly enough—is neither a sustainable nor effective approach. Best practices call for systematic methods that can be evaluated, replicated, and scaled up. Wise school-district leaders will insist that their schools work systematically toward expanding the capacities of general education classrooms to effectively educate a diverse student population.

The Systematic Support Planning Process, or SSPP, is designed to facilitate the type of creative problem-solving in which educators must engage to identify the supports their students with IEPs need in general education classrooms. Chapters of this book have focused on: (a) describing the SSPP and the types of assessment information that can inform decision-making, (b) providing strategies to answer the critical questions and implement the essential actions that comprise the SSPP, (c) highlighting the application of universal design for learning (UDL) principles to create classrooms that maximize accessibility, and (d) underscoring the importance of teaching students self-determination skills so that they learn how to become their own advocates. In this final chapter, cases that demonstrate how the SSPP has been applied in schools will be the focus.

The SSPP: Snapshots From the Classroom

The US Department of Education's Institute on Educational Sciences funded a multiyear project where teacher teams implemented the SSPP. Over 20 K–8 teacher teams from several states in diverse school settings have implemented the SSPP during the past 2 years. Although there is still much to be learned, all indicators are that the SSPP can be implemented with fidelity and teachers, school administrators, parents, and students perceive it as beneficial.

The students with IEPs who were identified as candidates for the SSPP project were either not included in general education classes previously, or were included but their teachers saw a need to expand the student's participation in classroom learning activities and/or progress in the general education curriculum. The purpose of this chapter is not to provide detailed findings or draw conclusions from statistical analyses on the impact of the SSPP. That will come at a future time when all data have been collected and specific knowledge claims can be made with confidence. At this time, however, it is possible to share stories of successes that exemplify what can be accomplished when supports are systematically planned and implemented. The following cases show how supports were provided to students and illustrate the types of practical solutions that arise when teachers

All indicators are that the SSPP can be implemented with fidelity and teachers, school administrators, parents, and students perceive it as beneficial.

focus on the three main questions driving the SSPP: *What to teach? How to teach? How to promote participation?*

Aamir

Background, strengths, and support needs. Aamir is in the first grade. He has been diagnosed with autism spectrum disorder and is eligible for special education services. He reads fluently at grade level. He speaks in short phrases to adults and peers about preferred topics, especially robots and dinosaurs. He needs supports that most other students do not require when asked to understand abstractions and to make inferences, especially in relation to the perceptions of others, and with social interaction and communication.

General education classroom instruction and learning expectations. The SSPP planning focused on supports for a language arts unit about characters in a story. Grade-level learning expectations included (a) making personal connections between self and characters in stories, and (b) making connections between characters in similar situations in different stories. A general education teacher and a paraprofessional were available to provide supports to students in the general education classroom, including Aamir, during language arts instruction.

What to teach? Teachers judged the grade-level content and learning goals for the unit to be appropriate for Aamir, although a modification for the expression of knowledge was needed for the learning goal of "making connections between characters in similar situations in different stories." Specifically, Aamir was asked to use visual supports to show his knowledge regarding connections between characters in different stories as opposed to writing or verbally explaining the connections. Additional goals to be taught during the class period that were specific to Aamir were focused on social communication with a peer and legible handwriting.

How to teach? Teachers indicated Aamir could learn through the same instructional activities provided to his classmates (i.e., whole-group discussion, think-pair-share, and stop and jot). The special educator developed the visual supports Aamir needed, and the general educator and paraprofessional applied them with

Aamir. Additionally, instructional procedures for his individual learning goals were develop by the special educator in collaboration with the general education teacher, and these were implemented by the general education teacher and paraprofessional within ongoing learning activities.

How to promote participation? Before instruction began, the general education teacher identified three learning activities to use during the language arts unit: whole-group discussion, think-pair-share, and stop and jot. The support plan emerging from the SSPP called for Aamir to participate in all of the classroom learning activities with accommodations. For the whole-group discussions, Aamir (with very minimal prompting from the paraprofessional), used visually supported response options developed by the special education teacher. Because whole-group discussion was somewhat unpredictable, during this time the paraprofessional had a white board to write answer options if Aamir needed this support. For think-pair-share, Aamir was provided a list of questions and prompts he could use to ask his partner. For stop and jot, Aamir was required to write one word of his answer legibly and then dictate the rest to the paraprofessional.

Support monitoring and evaluation. After implementing the supports for 2 weeks, the general education teacher reported Aamir was participating more in class than before the SSPP had been implemented. Moreover, the accuracy of his work had increased. After a month of the supports developed through the SSPP, it was evident that Aamir no longer needed direct support from the paraprofessional to participate in language arts class activities. Peers provided him with extra supports when situations arose where he needed them.

Elisha

Background, strengths, and support needs. Elisha is in the third grade. She meets criteria for special education services under IDEA due to diagnoses consistent with intellectual disability, visual impairment, and hearing impairment. She is very social and enjoys interacting with other students. She reads at the first-grade level. She enjoys sports and physical education class. She tries hard in school and always attempts all work requested of her in her academic classes. She needs supports that most other students do not require to complete academic work across all content areas. In particular, she needs supports to engage in discussions in academic classes with peers and educators, to attend to whole-group instruction, and to complete independent work.

General education classroom instruction and learning expectations. The SSPP planning focused on support needed for a math unit on fractions. The grade-level expectations included (a) understanding fractions as part of a whole, (b) drawing a bar model of fractions, (c) representing equivalent fractions using the bar model, and (d) comparing two fractions. The general education teacher and special education teacher were both present in the classroom during math instruction, with multiple coteaching opportunities available.

What to teach? After some discussion, the teachers agreed they expected Elisha to meet the expectations of the general education curriculum without modifications. However, the teachers also agreed Elisha needed to focus on a few additional learning outcomes outside the general education curriculum. In particular, she needed to work on communicating her thinking about a problem with a peer, identifying target vocabulary related to a lesson, completing her work independently, and attending to instruction in the whole-group setting.

How to teach? Elisha learned content through the same nine instructional activities provided to classmates (participation supports, described next, were provided to her during each learning activity). Elisha's special educator developed additional materials using strategies associated with explicit, systematic instruction to supplement instruction on the general education content. Instructional procedures for Elisha's individual learning goals were also developed by the special educator in collaboration with the general education teacher, and these were implemented by both teachers within ongoing learning activities.

How to promote participation? The general education teacher identified nine learning activities to teach the unit on fractions such as attending to a demonstration, whole-group discussion, investigating a concept, and interpreting a representation. The teachers agreed Elisha would participate in all of the learning activities with accommodations. The teachers identified two to four supports for each learning activity. For example, to support her in attending to a demonstration, the teacher provided Elisha with preferential seating, modeling of expectations, frequent verbal praise, and the option to have a break every 10 minutes. To participate in discussions with the teacher or peers, Elisha received modeling from a teacher or peer on how to use a complete sentence, sat near a peer buddy who provided the model, was visually supported to participate through enlarged answer options, and was provided with sentence starters.

Support monitoring and evaluation. After implementing supports for 1 week, the teachers met to discuss the effectiveness of the supports. Elisha's accuracy of work completed had improved, and she was remaining on task longer. Additionally, she was beginning to ask her peers questions before going to the teacher. The team continued to monitor Elisha's progress over the course of the unit, leaving all supports in place. She showed measurable academic growth; she was able to achieve the general education performance expectations with minor adaptations that included some verbal prompting and more explicit directions.

Oliver

Background, strengths, and support needs. Oliver is in the fifth grade. He receives special education services under the categories of intellectual disability and deaf and hard of hearing. Oliver has relatively strong communication skills, but experiences difficulty with articulation due to sensorineural hearing loss. He enjoys interacting with his peers but often needs prompts to stay on topic during conversations. He can identify numbers up to 100 and complete single- and double-digit addition problems with minimal support. He is also able to identify 200+ sight words and answer who, what, where, and when questions about a familiar passage.

General education classroom instruction and learning expectations. The SSPP planning focused on supports for a reading unit about nonfiction. The grade-level expectations for this unit included (a) identifying main ideas and supporting details from nonfiction texts and (b) comparing and contrasting the texts. During this time period, Oliver's classroom was staffed by his general education teacher and a paraprofessional.

What to teach? Oliver's general and special education teachers agreed that Oliver could meet the grade-level learning expectations with modifications, for example, identifying one main idea from a choice of four rather than two or more main ideas without choices. However, the teachers also agreed Oliver needed to focus on an alternative learning goal of remaining on topic during small groups with peers.

How to teach? The general education teacher identified nine learning activities she planned to use during the nonfiction unit, including making predictions, comparing and contrasting texts, participating in a book club, and participating in discussions with peers. The teachers agreed Oliver would benefit from participating in all of the learning activities with supports. For example, to support him in making predictions related to a nonfiction text, the special education teacher prepared visual supports including picture symbols and photographs of content from the text when asked to make a prediction. The teachers consulted with the speech-language pathologist to develop an instructional plan focused on teaching Oliver how to remain on topic during small-group activities. The team decided that Oliver would benefit from receiving tokens after the class period ended when he remained on topic by demonstrating appropriate communicative behavior and self-reflection (with support from a paraprofessional).

How to promote participation? Oliver was seated closer to the front of the classroom, nearer to where the teacher delivered most content; for small-group work, his group peers were carefully selected, particularly as the unit began. The teachers identified one to two supports for each learning activity to help keep Oliver fully engaged and participating in the class-wide learning activities.

Support monitoring and evaluation. After implementing the supports for a week, the general education teacher reported that Oliver was doing exceptionally well in the general education reading class. (He had been a student who had traditionally received much of his education in special education classrooms). Oliver was fully engaged and eagerly participating in all learning activities. The special education teacher also reported that the token system was proving to be effective, as he was staying on topic during small-group discussions. The team continued to monitor Oliver's progress over the course of the unit, leaving all supports in place.

The Future of Special Educators: A Profession of Problem-Solving Super Heroes

Occasionally, a concern will be raised regarding the future of special education teachers in the event schools become totally inclusive and all special education classrooms are eliminated (see Kauffman & Hornby, 2020). These chapters have, hopefully, made it clear that the profession of special education will flourish in an inclusive education context so long as special educators' expertise and efforts add value to general education classroom. Special education will be a profession that is widely respected and special educators will be in high demand if their efforts enhance the learning of students with IEPs and help establish general education classrooms that are good places for all students to learn.

This book began with a question: "What makes a great special educator?" The short answer was that great special educators are expert problem-solvers. In the vision for inclusive schools on which the SSPP is based, special educators are integral to an inclusive school's success. They are the go-to staff when it comes to coworking with general educators on implementing UDL principles to make classrooms more accessible, and when arranging supports to meet the needs of specific students. They also play a critical role in supporting students to become self-determined learners.

The profession of special education will flourish in an inclusive education context so long as special educators' expertise and efforts add value to general education classroom.

Neither the importance of special education services nor special education teachers decreases when there is a shift in providing services in separate settings to inclusive settings. What changes is the nature of the work of the special educator. The special educator is no longer charged with teaching a group of students who are removed from general education. Rather, the special educator is charged with collaborating with general educators to support classroom learning activities that promote learning and achievement for all students. And, don't worry, special educators still have plenty of opportunities to work directly with students within the context of the general education classroom, whether it be individually, in small groups, or in whole-class instruction.

In response to questions about what was different when using the SSPP from methods used before, practically every teacher team in the SSPP project mentioned that devoting time to collaborative problem-solving was one of the major reasons why they felt their efforts were successful. Furthermore, learning from one another was consistently mentioned to be one of the most rewarding aspects of the project. Of course, collaboration comes with some costs. The greatest cost of any collaborative effort is time—there is no getting around it. Due to the emphasis the SSPP places on collaboratively planning student supports, the demands on teacher time and effort must not be dismissed. School leaders wanting to implement the SSPP must allow teachers sufficient time to do the work that the process requires.

It would be great if there were a magic wand that could waved to instantly provide students with IEPs all of the supports they need. But, in the absence of a wand and instant gratification, there is collaborative problem-solving and long-term success. The SSPP is a process to help identify and arrange the supports that students with IEPs require to be successful in general education classrooms. All educators who to commit to the SSPP must be prepared to devote the necessary time and energy the process requires for successful implementation.

In one sense, the SSPP does require some magic. The magic lies within the imaginations of educators who put their minds to identifying and arranging supports that help students learn. When a workable, creative solution appears where none existed before, and when students with IEPs are learning in general education classrooms where they were unable to learn before, then—voilà!—teachers have accomplished something quite extraordinary. To all of the educators who have the courage, vision, and perseverance needed to implement the SSPP, there is but one thing left to say. Go forth, unleash your amazing, problem-solving super powers, and take joy in changing the world for your students!

Key Ideas From This Chapter

- Schools must take a proactive stance and work systematically towards expanding the capacities of general education classrooms to effectively educate a diverse student population.
- The cases presented in this chapter illustrate how the SSPP can be used to identify and arrange supports to students with different

disability characteristics, at different grade levels, and in different subject areas.

- An investment of time is essential to collaborative problem-solving, and collaborative problem-solving is essential to identifying the supports that students with IEPs need to fully benefit from instruction in general education classrooms.

Questions for Discussion

1. The three cases in this chapter show how educators who used the SSPP were able to come up with some good supports for students with different disability characteristics and at the different age/grade levels. We know that the supports were good ones because the student outcomes were positive. What else would you like to know about these students and their classroom experiences? Do these students remind you of any students with whom you have worked in the past? How so? What other supports do you think may have been useful?
2. Time is precious. Implementing the SPSS requires collaborative problem-solving, which takes time. Of course, collaborative problem-solving is a hallmark of other professions—for instance, medical doctors and lawyers are always meeting with one another to discuss cases and come up with good solutions. For the school leader who understands that teachers must devote time to collaborative problem-solving in an inclusive school, what practical solutions could free up time for teachers to collaborate?

References

Afacan, K., Wilkerson, K. L., & Ruppar, A. L. (2018). Multicomponent reading interventions for students with intellectual disability. *Remedial and Special Education, 39*(4), 229–242. http://doi.org/10.1177/0741932517702444

Alferink, L. A., & Farmer-Dougan, V. (2010). Brain-(not) based education: Dangers of misunderstanding and misapplication of neuroscience research. *Exceptionality, 18*(1), 42–52. https://doi.org/10.1080/09362830903462573

American Academy of Pediatrics. (2009). Learning disabilities, dyslexia, and vision. *Pediatrics, 124*(2), 837–844. https://doi.org/10.1542/peds.2009-1445

American Federation of Teachers (2014). [AFT Resolution]. Against standardized assessments for students receiving special education services. https://www.aft.org/resolution/against-standardized-assessments-students-receiving-special-education-services

Arias, V. B., Aguayo, V., Verdugo, M. A., & Amor, A. M. (2020). Differences in the support needs of children with developmental disabilities among groups of medical and behavioral needs. *Peer J.*, 8, Article e9557. https://doi.org/10.7717/peerj.9557

Assistive Technology Industry Association. (2021). *What is AT?* https://www.atia.org/home/at-resources/what-is-at/

Ayres, K. M., Lowrey, K. A., Douglas, K. H., & Sievers, C. (2011). I can identify Saturn but I can't brush my teeth: What happens with the curricula focus for students with severe disabilities shifts. *Education and Training in Autism and Developmental Disabilities, 46*(1), 11–21.

Bakken, L., Brown, N., & Downing, B. (2017). Early childhood education: The long-term benefits. *Journal of Research in Childhood Education, 31*(2), 255–269. https://doi.org/10.1080/02568543.2016.1273285

Barrett, C., Angel, J., Gilbert, M., Bouras, C., Thompson, K., & Singleton, E. (2005). Systematic processes for successful, sustainable practice development. *Practice Development in Health Care, 4*(1), 5–13. https://doi.org/10.1002/pdh.25

Baumgart, D., Brown, L., Pumpian, I., Nisbet, J., Ford, A., Sweet, M., Messina, R., & Schroeder, J. (1982). Principle of participation and individualized adaptations in educational programs for severely handicapped students. *The Journal of the Association for Persons with Severe Handicaps, 7*(1), 17–27. https://doi.org/10.1177/154079698200700211

Blanchard, M. R., Harris, J., & Hofer, M. (2011, February). Science learning activity types. Retrieved from College of William and Mary, School of Education, Learning Activity Types Wiki: http://activitytypes.wm.edu/ScienceLearningATs-Feb2011.pdf

Blaschke, L. M. (2012). Heutagogy and lifelong learning: A review of heutagogical practice and self-determined learning. *The International Review of Research in Open and Distance Learning, 13*, 56–71.

Bowman, J. A., McDonnell, J., Ryan, J., Coleman, O. F., Conradi, L. A., & Eichelberger, C. (2020). Effects of general education teacher-delivered embedded instruction to teach students with intellectual disability to solve word problems. *Education and Training in Autism and Developmental Disabilities, 55*(3), 318–331.

Brock, M. E., & Anderson, E. J. (2021). Training paraprofessionals who work with students with intellectual and developmental disabilities: What does the research say? *Psychology in the Schools, 58*(4), 702–722. https://doi.org/10.1002/pits.22386

Brock, M. E., & Huber, H. B. (2017). Are peer support arrangements an evidence-based practice? A systematic review. *Journal of Special Education, 51*(3), 150–163. https://doi.org/10.1177/0022466917708184

Bronfenbrenner, U. (1979). *The ecology of human development: Experiments by nature and design*. Cambridge: Harvard University Press.

Browder, D., Gibbs, S., Ahlgrim-Delzell, L., Courtade, G. R., Mraz, M., & Flowers, C. (2009). Literacy for students with severe developmental disabilities. What should we teach and what should we hope to achieve? *Remedial and Special Education, 30*, 269–282. http://doi.org/10.1177/0741932508315054

Browder, D. M., Spooner, F., Wakeman, S., Trela, K., & Baker, J. N. (2006). Aligning instruction with academic content standards: Finding the link. *Research and Practice for Persons with Severe Disabilities, 31*(4), 309–321.

Brown, L., Schwarz, P., Udvari-Solner, A., Kampschroer, E., Johnson,F., Jorgensen, L., & Gruenewald, L. (1991). How much time should students with severe intellectual disabilities spend in regular classrooms and elsewhere? *Journal of the Association for Persons with Severe Handicaps, 16*(1), 39–47. https://doi.org/10.1177/154079699101600105

Bruhn, A. L., Lane, K. L., Hirsch, S. E. (2014). A review of Tier 2 interventions conducted within multitiered models of behavioral prevention. *Journal of Emotional Behavioral Disorders, 22*(3), 171–189. https://doi.org/10.1177/1063426613476092

Butterworth, J., Smith, F. A., Winsor, J., Ciulla Timmons, J., Migliore, A., & Domin, D. (2015). *StateData: The national report on employment services and outcomes.* University of Massachusetts Boston, Institute for Community Inclusion. https://www.statedata.info/sites/statedata.info/files/files/statedatabook_2015%20_Final.pdf

Candy, P. C. (1991). *Self-direction for lifelong learning.* San Francisco: Jossey-Bass.

Carr, J. E., Nicolson, A. C., & Higbee, T. S. (2000). Evaluation of a brief multiple-stimulus preference assessment in a naturalistic context. *Journal of Applied Behavior Analysis, 33*(3), 353–357. https://psycnet.apa.org/doi/10.1901/jaba.2000.33-353

Carter, E., O'Rourke, L., Sisco, L. G., & Pelsue, D. (2009). Knowledge, responsibilities, and training needs of paraprofessionals in elementary and secondary schools. *Remedial and Special Education, 30*(6), 344–359. https://doi.org/10.1177/0741932508324399

Carter, E. W., Lane, K. L., Pierson, M. R., & Glaeser, B. (2006). Self-determination skills and opportunities of transition-age youth with emotional disturbance and learning disabilities. *Exceptional Children, 72*(3), 333–346.

CAST. (2018). *Universal design for learning guidelines Version 2.2.* Retrieved from https://udlguidelines.cast.org

Chamberlain, P. (2020). Knowledge is not everything. *Design for Health, 4*(1), 1–3.

Chang, R., Fukuda, E., Durham, J., & Little, T. D. (2017). Enhancing students' motivation with autonomy-supportive classrooms. In M. L. Wehmeyer, K. A. Shogren, T. D. Little, & S. J. Lopez (Eds.), *Development of self-determination throughout the life-course* (pp. 99–110). Springer.

Chazin, K. T. & Ledford, J. R. (2016). Preference assessments. In *Evidence-based instructional practices for young children with autism and other disabilities.* http://ebip.vkcsites.org/preference-assessments

Chene, A. (1983). The concept of autonomy in adult education: A philosophical discussion. *Adult Education Quarterly, 1*, 38–47.

Christenson, S. L., Reschly, A. L., & Wylie, C. (2012). *Handbook of research on student engagement.* Springer. https://doi.org/10.1007/978-1-4614-2018-7

Cohen, A., & Demchak, M. (2018). Use of visual supports to increase task independence in students with severe disabilities in inclusive educational settings. *Education and Training in Autism and Developmental Disabilities, 53*(1), 84–99. https://www.jstor.org/stable/26420429

Collins, B. C. (2012). *Systematic instruction for students with moderate and severe disabilities.* Brookes Publishing.

Conn, C., & McLean, R. (2018). *Bulletproof problem solving: The one skill that changes everything.* John Wiley & Sons.

Courtade, G. R., Lingo, A. S., Karp, K. S., & Whitney, T. (2013). Shared story reading: Teaching mathematics to students with moderate and severe disabilities. *Teaching Exceptional Children, 45*(3), 34–44. http://doi.org/10.1177/004005991304500304

Coyne, P., Pisha, B., Dalton, B., Zeph, L. A., & Smith, N. C. (2012). Literacy by design: A universal design for learning approach for students with significant intellectual disabilities. *Remedial and Special Education, 33*, 162–172.

Cramer, E., Little, M. E., & McHatton, P. A. (2018). Equity, equality, and standardization: Expanding the conversations. *Education and Urban Society, 50*(5), 483–501.

Dee, A. L. (2010). Preservice teacher application of differentiated instruction. *The Teacher Educator, 46*(1), 53–70. https://doi.org/10.1080/08878730.2010.529987

Delisle, J. R. (2015). Differentiation doesn't work. *Education Week*. Retrieved from https://www.edweek.org/teaching-learning/opinion-differentiation-doesnt-work/2015/01

Diedrich, J. (2021). The elusive nature of UDL. In K. A. Lowery (Ed.), *Critical issues in universal design for learning* (pp. 3–9). Orlando, FL: Knowledge by Design.

Duff, D., & Tomblin, B. J. (2018). Literacy as an outcome of language development and its impact on children's psychosocial and emotional development. In R. E. Tremblay, M. Boivin, & R. D. Peters (Eds.), *Encyclopedia on early childhood development* [online]. https://www.child-encyclopedia.com/language-development-and-literacy/according-experts/literacy-outcome-language-development-and-its

Dykens, E. M., Hodapp, R. M., & Finucane, B. M. (2000). *Genetics and mental retardation syndromes: A new look at behavior and interventions*. Paul H. Brookes.

Edyburn, D. L. (2010). Would you recognize universal design for learning if you saw it? Ten propositions for new directions for the second decade of UDL. *Learning Disability Quarterly, 33*(1), 33–41.

Edyburn. D. L. (2020). Universal design for learning and the landfill of revolutionary educational innovations. In S. L. Gronseth & E. M. Dalton (Eds.), *Universal access through inclusive instructional design: International perspectives on UDL* (pp. 332–342). Routledge.

Ehri, L. C., & Flugman, B. (2018). Mentoring teachers in systematic phonics instruction: Effectiveness of an intensive year-long program for kindergarten through 3rd grade teachers and their students. *Reading and Writing, 31*(2), 425–456. https://doi.org/10.1007/s11145-017-9792-7

Every Student Succeeds Act, 20 U.S.C. § 6301 (2015). https://www.congress.gov/114/plaws/publ95/PLAW-114publ95.pdf

Farmer-Dougan, V., & Alferink, L. A. (2013). Brain development, early childhood, and brain-based education: A critical analysis. In L. H. Wasserman & D. Zambo (Eds.), *Early childhood and neuroscience-links to development and learning* (pp. 55–76). Springer.

Ferguson, D. L., & Baumgart, D. (1991). Partial participation revisited. *JASH, 16*(4), 218–227.

Foegen, A., Jiban, C., & Deno, S. L. (2007). Progress monitoring measures in mathematics: A review of the literature. *The Journal of Special Education, 41*(2), 121–139.

Fowler, S. A., Coleman, M. R. B., & Bogdan, W. K. (2019). The state of the special education profession survey report. *Teaching Exceptional Children, 52*(1), 8–29. https://doi.org/10.1177/0040059919875703

Fuchs, D., & Fuchs, L. S. (2006). Introduction to response to intervention: What, why, and how valid is it? *Reading Research Quarterly, 41*(1), 93–99. http://www.jstor.org/stable/4151803

Fuller, B. (1981). *Critical path*. St. Martin's Press.

Fullan, M., & Quinn, J. (2016). *Coherence: The right drivers in action for schools, districts, and systems*. Thousand Oaks, CA: Corwin. https://us.corwin.com/en-us/nam/book/right-drivers-action#description

Gardiner-Walsh, S., Giese, K., & Walsh, T. P. (2020). Cued speech: Evolving evidence

1968–2018. *Deafness & Education International*. Advanced online publication. https://doi.rgo/10.1080/14643154.2020.1755144

Giangreco, M. F. (2021). Maslow's hammer: Teacher assistant research and inclusive practices at a crossroads. *European Journal of Special Needs Education, 36*(2), 278–293. https://doi.org/10.1080/08856257.2021.1901377

Giangreco, M. F., Cloninger, C. J., & Iverson, V. S. (2011). *Choosing outcomes and accommodations for children (COACH): A guide to educational planning for students with disabilities* (3rd ed.). Paul H. Brookes.

Great Schools Partnership. (2015, August 12). Curriculum. In *Glossary of Education Reform*. Retrieved month day, year, from https://www.edglossary.org/curriculum/

Goulet, M., Archambault, I., Janosz, M., & Christenson, S. L. (2018) Evaluating the implementation of Check & Connect in various school settings: Is intervention fidelity necessarily associated with positive outcomes? *Evaluation and Program Planning, 68*(1), 34–46. https://doi.org/10.1016/j.evalprogplan.2018.02.004

Great Schools. (April 5, 2010). *Implications of high-stakes testing for students with learning disabilities*. Retrieved on September 16, 2021, from http://www.greatschools.org/gk/articles/high-stakes-testing-learning-disabilities/

Hagiwara, M., Shogren, K. A., & Shaw, L. A. (2019) Examining the impact of respondent-level factors on scores on the *Supports Intensity Scale—Children's Version*. *American Journal of Intellectual and Developmental Disabilities, 124*(4), 309–323. https://doi.org/10.1352/1944-7558-124.4.309

Hallinger, P. (2018). Principal instructional leadership: From prescription to theory to practice. In G. E. Hall, L. F. Quinn, & D. M. Gollnick (Eds.), *The Wiley handbook of teaching and learning* (pp. 505–528). John Wiley & Sons. https://doi.org/10.1002/9781118955901.ch21

Harris, J., & Hofer, M. (n.d.). *Welcome to the learning activity types (LATs) Website!* College of William & Mary School of Education. Retrieved April 15, 2021, from https://activitytypes.wm.edu/

Hartmann, E. (2015). Universal design for learning (UDL) and learners with severe support needs. *International Journal of Whole Schooling, 11*(1), 54–67.

Hasbrouck, J., & Tindal, G. (2017). *An update to compiled ORF norms* (Technical report no. 1702). Behavioral Research and Teaching, University of Oregon. https://intensiveintervention.org/sites/default/files/TechRpt_1702ORFNorms%20FINAL.pdf

Haug, B. S. (2014). Inquiry-based science: Turning teachable moments into learnable moments. *Journal of Science Teacher Education, 25*(1), 79–96. https://doi.org/10.1007/s10972-013-9375-7

Haug, P., 2017. Understanding inclusive education: Ideals and reality. *Scandinavian Journal of Disability Research, 19*(3), 206–217. http://doi.org/10.1080/15017419.2016.1224778

Hehir, T., Grindal, T., Freeman, B., Lamoreau, R., Borquaye, Y., & Burke, S. (2016). *A summary of the evidence on inclusive education*. Abt Associates. https://www.abtassociates

.com/sites/default/files/2019-03/A_Summary_of_the_evidence_on_inclusive_education.pdf

Higher Education Opportunity Act of 2008, Pub. L. No. 110-315 § 122 Stat. 3078 (2008). https://www.govinfo.gov/link/plaw/110/public/315

Hogan, A. J. (2019). Moving away from the "medical model": The development and revision of the World Health Organization's classification of disability. *Bulletin of the History of Medicine 93*(2), 241–269. http://doi.org/10.1353/bhm.2019.0028

Hord, C., & Bouck, E. C. (2012). Review of academic mathematics instruction for students with mild intellectual disability. *Education and Training in Autism and Developmental Disabilities, 47*(3), 389–400.

Hott, B., Berkeley, S., Fairfield, A., & Shora, N. (2017). Intervention in school and clinic: An analysis of 25 years of guidance for practitioners. *Learning Disability Quarterly, 40*(1), 54–64.

Howery, K. L. (2021). The language we use to speak UDL. In K. A. Lowery (Ed.), *Critical issues in universal design for learning* (pp. 11–41). Knowledge by Design.

Hyman, S. L., Stewart, P. A., Foley, J., Cain, U., Peck, R., Morris, D. D., Wang, H., & Smith, T. (2016). The gluten-free/casein-free diet: A double-blind challenge trial in children with autism. *Journal of Autism and Developmental Disorders, 46*, 205–220. https://doi.org/10.1007/s10803-015-2564-9

Individuals With Disabilities Education Act, 20 U.S.C. § 1400 et seq. (2004). https://sites.ed.gov/idea/

Israel, M., Ribuffo, C., & Smith, S. (2014). *Universal design for learning: Recommendations for teacher preparation and professional development* (Document No. IC-7). Retrieved from University of Florida, Collaboration for Effective Educator, Development, Accountability, and Reform Center website: https://ceedar.education.ufl.edu/wp-content/uploads/2014/08/IC-7_FINAL_08-27-14.pdf

Jameson, J., McDonnell, J., Johnson, J., Riesen, T., & Polychronis, S. (2007). A comparison of one-to-one embedded instruction in the general education classroom and one-to-one massed practice instruction in the special education classroom. *Education and Treatment of Children, 30*(1), 23–44. http://www.jstor.org/stable/42899917

Janney, R., & Snell, M. E. (2013). *Modifying schoolwork* (3rd ed.). Brookes Publishing.

Jimenez, B., A., Browder, D. M., Spooner, F., & Dibiase, W. (2012). Inclusive inquiry science using peer-mediated embedded instruction for students with moderate intellectual disability. *Exceptional Children, 78*(3), 301–317. https://doi.org/10.1177/001440291207800303

Jimerson, S., Egeland, B., Sroufe, L. A., & Carlson, B. (2000). A prospective longitudinal study of high school dropouts examining multiple predictors across development. *Journal of School Psychology, 38*(6), 525–549. http://dx.doi.org/10.1016/S0022-4405(00)00051-0

Johnson, J. W., McDonnell, J., Holzwarth, V. N., & Hunter, K. (2004). The efficacy of embedded instruction for students with developmental disabilities enrolled in general education classes. *Journal of Positive Behavior Interventions, 6*(4), 214–227. https://doi.org/10.1177/10983007040060040301

Jonassen, D. H. (2011) *Learning to solve problems: A handbook for designing problem-solving learning environments*. Routledge.

Joyce, B., & Weil, M. (1980). *Models of teaching* (2nd ed.). Prentice Hall.

Kauffman, J. M., Hallahan, D. P., Pullen, P. C., & Badar, J. (2018). *Special education: What it is and why we need it*. Taylor & Francis.

Kauffman, J. M., & Hornby, G. (2020). Inclusive vision versus special education reality. *Educational Sciences, 10*(9), 1–13. https://doi.org/10.3390/educsci10090258

Kellems, R. O., & Morningstar, M. E. (2010). Tips for transition. *Teaching Exceptional Children. 43*(2), 60–68. https://doi.org/10.1177/004005991004300206

Kelly, A. V. (2009). The curriculum: Theory and practice (6th ed.). Sage.

Kirschner, P. A. (2017). Stop propagating the learning styles myth. *Computers and Education, 106*, 166–171. https://doi.org/10.1016/j.compedu.2016.12.006

Klemm, W. (2013, March 14). Why writing by hand could make you smarter. *Psychology Today*. https://www.psychologytoday.com/us/blog/memory-medic/201303/why-writing-hand-could-make-you-smarter

Kluth, P. (2010). *"You're going to love this kid!": Teaching students with autism in the inclusive classroom* (2nd ed). Paul H. Brookes Publishing.

Knowles, M. S. (1975). *Self-directed learning: A guide for learners and teachers*. Follett Publishing.

Konrad, M., Fowler, C. H., Walker, A. R., Test, D. W., & Wood, W. M. (2007). Effects of self-determination interventions on the academic skills of students with learning disabilities. *Learning Disabilities Quarterly, 30*(2), 89–113.

Kriegbaum, K., Becker, N., & Spinath, B. (2018). The relative importance of intelligence and motivation as predictors of school achievement: A meta-analysis. *Educational Research Review, 25*, 120–148. https://doi.org/10.1016/j.edurev.2018.10.001

Kurth, J. A., & Forber-Pratt, A. J. (2017). Views of inclusive education from the perspectives of preservice and mentor teachers. *5*(3), 189–202. http://doi.org/10.1352/2326-6988-$23.189

Kurth, J. A., & Gross, M. (2015). *The inclusion toolbox: Strategies and techniques for all teachers*. Corwin.

Kurth, J. A., & Mastergeorge, A. M. (2012). Impact of setting and instructional context for adolescents with autism. *Journal of Special Education, 46*(1), 36–48. https://doi.org/10.1177/0022466910366480

Kurth, J. A., McQueston, J. A., Ruppar, A. L., Toews, S. G., Johnston, R., & McCabe, K. M. (2019). A description of parent input in IEP development through analysis IEP documents. *Intellectual and Developmental Disabilities, 57*(6), 485–498. https://doi.org/10.1352/1934-9556-57.6.485

Lachapelle, Y., Wehmeyer, M. L., Haelewyck, M.-C., Courbois, Y., Keith, K. D., Schalock, R., Verdugo, M. A., & Walsh, P. N. (2005). The relationship between quality of life and self-determination: An international study. *Journal of Intellectual Disability Research, 49*(10), 740–744. 10.1111/j.1365-2788.2005.00743.x

Lambert, R., & Tan, P. (2017). Conceptualizations of students with and without disabilities as mathematical problem solvers in educational research: A critical review. *Education Sciences*, *7*(2), 51. https://doi.org/10.3390/educsci7020051

Lane, K., Oakes, W., Jenkins, A., Menzies, H., & Kalberg, J. (2014). A team-based process for designing comprehensive, integrated, three-tiered (CI3T) models of prevention: How does my school-site leadership team design a CI3T model? *Preventing School Failure*. *58*(3), 129–142. https://doi.org/10.1080/1045988X.2014.893976

Langberg, J. M., Epstein, J. N., Urbanowicz, C. M., Simon, J. O., & Graham, A. J. (2008). Efficacy of an organization skills intervention to improve the academic functioning of students with attention-deficit/hyperactivity disorder. *School Psychology Quarterly*, *23*(3), 407–417. https://doi.org/10.1037/1045-3830.23.3.407

Lawrence-Brown, D. (2004). Differentiated instruction: Inclusive strategies for standards-based learning that benefit the whole class. *American Secondary Education*, *32*(3), 34–62.

Lazonder, A. W., & Harmsen, R. (2016). Meta-analysis of inquiry-based learning: Effects of guidance. *Review of Educational Research*, *86*(3), 681–718. https://doi:10.3102/0034654315627366

Lee, A., & Gage, N. A. (2020). Updating and expanding systematic reviews and meta-analyses on the effects of school-wide positive behavior interventions and supports. *Psychology in the Schools*, *57*(5), 783–804. https://doi.org/10.1002/pits.22336

Lee, S.-H., Wehmeyer, M. L., & Shogren, K. A. (2015). Effect of instruction with the self-determined learning model of instruction on students with disabilities: A meta-analysis. *Education and Training in Autism and Developmental Disabilities*, *50*(2), 237–247.

Lee, S.-H., Wehmeyer, M. L., Soukup, J. H., & Palmer, S. B. (2010). Impact of curriculum modifications on access to the general education curriculum for students with disabilities. *Exceptional Children*, *76*(2), 213–233.

Lewin, K. (1943). Psychology and the process of group living. *Journal of Social Psychology*, 17, 113–131. http://doi.org/10.1080/00224545.1943.9712269

Lewis, T. J., Mitchell, B. S., Bruntmeyer, D. T., & Sugai, G. (2016). School-wide positive behavior support and response to intervention: System similarities, distinctions, and research to date at the universal level of support. In S. R. Jimerson, M. K. Burns, & A. VanDerHyden (Eds.), *Handbook of response to intervention* (pp. 703–717). Springer.

Levine, P., & Nourse, S. W. (1998). What follow-up studies say about postschool life for young men and women with learning disabilities: A critical look at the literature. *Journal of Learning Disabilities*, *31*(3), 212–233. https://doi.org/10.1177/002221949803100302

Lighter, L. (2018). Ultimate List of IEP Accommodations, modifications, and strategies. Retrieved September 29, 2021. https://adayinourshoes.com/wp-content/uploads/IEP-Accommodations-and-Strategies-printable.pdf

Lowrey, K. A. (2021). How far are the margins? UDL and students with intellectual disabilities. In K. A. Lowery (Ed.), *Critical issues in universal design for learning* (pp. 187–202). Knowledge by Design.

Lowrey, K. A., & Smith, S. J. (2018). Including individuals with disabilities in UDL framework implementation: Insights from administrators. *Inclusion*, *6*, 127–142.

March, R. E., Horner, R. H., Lewis-Palmer, T., Brown, D., Crone, D., & Todd, A. W. (2000). *Functional assessment checklist for teachers and staff (FACTS)*. University of Oregon.

Martin, J. E., Marshall, L. H., & Maxson, L. (1993). Transition policy: Infusing self-determination and self-advocacy into transition programs. *Career Development for Exceptional Individuals, 16*, 53–61.

Maslow, A. H. (1943). A theory of human motivation. *Psychological Review, 50*(4), 370–396. https://doi.org/10.1037/h0054346

McBride, D. M., & Cutting, J. C. (2019). *Cognitive psychology: Theory, process, and methodology* (2nd ed.). Sage Publications.

McConaughy, S. (2013). *Clinical interviews for children and adolescents: Assessment to intervention* (2nd ed.). Guilford Press.

McDermott, E. R., Donlan, A. E., & Zaff, J. F. (2019) Why do students drop out? Turning points and long-term experiences. *The Journal of Educational Research, 112*(2), 270–282. https://doi.org/10.1080/00220671.2018.1517296

McDonnell, J., & Hunt, P. (2014). Inclusive education and meaningful school outcomes. In M. Agran, F. Brown, C. Hughes, C. Quirk, & D. Ryndak (Eds). *Equity and full participation for individuals with severe disabilities: A vision for the future* (pp. 155–176). Baltimore: Paul H. Brookes.

McMaster, K., & Espin, C. A. (2007). Technical features of curriculum-based measurement in writing: A literature review. *The Journal of Special Education, 41*(2), 68–84.

Meyer, A., Rose, D. H., & Gordon, D. (2014). *Universal design for learning: Theory and practice*. CAST Professional Publishing.

Milner, H. R. (2013). *Policy reforms and de-professionalization of teaching*. National Education Policy Center. Retrieved from http://nepc.colorado.edu/publication/policy-reforms-deprofessionalization

Mithaug, D., Wehmeyer, M. L., Agran, M., Martin, J., & Palmer, S. (1998). The self-determined learning model of instruction: Engaging students to solve their learning problems. In M. L. Wehmeyer & D. J. Sands (Eds.), *Making it happen: Student involvement in educational planning, decision-making and instruction* (pp. 299–328). Paul H. Brookes.

Mithaug, D. E., Mithaug, D., Agran, M., Martin, J., & Wehmeyer, M. L. (2007). *Self-instruction pedagogy: How to teach self-determined learning*. Charles C Thomas Publisher.

Mithaug, D. E., Mithaug, D. K., Agran, M., Martin, J. E., & Wehmeyer, M. L. (2003). *Self-determined learning theory: Construction, verification, and evaluation*. Lawrence Erlbaum Associates.

Nancekivell, S. E., Shah, P., & Gelman, S. A. (2020). Maybe they're born with it, or maybe it's experience: Toward a deeper understanding of the learning style myth. *Journal of Educational Psychology, 112*(2), 221–235. https://doi.org/10.1037/edu0000366

Nelson, L. L. (2021). *Design and deliver: Planning and teaching using universal design for learning* (2nd ed.). Brookes Publishing.

Newton, P. M., & Salvi, A. (2020). How common is belief in the learning styles neuromyth, and does it matter? A pragmatic systematic review. *Frontiers in Education, 5*:60251. https://doi.org/10.3389/feduc.2020.602451

Nota, L., Ferrrari, L., Soresi, S., & Wehmeyer, M. L. (2007). Self-determination, social abilities, and the quality of life of people with intellectual disabilities. *Journal of Intellectual Disability Research, 51*, 850–865.

O'Neill, R. E., Albin, R. W., Storey, K., Sprague, J. R., & Horner, R. H. (2015). *Functional assessment and program development for problem behavior: A practical handbook*. Cengage Learning.

Paclawskyj, T. R., Matson, J. L., Rush, K. S., Smalls, Y., & Vollmer, T. R. (2000). Questions about behavioral function (QABF): A behavioral checklist for functional assessment of aberrant behavior. *Research in Developmental Disabilities, 21*(3), 223–229.

Parrish, A. M., Yeatman, H., Iverson, D., & Russell, K. (2012). Using interviews and peer pairs to better understand how school environments affect young children's playground physical activity levels: A qualitative study. *Health Education Research, 27*(2), 269–280. https://doi.org/10.1093/her/cyr049

Pennington, R., Flick, A., Smith-Wehr, K. (2018). The use of response prompting and frames for teaching sentence writing to students with moderate intellectual disability. *Focus on Autism and Other Developmental Disabilities, 33*(3), 142–149. https://doi.org/10.1177/1088357616673568

Pledger, C. (2003). Discourse on disability and rehabilitation issues: Opportunities for psychology. *American Psychologist, 58*(4), 279–284. https://doi.org/10.1037/0003-066X.58.4.279

Puckett, K., Mathur, S., & Zamora, R. (2017). Implementing an intervention in special education to promote social skills in an inclusive setting. *Journal of International Special Needs Education, 20*(1), 25–36. https://doi.org/10.9782/2159-4341-20.1.25

Qian, X., & Klemm, E. (2016, March 24). The intersection between check & connection and Positive Behavior Intervention Supports (PBIS). Check & Connects blog. https://attendengageinvest.wordpress.com/2016/03/24/the-intersection-between-check-connect-and-positive-behavior-intervention-supports-pbis/

Quenemoen, R. F., & Thurlow, M. L. (2019). *Students with disabilities in educational policy, practice, and professional judgment: What should we expect?* (NCEO report 413). University of Minnesota, National Center on Educational Outcomes.

Rabiner, D. L., Carrig, M., & Dodge, K. A. (2013). Attention problems and academic achievement: Do persistent and earlier-emerging problems have more adverse long-term effects? *Journal of Attention Disorders, 20*(11), 946–957. https://doi:10.1177/1087054713507974

Raley, S. K., Shogren, K. A., & McDonald, A. (2018). How to implement the self-determined learning model of instruction in inclusive general education classrooms. *Teaching Exceptional Children, 51*(1), 62–71.

Rao, K., & Cook, S. (2021). UDL implementation research: Building an evidence base. In

K. A. Lowery (Ed.), *Critical issues in universal design for learning* (pp. 67–87). Knowledge by Design.

Rao, K., Ok, M. W., & Bryant, B. R. (2014). A review of research on universal design educational models. *Remedial and Special Education, 35*(3), 153–166.

Reeve, J. (2002). Self-determination theory applied to educational settings. In E. L. Deci & R. M. Ryan (Eds.), *Handbook of self-determination research* (pp. 183–203). Rochester University Press.

Reeve, J., Ryan, R. M., Cheon, S. H., Matos, L., & Kaplan, H. (2021). *Supporting students' motivation: Strategies for success.* Routledge.

Reyes, E. N., Wood, C. L., Walker, V. L., Voggt, A. P., & Vestal, A. R. (2021). Effects of video self-modeling and system of least prompts on completion of transitional routines for a student with extensive support needs in inclusive settings. *Journal of Positive Behavior Interventions.* https://doi.org/10.1177/1098300721990291

Riley, S. (2018). *How to write a curriculum from start to finish.* Institute for Arts Integration and STEAM. https://artsintegration.com/2018/07/01/how-to-write-a-curriculum-from-start-to-finish/

Rimm-Kaufman, S. E., Storm, M. D., Sawyer, B. E., Pianta, R. C., & LaParo, K. M. (2006). The Teacher Belief Q-Sort: A measure of teachers' priorities in relation to disciplinary practices, teaching practices, and beliefs about children. *Journal of School Psychology, 44*(2), 141–165. https://doi.org/10.1016/j.jsp.2006.01.003

Riser-Kositsky, M. (2019). Special education: Definition, statistics, and trends. *Education Week.* https://www. edweek. org/teaching-learning/special-education-definition-statistics-and-trends/2019/12.

Rittel, H. W., & Weber, M. M. (1973). Dilemmas in a general theory of planning. *Policy Sciences, 4*(2), 155–169. https://doi.org/10.1007/BF01405730

Rodrigues, F., & Oliveira, P. (2014). A system for formative assessment and monitoring of students' progress. *Computers and Education, 76*(1), 30–41.

Rogers, C. R. (1951). *Client-centered therapy.* Houghton Mifflin.

Rose, D. H., & Meyer, A. (2002). *Teaching every student in the digital age: Universal design for learning.* Association for Supervision and Curriculum Development.

Ruppar, A., Afacan, K., Yang, Y., & Pickett, K. (2017). Embedded shared reading to increase literacy in an inclusive english/language arts class: Preliminary efficacy and ecological validity. *Education and Training in Autism and Developmental Disabilities, 52*(1), 51–63. https://doi.org/10.2307/26420375

Ryndak, D., Jackson, L. B., & White, J. M. (2013). Involvement and progress in the general curriculum for students with extensive support needs: K-12 inclusive-education research and implication for the future. *Inclusion, 1*(1), 28–29. https://doi.org/10.1352/2326-6988-$21.028

Schalock, R. L., Borthwick-Duffy, S., Bradley, V. J., Buntinx, W. H. E., Coulter, D. L., Craig, E. M., Gomez, S. C., Lachapelle, Y., Luckasson, R., Reeve, A., Shogren, K. A., Snell,

M. E., Spreat, S., Tassé, M. J., Thompson, J. R., Verdugo-Alonso, M. A., Wehmeyer, M. L., & Yeager, M. H. (2010). *Intellectual disability: Definition, classification, and systems of support.* (ED509596). ERIC. American Association on Intellectual and Developmental Disabilities. https://eric.ed.gov/?id=ED509596

Schwartz, I. S. (2005). Inclusion and applied behavior analysis: Mending fences and building bridges. In W. L. Heward, T. E. Heron, N. A. Neef, S. M. Peterson, D. M. Sainato, G. Cartledge, R. Gardner, L. D. Peterson, S. B. Hersch, & J. C. Dardig (Eds.), *Focus on behavior analysis in education: Achievements, challenges, and opportunities* (pp. 239–251). Pearson.

Shapiro, A. H. (2000). *Everybody belongs: Changing negative attitudes toward classmates with disabilities*. Routledge.

Sheve, J., Allen, K., & Neiter, V. (2010). *Understanding learning styles: Making a difference for diverse learners*. Shell Educational Publishing.

Shogren, K. A., Burke, K. M., Antosh, A., Wehmeyer, M. L., LaPlante, T., Shaw, L. A., & Raley, S. (2019). Impact of the self-determined learning model of instruction on self-determination and goal attainment in adolescents with intellectual disability. *Journal of Disability Policy Studies, 30*(1), 22–34.

Shogren, K. A., Little, T. D., Grandfield, E., Raley, S., Wehmeyer, M. L., Lang, K. M., & Shaw, L. A. (2020). The Self-Determination Inventory—Student Report: Confirming the factor structure of a new measure. *Assessment for Effective Intervention, 45*(2), 110–120. https://doi.org/10.1177%2F1534508418788168

Shogren, K. A., Lopez, S. J., Wehmeyer, M. L., Little, T. D., & Pressgrove, C. L. (2006). The role of positive psychology constructs in predicting life satisfaction in adolescents with and without cognitive disabilities: An exploratory study. *The Journal of Positive Psychology, 1*, 37–52. https://psycnet.apa.org/doi/10.1080/17439760500373174

Shogren, K. A., Plotner, A. J., Palmer, S. B., Wehmeyer, M. L., & Paek, Y. (2014). Impact of the self-determined learning model of instruction on teacher perceptions of student capacity and opportunity for self-determination. *Education and Training in Autism and Developmental Disabilities, 49*(3), 440–448.

Shogren, K. A., Raley, S. K., Burke, K. M., & Wehmeyer, M. L. (2019). *The self-determined learning model of instruction teacher's guide*. Kansas University Center on Developmental Disabilities.

Shogren, K. A., Shaw, L. A., Raley, S. K., & Wehmeyer, M. L. (2018). Exploring the effect of disability, race-ethnicity, and socioeconomic status on scores on the Self-Determination Inventory: Student Report. *Exceptional Children, 85*(1), 10–27.

Shogren, K. A., Wehmeyer, M. L., & Lane, K. L. (2016) Embedding interventions to promote self-determination within multitiered systems of supports, *Exceptionality, 24*(4), 213–224. 10.1080/09362835.2015.1064421

Shogren, K. A., Wehmeyer, M. L., Palmer, S. B., Forber-Pratt, A., Little, T., & Lopez, S. (2015). Causal agency theory: Reconceptualizing a functional model of self-determination. *Education and Training in Autism and Developmental Disabilities, 50*(3), 251–263.

Shogren, K. A., Wehmeyer, M. L., Palmer, S. B., Rifenbark, G. & Little, T. (2015). Relationships between self-determination and postschool outcomes for youth with disabilities. *Journal of Special Education, 48*(4), 256–267.

Shogren, K. A., Wehmeyer, M. L., & Singh, N. (2017). *Handbook of positive psychology in intellectual and developmental disabilities: Translating research into practice.* Springer.

Shogren, K. A., Wehmeyer, M. L., & Thompson, J. R. (2017). Person-centered and student-directed planning. In M. L. Wehmeyer & K. A. Shogren (Eds.), *Handbook of research-based practices for educating students with intellectual disability* (pp. 167–182). Routledge.

Shriner, J. G., & Destefano, L. (2003). Participation and accommodation in state assessment: The role of individualized education programs. *Exceptional Children, 69*(2), 147–161. https://doi.org/10.1177/001440290306900202

Shuster, B. C., Gustafson, J. R., Jenkins, A. B., Lloyd, B. P., Carter, E. W., & Bernstein, C. F. (2017). Including students with disabilities in positive behavioral interventions and supports: Experiences and perspectives of special educators. *Journal of Positive Behavior Interventions, 19*(3), 143–157. https://doi.org/10.1177/1098300716675734

Smith, M. (2007). Into the mouths of babes: Hyperactivity, food additives, and the reception of the Feingold diet. In M. Jackson (Ed.), *Health and the modern home* (pp. 304–321). Routledge.

Sparks, S. (March 13, 2019). Why teacher–student relationships matter. *Education Week, 38*(25), 7–8. https://www.edweek.org/teaching-learning/why-teacher-student-relationships-matter/2019/03

Special Education Guide. (2021). *Adaptations, accommodations, and modifications.* https://www.specialeducationguide.com/pre-k-12/inclusion/adaptations-accommodations-and-modifications/

Spooner, F., Knight, V., Browder, D., & Smith, B. R. (2012). Evidence-based practice for teaching academics to students with severe developmental disabilities. *Remedial and Special Education, 33*(6), 374–387. https://doi.org/10.1177/0741932511421634

Stage, S. A. (2001). Predicting student success on state-mandated performance-based assessment using oral reading fluency. *School Psychology Review, 30*, 407–419.

Snyder, P., Hemmeter, M. L., McLean, M., Sandall, S., McLaughlin, T., & Algina, J. (2018). Effects of professional development on preschool teachers' use of embedded instruction Practices. *Exceptional Children, 84*(2), 213–232. https://doi.org/10.1177/0014402917735512

Sugai, G. & Horner. R. R. (2006). A promising approach for expanding and sustaining school-wide positive behavior support. *School Psychology Review, 35*(2), 245–259. https://doi.org/10.1080/02796015.2006.12087989

Taylor, S. (2017). Contested knowledge: A critical review of the concept of differentiation in teaching and learning. *Warwick Journal of Education–Transforming Teaching, 1*(1), 55–68.

Thanheiser, E., & Jansen, A. (2016). Inviting prospective teachers to share rough draft mathematical thinking. *Mathematics Teacher Educator, 4*(2), 145–163. https://doi.org/10.5951/mathteaceduc.4.2.0145

Thompson, J. R., Bradley, V., Buntinx, W. H. E., Schalock, R. L., Shogren, K. A., Snell, M. E., Wehmeyer, M. L., Borthwick-Duffy, S., Coulter, D., Craig, E. P. M., Gomez, S. C., Lachapelle, Y., Luckasson, R. A., Reeve, A., Spreat. S., Tassé, M. J., Verdugo, M. A., & Yeager, M. H. (2009). Conceptualizing supports and the support needs of people with intellectual disability. *Intellectual and Developmental Disabilities, 47*(2), 135–146. http://doi.org/10.1352/1934-9556-47.2.135

Thompson, J. R., & DeSpain, S. N. (2016). Community support needs. In N. N. Singh (Ed.), *Handbook of Evidence-based Practices in Intellectual and Developmental Disabilities (pp.* 137–168). New York: Springer.

Thompson, J. R., Shogren, K. A., & Wehmeyer, M. L. (2017). Supports and support needs in strengths-based models of intellectual disability. In M. L. Wehmeyer & K. A. Shogren (Eds.), *Handbook of research-based practices for educating students with intellectual disability* (pp. 31–49). Routledge.

Thompson, J. R., Walker, V. L., Shogren, K. A., & Wehmeyer, M. L. (2018). Expanding inclusive educational opportunities for students with the most significant cognitive disabilities through personalized supports. *Intellectual and Developmental Disabilities, 56*(6), 396–411. https://www.aaiddjournals.org/doi/abs/10.1352/1934-9556-56.6.396

Thompson, J. R., Walker, V. A., Snodgrass, M. R., Nelson, J. A., Carpenter, M. E., Hagiwara, M., & Shogren, K. A. (2020). Planning supports for students with intellectual disability in general education classrooms. *Inclusion, 8*(1), 27–42. https://www.aaiddjournals.org/doi/10.1352/2326-6988-$21.27

Thompson, J. R., Wehmeyer, M. L., Hughes, C., Shogren, K. A., Seo, H., Little, T. D., Schalock, R. L., Realon, R. E., Copeland, S. R., Patton, J. R., Polloway, E. A., Shelden, D., Tanis, S., & Tassé, M. J. (2016). *Supports Intensity Scale—Children's version: User's Manual*. Washington, DC: American Association on Intellectual and Developmental Disabilities.

Timberlake, M. T., Thomas, A. B., & Barrett, B. (2017). The allure of simplicity: Scripted curricula and equity. *Teaching and Teacher Education, 67*(1), 46–52. http://www.mariatimberlake.com/wp-content/uploads/2017/07/the-allure-of-simplicity-TATE.pdf

Tomlinson, C. A. (2017). How to differentiate instruction in academically diverse classrooms (3rd ed.). ASCD.

Tomlinson, C. A. (1999). *The differentiated classroom: Responding to the needs of all learners*. Association for Supervision and Curriculum Development.

Tomlinson, C. A., & Moon, T. R. (2013). *Assessment and student success in a differentiated classroom*. ASCD.

Tremblay, P., & Belley, S. (2017). Individualized education plans in Canada: A comparative analysis. *International Journal for Corss-Disciplinary Subjects in Education, 8*(1), 3017–3024. http://dx.doi.org/10.20533/ijcdse.2042.6364.2017.0409

Turnbull, A. A., Turnbull, H. R., Erwin, E. J., Soodak, L. C., & Shogren, K. A. (2015). *Fam-*

ilies professionals, and exceptionality: Positive outcomes through partnerships and trust. (7th ed.). Pearson.

Turnbull, H. R., Turnbull, A. P., & Cooper, D. H. (2018). The Supreme Court, *Endrew*, and the appropriate education of students with disabilities. *Exceptional Children, 84*(2), 124–140. https://doi.org/10.1177/0014402917734150

Udvari-Solner, A., Ahlgren-Bouchard, K., & Harell, K. (2017). Instructing students with severe and multiple disabilities in inclusive classrooms. In F .P Overlove, D. Sobsey, & D. L. Giles (Eds.), *Educating students with severe and multiple disabilities: A collaborative approach*, (5th ed., pp 351–405). Paul Brookes Publishing.

US Department of Education. (2017). *Questions and answers (Q&A) on US Supreme Court Case decision* Endrew F. v. Douglas County School District Re-1. IDEA, Individuals with Disabilities Education. https://sites.ed.gov/idea/

van den Bosch, R.M., Espin, C.A., Chung, S. and Saab, N. (2017), Data-Based Decision-Making: Teachers' Comprehension of Curriculum-Based Measurement Progress-Monitoring Graphs. *Learning Disabilities Research & Practice, 32*(1), 46–60. https://doi.org/10.1111/ldrp.12122

Vilaseca, R., Gràcia, M., Beltran, F. S., Dalmau, M., Alomar, E., Adam-Alcocer, A. L., & Simó-Pinatella, D. (2017). Needs and supports of people with intellectual disability and their families in Catalonia. *Journal of Applied Research in Intellectual Disabilities, 30*, 33–46. http://doi.org/10.1111/jar.12215

Villa, R. & Thousand, J. (2016). *The inclusive education checklist: A self-assessment of best practices.* National Professional Resources, Inc./Dude Publishing. ISBN: 978-1-9385-3901-5

Walker, V. L., & Loman, S. (2021). Strategies for including students with extensive support needs in SWPBIS. *Inclusive Practices*. Advance online publication. https://doi.org/10.1177/27324745211000307

Wood, D., Bruner, J., & Ross, G. (1976). The role of tutoring in problem solving. *Journal of Child Psychology and Child Psychiatry, 17*(2), 89–100. https://doi.org/10.1111/j.1469-7610.1976.tb00381.x

Yates, P. A., Chopra, R. V., Sobeck, E. E., Douglas, S. N., Morano, S., Walker, V. L., & Schulze, R. (2020). Working with paraeducators: Tools and strategies for planning, performance feedback, and evaluation. *Intervention in School and Clinic, 56*(1), 43-50. https://doi.org/10.1177/1053451220910740

York-Barr, J., Sommers, W., Ghere, G., & Montie, J. (2016). Reflective practice for renewing schools: An action guide for educators (3rd ed.). Corwin Press. https://us.corwin.com/en-us/nam/reflective-practice-for-renewing-schools/book244056

Appendix A

Educator Generated SIS-C Supports Needs Report

Name & Age of Child Assessed: *Josiah, 7 years old*

Date of SIS-C Interview(s): *September 23, 2018*

Date of Family Friendly report: *October 7, 2018*

Interviewer's Name: *Harvey Thompkinson*

Respondents' Names and their relationship (how they know the child) to the child:

Becca Swearingen (Teacher)

Sabrina (Mother)

Nancy Lind (Paraprofessional)

Part 1: Results From the SIS-C Assessment

List all of the medical conditions that require extra supports (i.e., a rating of "1" or "2") from Part 1A of the SIS-C, record the rating, and describe in general terms the extra supports required.

MEDICAL CONDITIONS FROM SIS-C	RATING	SHORT SUMMARY OF SUPPORTS REQUIRED
Eating disorder	1	Josiah is a very picky eater, with very narrow food preferences. He likes chicken nuggets and mac & cheese, but rejects other foods, particularly fruits and vegetables. Parents must persuade him to take 2 bites of other foods that are offered, and he will usually do this willingly now, but in the past it was a huge struggle. His gastrointestinal issues concern chronic constipation. Soluble fibers and laxatives have helped. Also, managing his toileting schedule (making him try to go potty right after eating) has helped.
Gastrointestinal issues	1	

List all of the behavioral concerns that require extra supports (i.e., a rating of "1" or "2") from Part 1B of the SIS-C, record the rating, and describe in general terms the extra supports required.

Behavioral Challenges from SIS-C	Rating	Short Summary of Supports Required
Prevention of tantrums and emotional outbursts	2	Josiah has tantrums and these can escalate to what the family describes as meltdowns. When meltdowns occur, Josiah will begin to slap himself and bite his hand (while screaming and crying), and will throw toys and push over desks if these items are nearby. The introduction of sticker charts for good behavior and visual schedules to help him make transitions to new activities has helped reduce the incidences and intensity considerably, and parents have been coordinating behavior management strategies with the school for the past year. Josiah will wander away if not watched. He has a very limited sense of danger. He does not wander away to gain attention or make adults angry, he just starts roaming and forgets where he is going. Redirecting him is sufficient to get him to return.
Prevention of property destruction	1	
Prevention of self-injury	1	
Prevention of wandering	1	

Part 2: Results From the SIS-C Assessment

SECTION A: HOME LIFE ACTIVITIES	TYPE OF SUPPORT	FREQUENCY	DAILY SUPPORT TIME
1. Completing household chores	4 - full physical support	4 - always	1 - less than 30 minutes
2. Eating	3 - partial physical assistance	3 - very frequently	2 - 30 minutes to less than 2 hours
3. Washing and keeping self clean	3 - partial physical assistance	4 - always	2 - 30 minutes to less than 2 hours
4. Dressing	3 - partial physical assistance	4 - always	2 - 30 minutes to less than 2 hours
5. Using the toilet	4 - full physical support	4 - always	3 - 2 hours to less than 4 hours
6. Sleeping and/or napping	2 - verbal/gestural prompting	3 - very frequently	1 - less than 30 minutes
7. Keeping track of personal belongings at home	2 - verbal/gestural prompting	2 - frequently	1 - less than 30 minutes
8. Keeping self occupied during unstructured time (free time) at home	3 - partial physical assistance	2 - frequently	2 - 30 minutes to less than 2 hours
9. Operating electronic devices	4 - full physical support	4 - always	2 - 30 minutes to less than 2 hours
Total Score, Mean Rating, and Standard Score: Total Score is 74, Mean Rating is 2.74, Standard Score is 11			

Based on Section A, Josiah engages in home life activities with varying types of support, frequency in their delivery, and daily support time needed. Whereas Josiah requires minimal assistance to keep track of personal belongings at home, Josiah requires relatively more support in toileting and operating electronic devices. Below are recommendations for support strategies to promote Josiah's meaningful participation in home life activities, including natural and technological supports:

- Consistent support routines and procedures at the school and home for mealtime and toileting activities is important, and if progress slows or reverses, it is important for school and home to problem-solve solutions. Thus, support in the form of careful attention and communication to these areas at school and home should continue.
- Josiah could use an adapted cup, specialized utensils to ensure grip, or perhaps preferred dinnerware (e.g., plates and dishes with Pokémon on them) in efforts to reduce any frustration with eating and to make meals as motivating and enjoyable as possible. Although much of the support he requires during meals stems from the behaviors associated with being a resistant eater, the introduction of special cups, utensils, and dinnerware may serve as motivation and/or have a de-escalating effect on challenging mealtime behaviors.
- Josiah could use a play script (or a social narrative) to keep himself occupied during unstructured time at home.
- Josiah could use a sticker chart (with tokens of a cartoon character he likes) to use the toilet successfully.
- Josiah could also use video modeling supports and task analyses for self-care tasks, like washing and keeping himself clean.
- Because Josiah likes video games and electronics, it might be helpful to restrict access to those items until after mealtimes; first mealtime, then toileting, and then video games and electronics.
- Josiah's family could also ensure that the organization of the home is conducive to the activities and supports provided, including labeling the dressing area so Josiah can dress with less intrusive and intensive support from adults.
- Other modifications to the environment could be made like turning the water on while Josiah is in the restroom to increase the chance of success.

SECTION B: COMMUNITY AND NEIGHBORHOOD ACTIVITIES	TYPE OF SUPPORT	FREQUENCY	DAILY SUPPORT TIME
1. Moving around the neighborhood and community	3 – partial physical assistance	4 - always	2 - 30 minutes to less than 2 hours
2. Participating in leisure activities that require physical activity	3 – partial physical assistance	3 – very frequently	2 - 30 minutes to less than 2 hours
3. Participating in leisure activities that do <u>not</u> require physical exertion	3 – partial physical assistance	3 – very frequently	2 - 30 minutes to less than 2 hours
4. Using public services in one's community or neighborhood	3 – partial physical assistance	3 – very frequently	2 - 30 minutes to less than 2 hours
5. Participating in community service and religious activities	2 – verbal/gestural prompting	3 – very frequently	1 – less than 30 minutes
6. Shopping	2 – verbal/gestural prompting	3 – very frequently	1 - less than 30 minutes
7. Complying with basic community standards, rules, and/or laws	1 - monitoring	1 - infrequently	1 - less than 30 minutes
8. Attending special events in the community or neighborhood such as cookouts/picnics, cultural festivals, music/art fairs, or holiday-oriented events	2 – verbal/gestural prompting	2- frequently	2 – 30 minutes to less than 2 hours
Total Score, Mean Rating, and Standard Score: Total Score is 56, Mean Rating is 2.33, Standard Score is 8			

Section B provides insight into the supports Josiah needs in community and neighborhood activities. Josiah requires minimal assistance in complying with basic community standards, rules, and/or laws; however, his assessment results indicate he requires more support in moving around the neighborhood and community. As such, below are recommendations for support strategies to promote Josiah's meaningful participation in community and neighborhood activities, including natural and technological supports:

- Josiah could be taught to use a ring of behavior and communication visual cue cards to guide his participation and promote his safety in community and neighborhood settings and activities.
- Relationships could be established with natural supports in the community, such as a pool of neighbors who would feel comfortable and confident in intervening should they see that Josiah is not being safe in the neighborhood and peers who could help Josiah navigate the neighborhood such as walking with him to and from school.
- Josiah's family could consider getting a service dog who might be trained to bark whenever Josiah gets close to the street or to perform other functions to assure Josiah's safety.
- Josiah could use electronic technology with GPS that would let him know when has entered a place that is deemed "out of bounds" and could provide his family with information regarding his exact location.
- Josiah could have an ID bracelet that has his information like phone number and address, should he get separated.
- Josiah's family could put a bell on the door so they would be aware of when Josiah is leaving the house.
- Social narratives could be used to teach Josiah about community settings and activities, for instance, what church is about and what people do when they are there.

SECTION C: SCHOOL PARTICIPATION ACTIVITIES	TYPE OF SUPPORT	FREQUENCY	DAILY SUPPORT TIME
1. Being included in general education classrooms	3 - partial physical assistance	4 - always	4 - 4 hours or more
2. Participating in activities in common school areas (e.g., playground, hallways, cafeteria)	3 - partial physical assistance	3 - very frequently	2 - 30 minutes to less than 2 hours
3. Participating in cocurricular activities	3 - partial physical assistance	4 - always	2 - 30 minutes to less than 2 hours
4. Getting to school (includes transportation)	3 - partial physical assistance	4 - always	2 - 30 minutes to less than 2 hours
5. Moving around within the school and transitioning between activities	3 - partial physical assistance	4 - always	2 - 30 minutes to less than 2 hours
6. Participating in large-scale test-taking activities required by state education systems	3 - partial physical assistance	4 - always	4 - 4 hours or more
7. Following classroom and school rules	2 - verbal/gestural prompting	2 - frequently	2 - 30 minutes to less than 2 hours
8. Keeping track of personal belongings at school	3 - partial physical assistance	2 - frequently	1 - less than 30 minutes
9. Keeping track of schedule at school	3 - partial physical assistance	2 - frequently	1 - less than 30 minutes
Total Score, Mean Rating, and Standard Score: Total Score is 75, Mean Rating is 2.78, Standard Score is 9			

Based on Section C, Josiah would benefit from supports in several school participation activities. As such, below are recommendations for support strategies to promote Josiah's meaningful participation in school activities, including natural and technological supports:

- Josiah could use a visual schedule with pictures to keep track of school daily schedule and activities/tasks that have already been completed (e.g., first/then boards). As he becomes more adept at using visual schedules, he will be prepared to transition to visual guide apps on everyday technologies (e.g., smartphones).
- Josiah could use a technological device, like an iPod with the Reminders app, to keep track of his schedule.
- Josiah could use a labeling system to make sure that all of his items are in their correct place at the end of the day.
- Josiah's seat could be by the door so he could easily come in and leave the classroom, as needed.
- A buddy system could be used to help Josiah with transitioning from one class to another.
- Josiah could use sticker charts to set and work toward goals throughout school activities and tasks. Involving Josiah in the awarding of stickers and maintenance of the sticker charts would prepare him for developing self-management strategies.
- Josiah could be assigned a school job (e.g., putting the flag up every morning) with a peer buddy to promote social skills as well was learning sequences and routines. Small jobs would also be a good way to embed natural breaks in the day to help Josiah self-regulate.
- Different types of seating (e.g., yoga balls) could be explored to see if they positively impact Josiah's participation.

SECTION D: SCHOOL LEARNING ACTIVITIES	TYPE OF SUPPORT	FREQUENCY	DAILY SUPPORT TIME
1. Accessing grade-level curriculum content	2 - verbal/gestural prompting	4 - always	4 - 4 hours or more
2. Learning academic skills	2 - verbal/gestural prompting	4 - always	4 - 4 hours or more
3. Learning and using metacognitive strategies	2 - verbal/gestural prompting	4 - always	1 - less than 30 minutes
4. Completing academic tasks (e.g., time, quality, neatness, organizational skills)	3 - partial physical assistance	4 - always	4 - 4 hours or more
5. Learning how to use and using educational materials, technologies, and tools	2 - verbal/gestural prompting	4 - always	1 - less than 30 minutes
6. Learning how to use and using problem-solving and self-regulation strategies in the classroom	2 - verbal/gestural prompting	3 - very frequently	1 - less than 30 minutes
7. Participating in classroom-level evaluations, such as tests	2 - verbal/gestural prompting	4 - always	2 - 30 minutes to less than 2 hours
8. Accessing the health and physical education curricula	3 - partial physical assistance	1 - infrequently	1 - less than 30 minutes
9. Completing homework assignments	2 - verbal/gestural prompting	3 - very frequently	2 - 30 minutes to less than 2 hours
Total Score, Mean Rating, and Standard Score: Total Score is 71, Mean Rating is 2.63, Standard Score is 7			

Section D describes the supports Josiah would benefit from in school learning activities. An identified area of needed support is completing academic tasks, including tasks related to time, quality, neatness, and organization. As such, below are recommendations for support strategies to promote Josiah's engagement in school learning activities, including natural and technological supports:

- Josiah might benefit from modified school supplies (e.g., keyboards, weighted pencils); it would be important to find supplies that reduce his frustration with producing his schoolwork and enable him to submit his best work as well as communicate what he has learned.
- When Josiah has challenges with text materials, the use of a digital talking book format could be explored.
- Josiah could benefit from advance organizers and pre-teaching when receiving academic instruction in a group format.
- In math and science, Josiah could use a calculator to help with small computations.
- The use of an augmentative communication device or computer could help Josiah engage with the curricula.
- Josiah could benefit from extended time when he finds he needs it on a particular assignment; it is important for him to learn to realize situations where he needs a reasonable accommodation so he can learn to advocate for it.
- Josiah could use an oral presentation to demonstrate learning instead of traditional forms of learning assessments.
- Josiah and a few classmates could start a study group in classes that are difficult; a peer for notetaking might be helpful.
- Incorporating cooperative learning activities into instruction may support greater engagement and participation in learning activities

SUBSCALE E: HEALTH AND SAFETY ACTIVITIES	TYPE OF SUPPORT	FREQUENCY	DAILY SUPPORT TIME
1. Communicating health-related issues and medical problems, including aches and pains	2 – verbal/gestural prompting	1 - infrequently	1 - less than 30 minutes
2. Maintaining physical fitness	1 - monitoring	1 - infrequently	1 - less than 30 minutes
3. Maintaining emotional well-being	1 - monitoring	2 - frequently	1 - less than 30 minutes
4. Maintaining health and wellness	1 - monitoring	2 - frequently	1 - less than 30 minutes
5. Implementing routine first aid when experiencing minor injuries such as a bloody nose	2 – verbal/gestural prompting	4 - always	1 – less than 30 minutes
6. Responding in emergency situations	4 - full physical support	4 - always	1 – less than 30 minutes
7. Protecting self from physical, verbal, and/or sexual abuse	2 – verbal/gestural prompting	3 – very frequently	1 - less than 30 minutes
8. Avoiding health and safety hazards	2 – verbal/gestural prompting	3 – very frequently	4 – 4 hours or more
Total Score, Mean Rating, and Standard Score: Total Score is 46, Mean Rating is 1.92, Standard Score is 6			

Section E describes the supports Josiah may benefit from in health and safety activities. Josiah requires minimal support in maintaining physical fitness and an identified area of needed support is responding in emergency activities. As such, below are recommendations for support strategies to promote Josiah's meaningful participation in health and safety activities, including natural and technological supports:

- Josiah could be taught a song or a short rhyme that reminds him of information about what to do in emergency situations.
- A small informational card could be placed in Josiah's wallet for emergency situations containing his emergency contact.
- Social narratives could be used before emergency drills to teach Josiah what to do under those circumstances.
- Similarly, social narratives could also be used to teach Josiah measures to take to protect himself from physical, verbal, and/or sexual abuse.
- Josiah could engage in role-playing activities to practice how to respond in potentially abusive situations.
- Josiah could spend time with the nurse to learn how she implements routine first aid when students with minor injuries come into the nurses' office.
- A tracking device, such as TrackR or Tile, could be put into Josiah's backpack or he could even wear one on a necklace under his shirt (if he would tolerate it) to enable his location to be monitored should he get separated. If he was able to keep track of a phone, this would also be an option.
- Natural supports in the community (e.g., neighbors) and school (e.g., peers and teachers) should become aware of Josiah's special vulnerabilities, and informally monitor his interactions in various settings and activities to assure he is not being exploited.

SUBSCALE F: SOCIAL ACTIVITIES	TYPE OF SUPPORT	FREQUENCY	DAILY SUPPORT TIME
1. Maintaining positive relationships with others	2 - verbal/gestural prompting	2 - frequently	2 - 30 minutes to less than 2 hours
2. Respecting the rights of others	2 - verbal/gestural prompting	2 - frequently	2 - 30 minutes to less than 2 hours
3. Maintaining conversation	2 - verbal/gestural prompting	3 - very frequently	2 - 30 minutes to less than 2 hours
4. Responding to and providing constructive criticism	2 - verbal/gestural prompting	3 - very frequently	2 - 30 minutes to less than 2 hours
5. Coping with changes in routines and/or transitions across social situations	3 - partial physical assistance	4 - always	1 - less than 30 minutes
6. Making and keeping friends	2 - verbal/gestural prompting	3 - very frequently	2 - 30 minutes to less than 2 hours
7. Communicating with others in social situations	2 - verbal/gestural prompting	3 - very frequently	1 - less than 30 minutes
8. Respecting others personal space/ property	2 - verbal/gestural prompting	3 - very frequently	2 - 30 minutes to less than 2 hours
9. Protecting self from exploitation and bullying	2 - verbal/gestural prompting	3 - very frequently	4 - 4 hours or more
Total Score, Mean Rating, and Standard Score: Total Score is 63, Mean Rating is 2.33, Standard Score is 8			

Based on the results from Section F, there are supports Josiah would benefit in order to participate in social activities more fully. Below are recommendations for support strategies to promote Josiah's meaningful participation in social activities, including natural and technological supports:

- To help with coping with changes in routines, Josiah could be provided 1- or 2-minute warnings before transitions are about to take place throughout the day.
- As a school-wide measure that would also support Josiah, the school could initiate a bullying prevention program to help Josiah (and others) protect self from exploitation and bullying.
- To maintain conversations in social situations, Josiah could be equipped with and use a conversation ring with some generic conversation starters.
- There could also be some peers that could be designated to engage Josiah in some communication activities around a common area of interest (e.g., Pokémon) at natural breaks (e.g., lunch, recess) during the school day.
- Social narratives could be used to teach Josiah the principles of respecting others personal space and property.
- Josiah and peers could engage in role-playing to practice pragmatic communication skills as well as respect one another's personal space.

SUBSCALE G: ADVOCACY ACTIVITIES	TYPE OF SUPPORT	FREQUENCY	DAILY SUPPORT TIME
1. Expressing preferences	2 - verbal/gestural prompting	2 - frequently	2 - 30 minutes to less than 2 hours
2. Setting personal goals	2 - verbal/gestural prompting	2 - frequently	2 - 30 minutes to less than 2 hours
3. Taking action and attaining goals	2 - verbal/gestural prompting	3 - very frequently	2 - 30 minutes to less than 2 hours
4. Making choices and decisions	2 - verbal/gestural prompting	3 - very frequently	2 - 30 minutes to less than 2 hours
5. Advocating for and assisting others	3 - partial physical assistance	4 - always	1 - less than 30 minutes
6. Learning and using self-advocacy skills	2 - verbal/gestural prompting	3 - very frequently	2 - 30 minutes to less than 2 hours
7. Communicating personal wants and needs	2 - verbal/gestural prompting	3 - very frequently	1 - less than 30 minutes
8. Participating in educational decision making	2 - verbal/gestural prompting	3 - very frequently	2 - 30 minutes to less than 2 hours
9. Learning and using problem-solving and self-regulation strategies in the home and community	2 - verbal/gestural prompting	3 - very frequently	4 - 4 hours or more
Total Score, Mean Rating, and Standard Score: Total Score is 58, Mean Rating is 2.15, Standard Score is 7			

Section G describes the characteristics of supports Josiah needs in advocacy activities. This is an area in which Josiah requires support, but his age must be taken into consideration when considering advocacy activities. Below are recommendations for support strategies to promote Josiah's meaningful participation in advocacy activities, including natural and technological supports:

- Social narratives could be used to teach Josiah how to communicate his personal wants and needs. With the facilitation of a teacher, these stories could be developed by Josiah and his peers.
- Others in Josiah's environment, particularly his teachers and family members, should make sure Josiah has opportunities to initiate communication regarding his wants and needs as opposed to always asking him to respond to choices.
- Josiah's teacher might consider initiating class-wide instruction aimed at student goal setting and self-determination.
- Josiah could be paired with a peer with the intent that their job is to advocate and assist the other in various activities so he can practice advocating for and assisting others.
- Josiah's teacher could focus efforts on assuring that he has a meaningful role in educational planning; for instance, Josiah could be assisted in leading his IEP team meeting.
- Opportunities to practice and demonstrate self-determination skills should be incorporated into the daily curriculum and instruction (e.g., opportunities for choice-making regarding which assignment to complete first).

SUPPORT NEEDS PROFILE FROM SIS-C

Highlight the Standard Score for Each Activities Subscale and the SIS-A Support Needs Index

A. Home Life	B. Community & Neighborhood	C. School Participation	D. School Learning	E. Health & Safety	F. Social	G. Advocacy	SIS-C Support Needs Index
16	16	16	16	16	16	16	124 or more
15	15	15	15	15	15	15	120–123
14	14	14	14	14	14	14	116–119
13	13	13	13	13	13	13	112–115
12	12	12	12	12	12	12	108–111
11	11	11	11	11	11	11	104–107
10	10	10	10	10	10	10	100–103
9	9	9	9	9	9	9	96–99
8	8	8	8	8	8	8	92–95
7	7	7	7	7	7	7	88–91
6	6	6	6	6	6	6	84–87
5	5	5	5	5	5	5	80–83
4	4	4	4	4	4	4	76-79
3	3	3	3	3	3	3	72-75
2	2	2	2	2	2	2	68-71
0-1	0-1	0-1	0-1	0-1	0-1	0-1	67 or less

What are the three to five most important support strategies to implement for this student in the coming year?

1. **Supports for Meals and Toileting.** Josiah has made significant progress in his behavior at mealtimes, including his acceptance that he must try different foods. Also, his toileting process has improved, and his health has been better because of it. These have been big areas of stress for both Josiah and his family, but things have improved considerably over the past 9 months. Josiah's parents and teachers attribute the gains in these areas to the focus that has been placed on supporting Josiah through consistency in routines at mealtimes as well as toileting schedules, and it is critical that consistent efforts continue to be made at home and school. If Josiah continues to make progress in these areas, it is reasonable to believe that he will not require intensive support from adults for meals and toileting in the future. (The intensity of supports he currently needs would be quite intrusive for an older child.) Because this is the area of most concern for the family, the supports mentioned in Section A that have been established and the additional supports that may be helpful are the top priority for implementation. First and foremost, supports must include monitoring Josiah's progress in these areas and communicating progress between school and home, especially to assure the family continues to be able to access support from school professionals in terms of consultation and problem-solving.
2. **Supports for Peer Interaction.** Josiah's inclusion in the kindergarten classroom (last year) and first-grade classroom (this year) was a significant change from the early childhood special education classroom he attended before. An area of emphasis for Josiah's school participation are for him to be more engaged with his peers, including opportunities to be supported by his peers. Specifically, peer interaction and support will be increased in regard to: (a) in getting to and from school and (b) during the school day. Currently, adults provide most of the support Josiah needs at school. A concerted effort is needed to recruit and prepare neighborhood friends to walk with Josiah to and from school and support him to complete his morning "coming to school" routine (e.g., hanging up his coat, going to his desk) and his afternoon "leaving school" routines (e.g., getting his materials together to bring home).

There are older children in the neighborhood, as well as children in Josiah's grade who parents and educators believe would be willing to provide support and would be good at it, but adults will initially need to provide some guidance and direction to the peers and will need to monitor how things are proceeding as time moves forward. As for peer support during the school day, a specific support strategy of arranging opportunities for Josiah to spend short periods of time with a classmate each day completing routines was also identified as a priority for the remainder of this school year and the next. Two potential jobs were identified: watering the plants in the principal's office in the morning and checking the playground for discarded items (balls that were left out) in the afternoon. He and a peer friend will do these tasks, first with direct supervision from an adult but eventually the two friends will work collaboratively without direct supervision.

3. **Supports for Classroom Learning.** Josiah made progress in the general education curriculum during kindergarten and has also shown progress in first grade. However, the general education curriculum is getting more demanding as he progresses through first grade. It is clear to Josiah's educators that extra attention needs to be given to curricular adaptations for this school year. The curriculum needs to be broadened to include additional levels and types of academic skills that meet Josiah's learning needs. Specifically, Josiah's educators are going to infuse curricula that provide instruction in social skills that Josiah needs to learn. Also, Josiah explicitly needs to be taught study and organizational skills. A third focus for curricular adaptation will be on teaching Josiah introductory self-management skills. In addition to the aforementioned areas for curricular infusion, simplified academic skills and alternative academic targets that are aligned with the general education curriculum be identified for Josiah before the start of each new instructional unit. Personalized supports for his learning, such as providing him advanced organizers before instruction is delivered, will also be developed and implemented by the educational team. Making sure the curriculum is adapted so that general education classroom instruction remains relevant to Josiah's learning needs is a top priority of the educational team.

Index

About the Author

James R. Thompson, PhD, has over 40 years of experience in the field of developmental disabilities as a direct support professional, special educator, rehabilitation counselor, teacher educator, and researcher. He pioneered assessment and planning practices that are focused on understanding people with disabilities by their needs for extra support. He is the lead author of the adult and children's version of the Supports Intensity Scales, the first assessment tools to provide a standardized measure of the support needs of people with developmental disabilities. He currently serves at the University of Kansas as a Professor in the Department of Special Education, a Senior Scientist in the Beach Center on Disability, and an Associate Director of the Kansas University Center on Developmental Disabilities. He is the editor-in-chief of *Intellectual and Developmental Disabilities*, a professional journal of research, policy, and practice that is published by the American Association on Intellectual and Developmental Disabilities.